Fighting Vichy from Horseback

British Mounted Cavalry in Action, Syria 1941

Jonathan Washington

 Helion & Company Limited

To Georgina, Petra, Fergus, Hugo and to
Dr B, my favourite proof-reader ...

Helion & Company Limited
Unit 8 Amherst Business Centre
Budbrooke Road
Warwick
CV34 5WE
England
Tel. 01926 499 619
Email: info@helion.co.uk
Website: www.helion.co.uk
Twitter: @helionbooks
Visit our blog at blog.helion.co.uk

Published by Helion & Company 2023
Designed and typeset by Mary Woolley (www.battlefield-design.co.uk)
Cover designed by Paul Hewitt, Battlefield Design (www.battlefield-design.co.uk)

Text © Jonathan Washington 2023
Images reproduced by permission of the Cheshire Archives unless otherwise credited.
Maps drawn by George Anderson © Helion & Company Limited 2023

Every reasonable effort has been made to trace copyright holders and to obtain their permission for the use of copyright material. The author and publisher apologise for any errors or omissions in this work and would be grateful if notified of any corrections that should be incorporated in future reprints or editions of this book.

ISBN 978-1-915113-76-4

British Library Cataloguing-in-Publication Data.
A catalogue record for this book is available from the British Library.

All rights reserved. No part of this publication may be reproduced, stored in a retrieval system, or transmitted, in any form, or by any means, electronic, mechanical, photocopying, recording or otherwise, without the express written consent of Helion & Company Limited.

For details of other military history titles published by Helion & Company Limited contact the above address, or visit our website: http://www.helion.co.uk.

We always welcome receiving book proposals from prospective authors.

Contents

Acknowledgements		iv
Foreword		ix
Introduction		xi
1	Two-Legged Yeomanry	33
2	Embarkation	46
3	Palestine, Training and Official Scrutiny	52
4	Coming to Scratch	77
5	The Horse Soldiers Fight	95
6	The 5th Cavalry Brigade	125
Conclusion		161
Epilogue		168

Appendices:
I	Allied Chain of Command, Syria 1941	172
II	Syria Branch – Spears Mission	173
III	Lieutenant Alwyn Clark Recollection	176
IV	North Somerset Yeomanry Casualty Return Following the Assault on Jebel Mazar	178
V	Postscript	180

Bibliography	182
Index	186

Acknowledgements

There are very many different reasons why someone writes a book. Probably most of which do not apply to how this one came to be written. At the time I committed to writing this book, I certainly had no pressing academic reason. Until six months before putting proverbial pen to paper I didn't have any inclination either. The fact this has been written is therefore a testament to both the inherent interest value of the topic (the fact that the British used mounted cavalry in war in 1941), and to the accounts, testimonials, sources and regimental histories accumulated before me. Without their hard work - my attempt at putting this history together would not have been possible.

The crucial ingredient in my beginning this project is the inherent interest value in discovering that the British army sent horsemen into combat in the Second World War. Although anyone who taught me history at university might be somewhat surprised to see that I have had a book published, the fact remains that the subject has always drawn me inexorably. For this I have to thank my parents. As the product of a military background, it is fairly inevitable that military history has always drawn a significant amount of my attention. I should also add that although never supremely interested in horses, I have generally been within fairly close proximity to them. More importantly, as a former yeoman (the name for cavalry of the Territorial army - now Army Reserve), my eye has always been caught by any references to the yeomanry in print.

All of this meant my interest was sparked at a lunchtime reunion with some old friends – all of whom shared the same Territorial Army and university background as myself – and upon whom I was eavesdropping while I tried to reason with a small child. Noting that my friends were crowding around a large hardback with pictures, I broke off negotiations and drifted across the room whereupon my eyes fell upon the open copy of Janusz Piekalkiewicz's *The Cavalry of World War II*. The photos were fantastic. One even had a Wehrmacht cavalryman daubing his mount in camouflage paint. I spent the next twenty minutes – after my friends and the persistent child had gone through to be sociable – leafing through one astonishing vista after another. I already knew that the Germans and Soviets had deployed horses extensively during 1939-45 (though not much beyond that) so the only reaction at this stage was to self-indulgently keep leafing through the photographs while everyone else was being civilised. I was genuinely surprised though to turn the page upon pictures of British cavalry in the Second World War. I was still further surprised to read through the anecdotes that attended them; about coming under machine gun fire as they crossed the Litani (a river I myself crossed a few times whilst living in Lebanon in 2007), and "Spencer's ride". This was mind-blowing – to me at least .

The result was that that evening, when I no longer needed to be sociable, I browsed and browsed in search of a history about Britain's cavalry in combat during the Second World War. It didn't exist. Even the pages of Wikipedia failed to produce much more than the fact that the Cheshire Yeomanry and the Yorkshire Dragoons both deployed on horses briefly in 1941. There is now I notice, a marginally better coverage of the topic out there on the internet, and possibly I would have been duly satiated if the current coverage then existed. There wasn't in 2016 however, and it certainly seemed a shame.

About three months later, my wife got promoted. The promotion took us out to Slovakia for three years and, not speaking Slovak, this was probably going to limit my chances of employment over those three years. Besides, Fergus our youngest would be too little to begin at the British International School, and so I would have to be at home to look after him. This would mean that I was going to have some time on my hands; at least for the first year. After all, nap time could sometimes take up to three hours a day.

The issue of what to do with this time was suggested to me by my sister-in-law and her husband. They have always expressed polite admiration for my capacity for tedious historical detail - while simultaneously courteously ignoring the lack of any significant historical accomplishment. Their suggestion was that I use my time to turn some of my minutiae into a book of some sort. They even knew of a publisher that was taking unsolicited manuscripts on all historical topics just then – they'd be bound to publish some of my pseudo-wisdom. "Why not?" they encouragingly asked. "What areas could you write about most comfortably?". I scrabbled around in my brain for something that covered an area not already inundated with published literature, and British cavalry during the Second World War appeared to be the stand-out candidate. The main problem of course, was that I did not know anything about this particular area. However, it seemed at the time that a few regimental histories and a trawl of the war diaries (which I assumed would be digitised) would provide enough material to regurgitate and turn into a book at some point in the following year. This was in 2017.

Technically the blueprint for research indicated in the previous paragraph has held true. I did end up finding a great deal in regimental histories and in the war diaries. The fact that the unit war diaries were only held physically and at Kew is a fact for which I will always be grateful, as I immediately loved the process of picking through pages written or printed over eighty years before, and since touched by very few other hands. I would also add that those sources provided detail on horses and men in battle in the same war that my grandmother and great uncles served. To say it was absorbing would at least succinctly explain why I have persisted with this project and tried my best to turn it into a coherent history of a very surprising phenomenon.

Effective or otherwise, researching this book has called in a significant amount of good will. I might also add at this stage that it would be impossible to effectively comment on British cavalry in Operation "Exporter" without relying heavily on the material concerning the Cheshire Yeomanry. It was they after all who did the most fighting out of all the British horsed cavalry involved. It has been fortunate then that the Cheshire Yeomanry Regimental Association has been invariably; authoritatively knowledgeable, magnanimous and efficient at every step. They supplied me with a copy of their regimental history at little more than cost price where many more expensive ones were available to the unwary, they have granted me permission to use their extensive range of material, not least their photographs, and they have liaised where appropriate with the likes of the Chester Archives who in turn were welcoming, gracious and expert. Robert Gladding has been my primary contact at CYRA and I thank him deeply. Mention should also go to Alex Siddell who put me in touch with him. Special mention also goes to Chris Seaton, Officer Commanding at time of writing of the squadron descended from the Cheshire Yeomanry (more on him later). Essentially, this book relies in many ways on Cheshire's finest, both native and adopted.

The actual writing of my first draft however was not conducted in Cheshire, but off British soil, in Slovakia, while Fergus napped. At times I attempted it while all my children were awake. But Hugo and Petra were not interested in writing without pictures and by this stage could operate the TV remote themselves. Their forbearance is gratefully noted, and so too is that of my wife Georgina. She after all was willing to work, and to look after house and children single-handed while I gallivanted off to the archives at Kew, and to Chester among other destinations. I must also thank Gill Hoffs, who is actually a proper writer and historian. She gave me encouragement and sage advice on the process from day one.

As indicated above, the extent of gratitude owed goes beyond this short list. A notable feature of historical research is that it involves not only time in the archives, but extensive periods of time on the phone. There are probably dozens of forgotten names out there, all helpful and resourceful, who have indulged my questions, pointed me in the right direction, and recommended appropriate titles. In some cases I have been able to work out who I owe thanks to, simply by going through my email inbox. Robert McIntosh of the museum of Military Medicine falls into this list because he got closer than anyone else into identifying what happened to the horses of 1st Cavalry Division and in particular those of 5th Cavalry Brigade after March 1942. But trawling my emails also reveals many other individuals who had no reason to help and yet offered their time and support. Jane Bevan for example, sent me copies of an unpublished manuscript regarding her father's unit, the North Somerset Yeomanry and also offered me a variety of contacts. For gestures such as this I am truly grateful.

There are thankfully more quantifiable measures of gratitude which I owe. The most obvious of these is to Duncan Rogers and the team at Helion who took my project on. For the record, I should add that Helion is not the publisher my sister-in-law originally recommended to me, when she was persuading me to write a book.

Helion, since taking on my project, have provided a focus and line of guidance that has transformed my original research attempt into something altogether more readable and useful. Take from that what you will about my early attempts at writing this book. Dr Michael LoCicero in particular has been a mainstay of intellectual support. His feedback has been useful, digestible and gracious. His air of calmness and his practical approach has also opened my eyes to what the publishing process can achieve. For calm, efficient enthusiasm, as well as wealth of knowledge, I must also once again identify Chris Seaton of the Cheshire Yeomanry. His advice on regimental details, as well as general technical overview have been a pleasure to make the most of. 2023 is the 226th anniversary of the Cheshire Yeomanry, and their descendants in C Squadron Queen's own Yeomanry. I wish them all the best and thank them for their help and enthusiasm.

An enduring legacy, for me, of writing this book has been the privilege to get to know the historical intricacies of a fascinating undertaking. That undertaking extends well beyond the start and end of Operation Exporter in 1941.The rich depths of regimental histories, diaries, photographs and official records has animated the tale of a group of people and animals on a scale that has astonished me. These records have imbued the object of my research with a compelling vivacity. They have brought life to the project. Whether it is the details of an entire cavalry division travelling by train, or of the veterans of Exporter leading their equine comrades in arms to the euphemistically named remount depots in 1942. Although I have tried my best to do justice to these tales, my attempts inevitably pale in contrast to the raw source material.

As impregnably ill-qualified as I am to write this book, I am under no illusions about how much I owe to my sister-in-law Fliss, her husband Kev, Fergus who is now 7, Robert Gladding and the Cheshire Yeomanry Regimental Association (and of course Chris Seaton), Duncan Rogers and Michael Locicero at Helion, my wife Georgina and to my sister, Dr Washington. Finally, this book would not have been possible without the gracious assistance and permissions of the Cheshire Yeomanry Regimental Association. Their contributions were fundamental in ensuring this book sees the light of day. It is with deep and biting embarrassment that I also realise there are other people who should be acknowledged here and also those who should be acknowledged better. I would also like to take the opportunity to recognise the truly magnificent work that has gone before me; especially that of Lt. Col. Verdin, the nameless trojans at the Australian War Memorial who digitised all of their collection and made it so easy to navigate, the staff at the National Archives, and of course the team at Helion. If I have inadvertently infringed copyright I deeply apologise.

Trooper Mullen of the Cheshire Yeomanry and his equine charges at Acre c.1940.

Foreword

Horse-mounted cavalry's importance on the battlefield was always going to decline as the world began to mechanise in the early decades of the 20th century, but the shape of that decline may be very surprising to many readers. People may question how the British Army – a leading, modern army – might have resorted to using horse-mounted cavalry during the Second World War. As the present-day Squadron Leader of the Cheshire Yeomanry, the British regiment with the most mounted warfighting experience of any British regiment in the Second World War, these twilight years of cavalry are a fascinating part of our history and demonstrate how the use of cavalry did not become obsolete overnight. The scholarship in this book outlines, contextualises, and evaluates precisely how this came to be. In retrospect, given the scarcity of the resources and the challenging terrain facing allied forces in the Middle East, it is less surprising that horsemen were deployed for combat. This is certainly the view of modern-day Cheshire Yeomen who have a long and varied history to look back on.

Our experience with the final days of mounted cavalry in the Second World War are just one part of the Cheshire Yeomanry's journey towards a final dismounting, and Cheshire Yeomen have often found themselves in counter-intuitive engagements that would confound many people's understanding of the progression of military technology in the last century. We went into the First World War exercising on a confusing mixture of bicycles and horses[1], but we were eventually tasked on horseback to defend Norfolk from bombing raids by airships and early aeroplanes. Our first action of the War as a mounted regiment was engaging a German plane with our machine guns in February 1915[2]. As trench warfare commenced on the Western Front, the 2nd Duke of Westminster, a Major of the Cheshire Yeomanry[3], but working with the Royal Navy, was among the first to experiment with the idea of armoured cars. Inspired by armoured trains in South Africa, he bought Rolls-Royce cars at his own expense and tested a squadron of the "infernal motors" in an exercise against our horses at Beccles in Suffolk on New Year's Day 1915. Finding them successful – "we did not

---

1   Verdin, p.40.
2   Verdin, p.59.
3   Fletcher, p.29 and newspaper clipping of him in uniform.

have a chance"[4] – he was the first to deploy them overseas, using them in anger first at Ypres, and most daringly in a 120-mile raid to rescue shipwrecked British sailors from Senussi tribesmen at Bir Hakeim, where he won the Distinguished Service Order. After moving to Egypt, members of the Cheshire Yeomanry also fought in the Camel Corps, before in the latter stages of the First World War the first line of the Cheshire Yeomanry were converted to infantry[5] and the second line back to bicycles[6], but following the war we were fortunate enough to regain our horses in contrast to most of the British Army which was being mechanised. As Jonathan deftly explains in this volume, having experimented with motors and armour as early as 1915, during the Second World War we astonishingly had yeomanry back on camels and even fought aircraft as cavalry 26 years after we had first done so against airships. We went on to retain the horses late into the Second World War, operating from horseback in contact with the enemy in the Lebanon as recently as June 1941[7], becoming the "last regiment to fight on horses."

Eighty years after our last mounted action, the Cheshire Yeomanry are today one squadron of the wider Queen's Own Yeomanry, mounted on Jackal wheeled fighting vehicles and still working in the light cavalry role. Just as in the Second World War when we were on horseback, our job remains to screen either to the front or on the flanks of a larger force, finding the enemy and conducting raids when opportunities present themselves. The fighting platform we use may have changed many times and will undoubtedly keep changing in the future, but the role and fundamental tactics today of the British light cavalry very closely resembles that of our predecessors as described in this book.

Cheshire Yeoman past, present, and future are indebted to Jonathan for the scholarship he presents here, and his fascinating explanation of how the British came to be deploying horses so late in the 20th century.

Major Chris Seaton
Squadron Leader
C (Cheshire Yeomanry) Squadron
The Queen's Own Yeomanry

4   Verdin, p.50.
5   Verdin, p.80.
6   Verdin, p.172.
7   Verdin, p.318.

Introduction

The fact that Britain sent horse soldiers into combat during the Second World War has been almost entirely forgotten. To many the idea is risible. This is the inevitable result of how the historiography of warfare in the 20th century has evolved and will be covered in more depth below. In brief though, there are two notable trends in the study of cavalry[1] in particular during the 20th century: firstly, how widely and for how long cavalry were criticised for being ineffective in the First World War, a view predominant for many years and originally traceable to British official historian Brigadier General Sir James Edmonds; second, that the huge extent to which cavalry were employed in 1939-45 has been largely ignored. It is recognised that the Soviets and the Wehrmacht employed horse drawn transport extensively, but less attention is paid to the horse-mounted soldiers that almost all armies, including the British had under arms. Cavalry are generally regarded to have performed an unimportant role, and one that was only accorded them because of a lack of sufficient vehicles. Many have suggested with varying degrees of certainty, that generals in the 20th century only persisted with cavalry out of sentimental attachment. Even as highly a respected historian as Tim Travers has framed his disapproval of Haig in terms of the C-in-C's alignment with the use of cavalry.[2] Since Edmonds set this particular school of thought in motion, the work of Basil Liddell-Hart and J.F.C. Fuller, for example, have since squared all approval of cavalry post 1914 in the realms of reactionary and incompetent cavalry generals being emotionally bonded to cavalry glories of the past. By extension, the existence of British cavalry at the start of the Second World War is therefore easy to file under this heading - and has been done so. This

---

1   The term cavalry is employed here to denote mounted soldiers, not units who were once upon a time mounted soldiers, like the 11th Hussars or the Royal Scots Greys. These units, where appropriate are deemed armoured or mechanised, unless explicitly explained otherwise in that particular example.
2   As cited in David Kenyon, *Horsemen in No Man's Land: British Cavalry and Trench Warfare 1914-1918* (Pen and Sword: Barnsley, 2011), p.3, fn.8. See Tim Travers, *The Killing Ground:* The British Army, the Western Front and the Emergence of Modern Warfare 1900-1918 (London: Allen & Unwin, 1990) and *How the War Was Won, Command and Technology in the British Army on the Western Front, 1917-1918* (London: Routledge, 1992).

cavalry-traditionalist resistance to change is now termed 'The Liddell-Hart Paradigm'[3] and has continued with the likes of David Roberts in *The Storm of War*.[4] In the realms of public opinion, these persisting strands of thought appear to have become firmly ossified; and entangled. As such the historiography of 1914-18 cavalry and of 1939-45 cavalry needs to be addressed specifically and disentangled, given the current trend of academic opinion.

In part, the historiography of cavalry in the 20th century has become fairer and more rigorous. This has mainly developed since around the end of that century[5] as the understanding of First World War cavalry on the western front has become clearer. The Marquis of Anglesley wrote "Justice has never been done to the part played by the cavalry in France and Flanders during the years 1915 to 1918"[6]; and this was certainly true at the point he finished writing his eight-volume *History of the British Cavalry* in 1997. Described by David Kenyon as a "literary monument to the arm", Anglesey provided a balanced and detailed narrative account of the British cavalry in war and peace - most notably on the western front. It countered the vast majority of literature, and broader historical understanding which mainly regarded the use of cavalry in this theatre as anachronistic and futile. However, it was not the very focussed, analytical contribution that a fair hearing of the efficacy of cavalry in battle on the western front required, which in turn would allow the same service to be done for the cavalry of the Second World War. A more modern, analytical investigation into First World War cavalry was provided by Kenyon himself in 2011.[7] Kenyon's work – the most substantially analytical and the current leading title on the topic – built on the work of Steven Badsey.[8] Most notably Kenyon identified the tactical value of cavalry on the 1914-18 battlefield. This is significant both because cavalry were primarily seen, at least by Haig until mid-1918, as having a key operational rather than tactical role, and because their tactical contribution on the western front was potent when they were deployed effectively, as they were by Rawlinson at Amiens in 1918 – despite all the available technology later deemed as rendering them useless. The tactical successes of cavalry on the western front did not contribute to a wider recognition either then or after because there simply weren't enough of them being allowed to operate in the way in which they were most effective, and because Edmonds's view was quickly

---

3   Timothy Harrison-Place, *Military Training in the British Army 1940-1944: From Dunkirk to D-Day* (London: Frank Cass, 2000), p.95.
4   David Roberts, *The Storm of War* (London: Penguin, 2010).
5   A notable exception is Stephen Badsey's 1982 *Fire and the Sword: the British Army and the Arme Blanche controversy 1871-1921* (Doctoral thesis) (University of Cambridge: 1982).
6   Marquis of Anglesley, *A History of the British Cavalry*, Vol. VIII (London: Leo Cooper, 1997), p. xix. This quote is also cited by David Kenyon in his introduction to British cavalry in trench warfare.
7   David Kenyon, 2011.
8   Stephen Badsey, *Doctrine and Reform in the British Cavalry 1880-1918* (Aldershot: Ashgate, 2008).

adopted. The tactical value of cavalry in Palestine under Allenby in 1918 has been more widely recognised and is explicitly covered by Anglesey, and also by Cyril Falls whose 1964 *Armageddon* provides significant detail on British cavalry in Palestine during the First World War.[9] Falls's[10] work on the western front is scrutinised by Kenyon. What both Kenyon and Falls clearly identify and explain the effect of, is the fact that weaponry that could be used against the cavalry could also be used by the cavalry. Falls for example provides examples of Allenby's cavalry in Palestine in 1918 employing machine guns and armoured cars to suppress enemy soldiers, while sub-unit commanders (the squadron leaders) independently took the initiative to charge with lances and rout their enemy; a textbook example of this was performed at Musmus Pass by the 2nd Lancers under Captain Davidson. As has been made clear by Kenyon, the license to act swiftly was vital for cavalry to be successful, as they were most effectively used in swiftly exploiting the local successes of other arms. Kenyon also provides great detail on the effect of cavalry with their own machine guns and organic brigade horse artillery. Even on the western front this weaponry crucially allowed them to suppress positions that could then be either subsequently or simultaneously charged, when circumstances allowed them to use their initiative and exploit their maneuverability. Speed was also a feature that also helped a great deal in crossing exposed ground and incurring fewer casualties than slower-moving infantry.

Normally the cavalry on the western front were hampered by their view by Haig as being an operational asset; and therefore being designated as corps or army troops, who could therefore only act on the orders of corps or army commanders. These commanders in turn were only able to pass down the orders to take tactical objectives when the opportunity for cavalry to be used effectively had long since passed (and this did lead to massacres). Furthermore, it was not German machine guns that proved insurmountable obstacles to British cavalry - it was German machine guns in prepared positions. Machine guns that had been moved quickly and not had time to entrench were still vulnerable to cavalry acting under local initiative.

These key features of cavalry in 20th century warfare have only received reasonable scrutiny recently. This scrutiny is very much a phenomenon of modern military history; and it is only this recent perspective that has allowed the trend of historiography, which once designated cavalry as so anachronistic, to be recalibrated. It is also this hitherto widely accepted school of thought that has influenced any coherent understanding of cavalry in the Second World War.

---

9   Cyril Falls, *Armageddon 1918* (London: Weidenfeld and Nicolson, 1964).
10 Cyril Falls (ed.), *Military Operations France and Belgium 1917*, Vol. I (London: Macmillan, 1940).

In the interests of clarity, understanding the comparative dearth of scholarship on cavalry in the Second World War, begins with first addressing the aphorism that the potency of cavalry was buried in the trenches of the First World War. Kenyon has traced much of the historiographical bias against cavalry back to Edmonds.[11] In particular:

- The myth that British high command was dominated by incompetent cavalry officers (the Work of Prior and Wilson, Terraine, Sheffield and Travers et al has, at least within academic circles, disestablished this particular dogma).
- The 'last machine gun' myth; the use of cavalry was suicidally futile if the enemy still possessed even one working machine gun.
- The 'fodder' myth; supporting the cavalry corps during the First World War was a logistic millstone around the necks of an already hard-pressed British echelon and shipping infrastructure that drew supplies away from other more useful arms.[12]

Rigorous academic research, beginning with Terraine in the mid-1950s has dealt with the cavalry generals myth, that owed its existence in a great part to the memoirs of David Lloyd George. Kenyon has dealt with the other myths. But this has only served to deal with the misconceptions concerning cavalry during the First World War. Those concerning the Second World War, unchecked by the likes of Kenyon and Paddy Griffith, have persisted, benefitting from the fertile and deceptive ground soil laid originally by Edmonds.

This legacy was compounded into the wider interpretation of cavalry in the Second World War, by the Polish lancer myth of 1939. If taken at face value, this supports the Edmonds interpretation that the usefulness of cavalry was proven to have expired by the First World War and should never have been considered again. This Polish lancer myth began as Goebels inspired propaganda, most notably in the Nazi propaganda film *Kampfgeschwader Lützow*, in which Slovak soldiers dressed up as Polish cavalry.[13] The point of this propaganda was to highlight the comparative sophistication of the Third Reich against, in this case, Polish people.

---

11 J.E. Edmonds, (ed.), *History of the Great War Based on Official Documents, Military Operations France and Belgium 1918,* Vol V (London: HMSO 1945), p.196.
12 David Kenyon, *Horsemen in No Man's Land: British Cavalry and Trench Warfare 1914-1918* (Barnsley: Pen and Sword, 2011), p.3.
13 Stuart Dowell, 'Charge of the fake brigade: An enduring myth of the 1939-45 war is that Polish cavalry charged German tanks. They didn't' See *The First News* <https://www.thefirstnews.com/article/charge-of-the-fake-brigade-debunking-the-myth-of-the-wwii-cavalry-charge-against-german-tanks-2131> (accessed 6 August 2021).

The legacy of this film remarkably remains, and it is that most western history is still suspicious about the employment of cavalry in the Second World War. The surest evidence for this attitude lingering in British academic circles is that there has been no thorough investigation into the operational deployment of British cavalry – not even from Stephen Badsey or Roger Salmon who has written so effectively on the mechanisation of British cavalry (a process only completed in 1942).[14] As Janusz Piekalkiwicz wrote: "The role of cavalry in World War II has rarely been given the attention it deserves. The overriding impression from most histories and memoirs is of the clash of tank forces".[15] This is not a complete picture.

The evolution of the historiographical understanding of cavalry during the First World War is relevant to the second point of misunderstanding raised in the opening to this chapter - and the area in which this book falls. Namely the lack of analysis on cavalry in the First World War. With so much negative literature on the use of cavalry during 1914-18, until Badsey and Kenyon, it is perhaps no great surprise that so little interest was paid to the use of cavalry in an even more technology-dominated war a generation later. A noteworthy exception to this trend is Piekalkiewicz in his own detailed and descriptive account of cavalry. When Piekalkiewicz wrote *The Cavalry of World War II*,[16] he expressed that in all the histories then available (writing initially in 1976), there remained a historiographical gap. Namely the study of the use of cavalry, and this is still broadly the case - not least because Piekalkiewicz's work is far from being mainstream. That is not to say that some corners of the internet now recognise the role of cavalry during 1939-45, and in a commercially successful history, Colin Smith specifically mentions the contribution of British cavalry in Syria in 1941 in his history of the fighting against Vichy France and its colonies.[17] But the lead has not been followed.

Notwithstanding the contribution of the internet, Piekalkiewicz did for cavalry in the Second World War what Anglesey did for British cavalry in the First World War. However, Piekalkiewicz in terms of depth still stands almost alone on the topic, and his work, while detailed and narrative, is not a modern analytical investigation - though some of the interviews he uses in the book reveal fascinating accounts of the evolution of cavalry tactics of the Second World War, especially with the Red Army in Operation Bagration.

What most historians have ignored so far is that the British were also capable of effectively developing realistic tactics for cavalry in the 20th century. For example, after the Syria campaign in the summer of 1941, the British planned a role for mortar

---

14 Roger Salmon, *The Management of Change*: Mechanizing the British Regular and Household Cavalry Regiments 1918-1942. Roger Salmon. (Thesis for the University of Wolverhampton 2013).
15 Janusz Piekalkiewicz, *The Cavalry of World War II* (London: Orbis, 1979).
16 Janusz Piekalkiewicz, *The Cavalry of World War II* (London: Orbis, 1979).
17 Colin Smith, *England's Last War Against France: Fighting Vichy 1940-1942* (London: Phoenix, 2010).

and machine gun-armed cavalry to operate from mountains in the enemy's rear area and be resupplied by aircraft, although German failures in the USSR meant that this role never had to be tested. Logically it should not be a surprise though that cavalry tactics continued to develop throughout the Second World War, just as the tactics of other arms did. But nor was this merely a development forced on planners by the strictures of war. Throughout the interwar period, the British for example had been refining the operational role of cavalry, albeit with certain caveats.

Evolution of British Cavalry between the Wars

In broad military terms, the evolution of British operational procedures, between 1920 and 1935, is easily charted through the four interwar editions of its doctrine document, *Field Service Regulations*. The general staff also issued two further manuals at the end of the 1920s: *Mechanised and Armoured Formations* (1929) and *Modern Formations* (1931). These envisioned the British army as composed of brigade-sized building blocks: infantry brigades, cavalry brigades, light armoured brigades and mixed armoured brigades. All-arms capability would be achieved by putting these into divisions. The two types of division were infantry division and mobile division. Both would be all-arms and both would require cavalry. The recognition of cavalry brigades very clearly recognises the tactical value of cavalry for combat (on any battlefield), albeit in the absence of anything better. The cavalry brigade would be considerably more capable of cross country movement than the bussed infantry. The reconnaissance capability would of course be affected by the slow pace of modernisation over the *interbellum* years.

Given these hampering factors, and the overall vision for Britain's cavalry regiments, it is not surprising that the cavalry units committed to action in 1941 were yeomanry regiments of the Territorial Army. Furthermore, as explicable as the logic for retaining them was, it still failed to convince many, and Churchill was still demanding answers as to why they had been mobilised with horses in 1939, many months after he took office.

However, the recognition of cavalry as an operational asset remains valid. But it did come with two caveats: 1. There was no discernable tactical innovation for British cavalry between the wars. This should not hide the fact that the use of cavalry units was scrutinised. As with the rest of the army, the use of unit and sub-unit drills was not addressed. This lack of innovation was largely because: 2. The army had shown it had no intention of maintaining horsed cavalry long-term ever since 1921[18] as for example denoted when Archibald Montgomery-Massingberd, who later was to become GIGS, had accepted as such.[19] But in a conceptual context, the British

---

18   David French, *Raising Churchill's Army: The British Army and the War against Germany 1919-1945* (Oxford: OUP, 2000), p.37.
19   French, *Raising Churchill's Army*, p.37.

army specifically avoided laying out standard tactical drills for any of its units anyway, trusting to the initiative of unit commanders.[20]

Roger Salmon's research into British mechanisation[21] also identifies the official recognition of cavalry's operational role in British doctrine. In February 1938, with mechanisation still far from being complete, ongoing research was still yet being carried out into what kind of vehicle could be built to allow the British cavalry to execute their "multifarious duties… under the new conditions which will exist in the movement and engagement of modern mechanised armies."[22] The 'multifarious duties' needed to include the traditional (light) cavalry roles of close and distance reconnaissance, protective duties, pursuit and covering withdrawals, raids, and acting as a mobile reserve.[23] Although unsigned, the document detailing this appears to be the draft design of a 30mph machine-gun carrier.[24] As Salmon identifies, "The document is significant as it acknowledged the role of cavalry under 'modern' battle conditions", and Vickers's (severely hampered) effort to design a satisfactory vehicle[25] to replace it. Evidently the role of cavalry was still securely, if narrowly, established in British army operational doctrine, and of course the *FSR* officially enshrines this. The lingering need to maintain cavalry in the absence of sufficient vehicles also explains why the army issued the *Manual of Horsemastership, Equitation and Animal Transport-1937*, and why, as the government-published *Spitfire Manual 1940* was rolled out, so too was *Web Equipment, cavalry, pattern 1940*.

The mechanisation process was not yet complete, but this still is a lucid explanation for the existence of cavalry on the British ORBAT and should not be taken as evidence of sentimental attachment to horses. This then provides a firmer explanation as to why the War Office in 1939 mobilised the yeomanry with their horses; there *was* a clear operational role for them, and even if nobody wanted them to fulfil it, it would have been remiss if a gap that could be filled with available resources was left unfilled. Since the 1920s, the roles mentioned above were clearly being given over, more and more, to mechanised units, as funding arose. The army clearly regarded this metamorphosis of the cavalry as ineluctable, but it was still incomplete and this did not go unnoticed. There still weren't enough mechanised units; so some cavalry had to stay on the ORBAT for now. The gap in mechanised capability could not be allowed

20 French, *Raising Churchill's Army*.
21 Roger Salmon, *The Management of Change*: Mechanizing the British Regular and Household Cavalry Regiments 1918-1942. (University of Wolverhampton: 2013).
22 Vickers historical document 744; 'Cavalry Tank', unsigned draft, 25 February 1938. As cited in Salmon, *The Management of Change*.
23 Salmon, *The Management of Change*, p.281.
24 Vickers historical document 744; 'Cavalry Tank' as cited in Salmon, *The Management of Change*: *Mechanizing the British Regular and Household Cavalry Regiments 1918-1942*. (University of Wolverhampton: 2013).
25 Salmon, *The Management of Change*, p.281.

to mean a gap in overall operational capability. This was still the case, albeit due to unforeseen circumstances post-*Blitzkrieg*, in 1941.

Salmon's scrutiny of British Army mechanisation throughout the interwar period and into 1942 shows a very precise focus upon cavalry deployment, and one that is even more relevant to the subject of this book. He finds that in Egypt in the late twenties, the 12th Lancers' "role in war was chiefly reconnaissance, but by dismounting, three-quarters of a troop could carry out an infantry role [one in four men being tasked as horse-holders] working with other arms and getting around the flank of an enemy to pin them."[26] These are precisely the two duties that the yeomanry in 1941 were called upon to perform repeatedly in their war. The 12th Lancers' unit drills it should be pointed out, did not differ from those of other cavalry units, including the yeomanry in 1941, and this was despite the fact that the army was deliberately allowing local commanders to create their own tactical solutions.

On top of general war-fighting roles, there were other tasks that cavalry were well-equipped to do. Colonial security duties in Trans-Jordan and mandated Palestine involved the use of horsemen for the time being (i.e. between the wars). Horsed units were also maintained in British India, where in fact Arthur Sandeman led a doomed cavalry charge in 1942.[27] The main reason for the horse's continued use in these places was clearly the slow rate of mechanisation. The underlying cause behind this protracted modernisation process however is disputed. Nonetheless Roger Salmon and David French amply demonstrate that the slow mechanisation was evidently not the result of the Liddel-Hart paradigm.

Any interpretation of British Army equipment and deployment between 1918 and the late thirties must be scrutinised first through the lens of chronic under-investment.[28] Consequently the British maintained cavalry in far flung corners of the empire, (probably) not because of determined conceptualisation, but because it was cheaper and easier to keep these units mounted, until the funds materialised for armoured cars and the time to retrain presented themselves. Futhermore, the fact that horsed cavalry did the job sufficiently well, without being mechanised, was salient and undoubtedly counted against rapid mechanisation throughout the empire. The whole issue in microcosm is captured in the following statement:

---

26 Salmon, *The Management of Change*, p.103.
27 As members of the Indian army, Sandeman's cavalry brethren are not covered in this book.
28 Investment in the army after 1936 extended to creating a BEF for fighting on mainland Europe in the approaching war ... and virtually nothing else. Not even a larger reserve force – which would have been a comparatively cheap undertaking. See French and Salmon.

"In 1928 ... 'the main trouble in the way of mechanisation [sic] is the capital cost... that had frightened off "His Worthiness" [Sir Laming Worthing-Evans, Secretary of State for War]'.[29]

Coming from the Director of Staff Duties (whose key role involved overseeing the evolution of FSR), this strongly reinforces the view of French and Salmon. Mechanising the cavalry, in short, was not an issue any 20s or 30s Secretary of State for War could ever persuade the treasury was worth notable immediate investment. The issue of re-equipping the army was simply not a priority in the late 1920s, nor was it politically advisable. By the time that war was on the horizon in the mid-1930s, strategic policy was pushing the British army ever further down the list of priorities. The new pillars in national defence were the RAF, RADAR, the Royal Navy and the French army.[30] And if this meant a lowering of priority for the army as a whole, then it was doubly so for the cavalry.[31] One of the best indicators of the pressure on the treasury, either in the pacifist 1920s, or the volatile 1930s, is the exiguous rate of mechanisation; despite the fact that since 1920 the express plan had been to eventually mechanise all the cavalry. It took a general European war (and nothing less) in 1939 for the last of the regular units, and even then *only* these, to be mechanised. When British cavalry committed to action in 1941, they didn't even have the 1940 cavalry pattern webbing, which had been cancelled at the last minute, nor did they have Bren guns and had to make do with the older Hotchkiss guns. In fact the only discernible differences between them and the cavalry of 1907, was the lacing on their boots and the fact that their sabre grips had been upgraded to rubber. The continual trade-off nature of cavalry's place in the modernisation versus threat see-saw is exemplified in the words of the Chief of the Imperial General Staff, Field Marshal George Milne (C.I.G.S. 1926-1928), when he wrote to Sir Laming Worthington-Evans, the then Secretary of State for War:

> The Army in war must have some fast moving troops which will be able to protect it, and to perform the close reconnoitring duties which aeroplanes cannot do. Both these functions must be performed for the present by cavalry

---

29 LHCMA – LH11/1928/2, 'Talk with Colonel CNF Broad Director of Staff duties, Army and Navy Club', 2 February 1928. As cited in Salmon,, p.83, fn.130.
30 French, *Raising Churchill's Army*, p.275.
31 TNA WO 32/2842 Army Organisation: Cavalry (Code 14 (D)): Cavalry Committee: Final report 1926-1927; 20/Cavalry/612 no.6, 17 November 1927; also TNA WO 32/2845 Army Organisation: Cavalry (Code 14 (D)): Future organisation of the Cavalry: Sub-committee of Imperial Defence 1927-1928; 20/Cav/612 minute 19, 8 June 1928. As cited in Salmon, *The Management of Change*, p.100, fn. 201.

until we can afford mechanisation [sic]. You have cut them down, to what you consider, and what you have accepted, as the closest margin of safety.[32]

By the end of the inter-war period that margin of safety was the nine regiments of the yeomanry, and three regular regiments still kept as mounted cavalry.

The yeomanry, Britain's part-time cavalry, had no problem with remaining in a horsed role between 1919 and 1939 – they enjoyed it. And they never expected to do a serious job with the horses. Like all the other volunteers of Britain's Territorial Army, the yeomanry had been neither trained intensively, nor had they been expected to contribute to Britain's fighting strength since 1918. Although the war-clouds had started to loom well before September 1939, the yeomen were happy to mark time with the horses and a fun weekend role, until a more modern role was designed for them. Given their lowly level of priority, underfunding was naturally a decisive ingredient in creating this situation, as with all decisions that had been made about the yeomanry. One day, it had been assumed, they would no doubt be mechanised; but not before the chancellor's next budget. This theme was as true in 1939 as it had been in 1920. Consequently, their tactical repertoire did not evolve during this time-period either, despite the elucidating of operational doctrine identified in the above mentioned documents. A general reflection of the lowly priority the T.A. endured, is nicely encapsulated by Laurence Carr, the Director of Staff Duties at the War Office, who keenly felt the pressures of others' apathy and narrow-focussed investment. Possibly in response to the armoured evangelism of Percy Hobart and his rather grating ardour, Carr wrote to him in June 1939 through gritted teeth:

> You will recall that in April 1938 we received a charter to prepare a [Field Force] of 4 divs [divisions] and a mobile div to be rearmed for a war in the Middle East… The T.A. did not come in [to this charter] except for the necessity of providing them with a bare minimum training equipment.[33]

Apart from showing the lack of thought given to the T.A., this paucity of equipment is symbolic of the general dearth of attention and funding for the army as a whole; and the T.A. in particular. It should be noted that it had been even worse before the April 1938 spike in investment that came with the "charter" Carr mentions (the T.A. was actually able to start recruiting more widely as well). The bite of economy measures before that point was so severe that Territorial Army units were permitted to recruit only up to 60% of their wartime establishment. The result was a lack in credibility

---

32 WO 32/2846 Register 16/General/5558 Minute 14; Milne to Sir Laming Worthington-Evans, 3 November 1927. As cited in Salmon, p.94, fn. 177.
33 L.Carr to P.C.S Hobart, 2 June 1939, Hobart correspondence with Liddell-Hart (folder 1), Liddell-Hart Papers as cited in Salmon and in Allan R. Millett and Williamson Murray (eds.) Military Effectiveness: Vol. 2, The Interwar Period (Cambridge: Cambridge University Press, 2010), p.123, fn. 122.

and morale so that they were in fact only able to achieve 80% of this projected 60% strength.³⁴ David French is undoubtedly accurate when he indicates that government neglect of the force did little to encourage recruitment.³⁵ French asserts that The T.A. failed to recruit sufficiently and to attract sufficient quality until Hore-Belisha's reforms took hold. Then the quality changed markedly, despite the lack of quality equipment and instructors.³⁶ The yeomanry benefited as much as anyone else from this process - the best didn't want to go into the infantry. They had heard about the trenches from their fathers.

This meant that one undoubted asset the yeomanry possessed, unlike the regular army, was high-quality manpower. When the T.A. was expanded in April 1939, its doors were swamped with keen new recruits who realised that war was coming. Many of those who didn't want to be in the trenches went for units that everyone assumed would serve in the coming war as mechanised, artillery or signals units. Consequently, many astute young urban workers opted for the yeomanry cavalry without having ever ridden before - and were accepted by units who assumed they would not need skills in horsemastership when they were put onto a war-footing. The recruiters were mainly swayed by the recruits' clerical, and trade skills; prime material for conversion to technical roles in the swiftly metamorphosing army. The evidence for this stream of promising recruits comes from the regimental histories and personal memoirs of the yeomanry.³⁷ This stands in stark contrast to the recruiting experience of the T.A. prior to Leslie Hore-Belisha's rapid expansion of it in response to Chamberlain's token commitment to raising a continental army. When the real deluge of recruits descended upon the T.A. in 1939, most yeomanry units for example ended up doubling their numbers by taking on complete novices to horsemanship. Thus, when the territorial regiments were mobilised in September, around 50 % of the T.A. had completed a mere 20-35 training days when they were mobilised; the units were still classed as operational. This created a cavalry force that was evidently not envisioned to fight. As made clear by Salmon, French and Badsey, these cavalrymen would only remain mounted until the vehicles became available.

Although the British had been developing armoured tactics since 1919, lack of funding and the consequently slow development of armoured technology had meant a conceptual placeholder role for cavalry still had to be retained. It came as a surprise that this placeholder role was still being occupied in 1941.

The British, as is clear, did not want to be moving forward with cavalry on their ORBAT. French admirably clarifies the purpose and remit of the British army by 1939 and the strategic vision that guided it. He also makes clear that the purpose and

---

34   Anon., Military Notes, *Journal of the Royal United Services Institute*, 65 (1920), p.421.
35   French, *Raising Churchill's Army*, pp.54-55.
36   French, *Raising Churchill's Army*, pp.54-55.
37   Fitzgeorge-Parker, *No Secret so Close*; Verney *Going to the Wars*; Verdin. *The Cheshire (Earl of Chester's) Yeomanry*. The last British regiment to fight on horses, and Flanakin, *The Teddy Bear Lancers*.

remit of the British army was fundamentally different from those of other armies. It is therefore not such a surprise that other European armies retained cavalry. Nor is it a surprise that tactics for mounted soldiers outside the British army *had* changed in the 20th century. Existing historiography does not widely reflect the general developments in cavalry tactics, but the original source material does.

A reasonably detailed investigation into the use of cavalry during the Second World War reveals the extent and efficacy of their use. The Wehrmacht for example had mounted reconnaissance units in each infantry division, while the Soviets developed combined operations with armour, aircraft and cavalry that exploited the strengths of each arm. The British – for very particular reasons – used cavalry for flank protection and reconnaissance in the invasion of Vichy-held Syria. Yet so little recognition has been attributed to the tactical value of cavalry during 1939-45, beyond Piekalkiewicz.

It is of course important to note that Second World War cavalry were not the tactical equals of armour and contemporary infantry in all situations. The value of cavalry persisted because specific tasks in specific environments could still be done better by cavalry than by vehicles or foot soldiers. A more modern example of this set of circumstances that saw the use in Afghanistan of mounted men during the 21st century with the ODA 595 special forces group.[38] The fact that this was in very specific circumstances corresponds well with the point about 1939-45 cavalry; they were useful and contributed significantly in very specific circumstances. But they are also enshrined in the development between the wars of the British army's *FSR*. This is fundamentally because at no point did the British try to eradicate all their cavalry in a clean sweep[39]; even though in May 1919 the General Staff decided it wanted an army with "a good proportion of tanks in it".[40] Tanks themselves had of course been introduced piecemeal and had proved faulty technology. In fact the communications issues between different crews working in the same sub-unit during the First World War had only been solved by putting the company commander on a horse so that he could easily move back and forth between the crews as they engaged the enemy. This is merely one example of the overlap between horse and vehicle on the same battlefield, but it serves as a reminder that the emergence of one arm did not automatically precipitate the end of another. Tanks after all were not a direct replacement for cavalry.[41]

---

38   Anon., 'Interview: U.S. Special Forces ODA 595' *Frontline* (Date unknown) <https://www.pbs.org/wgbh/pages/frontline/shows/campaign/interviews/595.html> (accessed 12 August 2021).
See also, *How the 'Horse Soldiers' helped liberate Afghanistan from the Taliban 18 years ago* <https://www.militarytimes.com/news/your-military/2019/10/18/how-the-horse-soldiers-helped-liberate-afghanistan-from-the-taliban-18-years-ago/> (accessed 13 August 2021).
39   French, *Raising Churchill's Army*
40   French, *Raising Churchill's Army*, p.28
41   Kenyon, *Horsemen in No Man's Land*

As with the presence of mounted US soldiers in Afghanistan, the fact remains that cavalry, by virtue of their innate qualities contributed usefully to the course of the Second World War. These attributes included being faster than dismounted men, capable of crossing ground vehicles couldn't, capable of transporting and using exactly the same weapons that infantry employed. A more significant point though is that formations in other armies using cavalry with supporting arms *did* prove themselves the equals of mixed arm formations composed of other arms. For this the extensive research of Piekalkiewicz is invaluable, but so too is Général of the Army Henri Niessel's contribution "Cavalry" in the Basil Liddell-Hart edited *The Soviet Army* (1956).[42] Although the chapter and the book are about the Soviet Army as it stood in 1956, the compilation inevitably draws heavily on the experiences of 1939-45, hence the contributions of experts like Von Manstein, Student and Weygand. Niessel, commenting specifically on cavalry, was a fluent Russian speaker who knew Russia intimately and, as well as having served as the French Army's senior liaison officer to the Tsarist army, came to be regarded as the foremost French expert on the Russian/Soviet military. His contributions are specific and offer invaluable perspective on the Red Army cavalry. For the use of German cavalry in the war, the main source used here is Piekalkiewicz's book.

German cavalry is taken here as the first point for comparison, because it was Germany which had developed the use of armour and dive-bombers in mixed arm attacks the most effectively during the *interbellum*. The fact that Germany was also deploying cavalry, and doing so far more readily than Britain is therefore notable. German persistence with horses during the Second World Was was overwhelmingly not a product of arcane Prussian *Junker*-type officers holding up progress. It was because firstly, they lacked the full mechanised capacity required for an army of 98 invading divisions,[43] and secondly, for the uses and conditions of warfare that the Wehrmacht faced, cavalry were of considerable value. Note also that while the soviet army employed around 3 million horses during the war, the notably smaller German army used over 2.5 million – a figure not dissimilar – and therefore had a higher ratio of men to horses.[44] Nor were these all transport animals. The German army employed horsemen both in a cavalry division in its own right – some of which it deployed sword on sword against Polish adversaries in 1939 – and throughout the rest of the army; predominantly scouting for the infantry divisions. If this sounds anachronistic, then consider that infantry divisions moved at the speed of marching men, as most were not motorised. This meant that any forward troops of theirs did not necessarily need to go as fast as a speeding motorcycle; merely faster than the average man weighed down with kit. There are of course further tactical reasons that cavalry were effective

---

42 Henri Niessel, 'Cavalry', in B.H Liddell-Hart (ed.), *The Soviet Army* (London: Weidenfeld and Nicolson, 1956), pp.347-343.
43 Some 98 divisions invaded Poland in September 1939.
44 Piekalkiewicz, *The Cavalry of World War II.*

when operating ahead of infantry and armour, but these will be explored later. The most important reason that the Germans used cavalry extensively is that, over the terrain that they had to negotiate in Russia, cavalry were by far the most mobile arm and the best suited to negotiating swampland, steppe and mountainside in the absence of roads. They could go where vehicles couldn't, and they do it faster than men.

As Piekalkiewicz points out, despite contemporary technology, cavalry often proved themselves an "indispensable branch of the armed forces", and of key tactical and operational value.[45] That is not to say that they were not misused and tasked with charging prepared defences unsupported, but that their role was of significant value and was unique – it could only be done by cavalry. As a result, their extensive use by the Germans should not be surprising.

During the Russian campaign, every Wehrmacht infantry division had a mounted reconnaissance battalion, and their horsemen were ideal for reconnaissance in many different terrains. They were in fact used very heavily; they not only patrolled the division's main line of advance, but also covered each flank, and therefore they had to be on the move right round the clock. While some patrols would return to the division around 11 o'clock at night, others would remain out on task for days at a time, redeploying each day according to radio-issued orders. The seemingly endless availability of grass for their horses presumably facilitated this. Given these characteristics of German cavalry, it should be less of a surprise that the British sought to use their own cavalry too, in more rocky terrain and for exactly the same roles.

There are two points though to be made about the German cavalry. First, even after the success of *Blitzkrieg* in 1940, there was still plenty of hostility within the Wehrmacht's officer class to the newfangled way of fighting.[46] On one occasion a contemporary of Guderian, the father of Blitzkrieg, said of tanks 'To hell with combat! They're supposed to carry flour!'[47] So it is conceivable that there might have been some entrenched thinking linked to cavalry. Secondly, although the Germans disbanded their cavalry in 1942, they soon recognised their mistake and found themselves scrabbling to recruit a new cavalry arm from anti-communist Cossacks. In other words, just as the British did not have the capacity to wholesale replace cavalry with tanks in the First World War, not that they ever countenanced it, so the Germans were unable to do so effectively when they tried during the Second World War. Those disputing the effectiveness of the troops on the ground though should refer not only to the speed with which a cavalry arm was re-raised in 1943, but to the fact that in 1939 Polish casualties included not just those suffering from machine-gun bullets and shrapnel, but also those suffering from the cuts of German cavalry sabres.

---

45 Piekalkiewicz, *The Cavalry of World War II*.
46 Heinz Guderian, *Panzer Leader*, trans. Constantine Fitzgibbon, (London: Penguin, 2009).
47 Heinz Guderian, *Panzer Leader*, p.21.

Red Army Cavalry

Those who took on Stalin's cavalry discovered an even wider range of wounds was possible. This is because the Red Army used a wide variety of weaponry in its cavalry divisions and had a far more aggressive role for its horsemen.

The Red Army has become notorious for a scant regard to the lives of its soldiers and stories of penal battalions abound, as do those of NKVD battalions machine-gunning suspected deserters *en masse*. However, Soviet reasons for using cavalry were not because they were happy to commit hapless soldiers and expendable animal transport to their deaths for marginal gains using primitive tactics. First and foremost, they used cavalry because no other arm was capable of handling the Russian terrain as well. But there were also key tactical elements that the presence of cavalry gave to mixed arm groupings, even those that included mechanised units. Each cavalry division also contained lorry-borne units, much as each German cavalry regiment maintained platoons of Adler scout cars, and British yeomanry regiments Motor Transport sections and motorcycles. Horses and vehicles both contributed different strengths to mixed units and in the Soviet forces, and despite lacking an apparent strategic role, cavalry had a clear tactical point of difference when it came to combat.

The recognition of cavalry's unique value is seen in the Order of Battle (ORBAT) of Soviet cavalry divisions. These divisions also included supporting tanks and artillery complete with specialist cross-country vehicles thus enabling the motorised elements to keep up with the cavalry.

In any one Soviet cavalry regiment (using soviet naming conventions) there were:

- 4 squadrons of horsemen (about a 100-120 each), with 8 light machine-guns; 6 anti-tank rifles, and a large number of sub-machine-guns;
- 1 squadron armed with 16 machine-guns (presumably belt-fed maxim-type guns)
- 1 battery of 76mm Field guns (light artillery comparable to mountain warfare guns);
- 1 battery of 45 mm anti-tank guns (eminently respectable throughout the war);
- 1 squadron armed with 12 medium mortars (82mm – the same sort of weapon was issued to most infantry battalions in most of the armies in the Second World War to significantly enhance a battalion's fire-power);
- 1 anti-aircraft troop (machine-guns)
- 1 Signal troop
- 1 Reconnaissance troop;
- 1 Pioneer troop
- 1 Chemical troop

The considerable fire-power of these units was augmented by the additional fire-power of the cavalry division to which each regiment belonged. The divisional assets included a battalion of tanks, an artillery regiment armed with 76 mm guns and two batteries of 120 mm mortars and further anti-aircraft weaponry.[48]

In simple terms, a Soviet cavalry formation, of any size, was equipped to not just reconnoitre, but to fight through and launch diversionary or preliminary attacks, and to do it against anything the enemy could bring to bear. As such they had to be formidably armed. However, despite their fire-power, and the fire-power likely to be opposing them, there was clear recognition that deploying extensive numbers of horse-mounted soldiers was principally to exploit the terrain and tactical environment rather than just destroy enemy fighting units. The latter could be done though, and the horses made all this fire power more manoeuvrable than it would otherwise be. Notably, the ORBAT of a cavalry division included tanks specifically *in order* to allow the horsemen to carry out their role better.

By way of comparison, the ORBAT of a British yeomanry regiment began the same way; with 4 squadrons of horsemen and a similar quantity of light-machine guns, anti-tank rifles (though these were useless against anything other than scout-cars) and the sub-machine guns. The next item on the list was very similar – the yeomanry regiments each boasted a highly effective machine-gun troop, though equipped with only four Vickers guns, (belt-fed, water cooled medium machine guns mounted on a tripod and requiring a crew of three). But that is where the similarities – and the fire-power of a yeomanry regiment – stopped. In other words, they were nowhere near as well equipped to fight with the enemy and were very much reconnaissance troops. This is reflected in the fact that the British use of cavalry was virtually identical to that of the reconnaissance battalions in German infantry divisions. Inevitably, the German reconnaissance "battalions" were in fact only around 200 men and horses each; and only equipped for reconnaissance rather than fighting through. But then again, the Soviet forces had a very different approach to reconnaissance, preferring to fight the enemy to find out their strength.

The Soviet forces in Russia were invariably fighting where there was space to deploy cavalry to the rear of the enemy lead units that were being engaged by Soviet armoured groups. The crucial point here is that the Red Army developed doctrines for the cavalry to operate *with* tanks, and never as a replacement *for* tanks. Cavalry were not a stop-gap, as they were in the British army. The basis of the doctrine was that cavalry would either screen and link between advancing columns of armour and infantry; or that armour would create the breakthrough and cavalry would then rush through into the rear to exploit the space. This is a role Haig is now vilified for planning during the First World War (his mistake was believing that cavalry were an operational asset for exploiting major breakthroughs rather than a tactical asset for exploiting local breakthroughs). Niessel continually refers to the formations in which cavalry were employed large scale as "mobile formations".[49] In short, regardless of the technology

---

48 Niessel, *Cavalry* pp. 337-8.
49 Niessel, *Cavalry* pp. 337-8.

available to the Red Army at any stage of the war, horsed cavalry performed a unique movement capability that the Soviets still needed.

Given the clearly defined role of cavalry within Stalin's military machine, and the difficult terrain with few roads, it is unsurprising that the Soviets continued to maintain cavalry divisions after the war. After all, there were plenty of civilian Soviet horses to call on. By 1951 there remained 12 divisions, though by 1956 these had been further cut; albeit while maintaining a separate 10 Mongolian cavalry divisions in Outer Mongolia.[50] Consider further the use of horses in Afghanistan against the Taliban. Terrain is the inherent determining factor in the efficacy of cavalry.

The Red Army of the Second World War exploited the mobility of cavalry for significant operations; such as using an entire corps of cavalry to advance 170km behind a large German formation, and then to hold ground there for five days. Similar feats were repeated on a number of occasions. This also shows the defensive capabilities of cavalry; just as when Soviet cavalry were detailed to fight two large-scale rearguard actions at Stalingrad and Kharkov. In the latter, three Soviet cavalry divisions took on two German armoured divisions and an infantry division. After nine days of fighting, the Germans pulled back when Soviet infantry reinforcements were able to link up.[51] No doubt the mobility and concealment properties of cavalry went a long way to helping a Soviet formation protect an area in-depth, but the considerable fire-power of a Soviet cavalry division was undoubtedly the predominant factor in their survival.

In this case, cavalry presented the theatre commander with an operational asset, as well as a tactical one. That said, horses are a trickier logistical challenge than vehicles, being neither as robust nor as capable over great distances while retaining unit cohesion. At least this was the experience of the Soviets who, like everyone else, found the logistics of cavalry difficult, and sometimes had to resupply them by air when cavalry columns couldn't be diverted quickly enough to meet their resupplies. As tempting as it is to categorise this combination of cavalry with air-drop as a measure of the Soviet genius for exploiting their benefits, the fact remains that the air-drop option was as much the product of cavalry's failings.[52]

Red Army cavalry doctrine, while impressive, was not actually a product of the response to Operation 'Barbarossa'. Cavalry offensive operations, inevitably because of similar operational conditions, closely reflected those of General Büdenny (specifically

---

50 Niessel, *Cavalry* pp.343
51 Niessel, *Cavalry* pp.341-3
52 The Red Army came to draw some conclusions about horse stamina from the colour of the animals: Brown horses were prone to go lame more than average and suffered badly from bruises, black horses lacked the same stamina of other colours, and whites were the most trouble free. See Piekalkiewicz *The Cavalry of World War II* pp.243-244. Ultimately the conclusions about black horses lacking stamina are the least convincing, as other factors would have muddied the waters so much – breed of horse, diet, quantity of rations, conditioning (long-term and short-term).

dismissed by Falls as mounted infantry, rather than cavalry[53]) in the 1920 Polish war. The units involved also showed strong similarities in terms of unit organisation and equipment, corps ORBAT and doctrine.[54] They also conceptualised a mixed cavalry and tank army for the Finnish war,[55] specifically because of the singular terrain, although they never actually deployed it. In short, the Red Army had always seen cavalry as a worthwhile component of their forces – even while they developed a scheme for paratroopers in the 1920s.

By summer 1944 the Soviets had developed cavalry tactics to complement their impressive armoured capabilities. This is evident in the divisional tactics of the Red Army's cavalry during Operation Bagration:

> As we were planning our assault on the river Dvina positions we debated the problem of how to put the cavalry corps to their most effective use. In modern warfare, with extensive use made of tanks and automatic weapons, the cavalry is highly vulnerable. After analysing the difficulties from all points of view we decided to protect them against the enemy armoured attacks with a diamond-shaped formation of armoured units.[56]

With the role of both tanks and cavalry clearly defined, the tanks would destroy enemy hardware, especially armour and gun positions, while the latter would pursue the retreating infantry. This would firstly destroy supporting infantry units, and at the very least would ensure that there was no time for them to reorganise and establish snap ambush positions against the Soviet tanks. German infantry were prone to counter-attacking from anywhere, even against armour, and the Soviets' immediate flushing through of cavalry would prevent this. Where the enemy had effective machine-gun positions, the cavalry would wait merely until Red Army infantry arrived, before pushing on. Essentially this ensured speed of advance, as the armour could continue at a fairly steady rate. It should be noted that the Red Army here planned for using cavalry in a far more congested battlefield than the British were to in Syria, and on a very different scale.

The Soviets had also learned that pushing on to exploit with cavalry could be overdone and that their daily fighting capacity was limited:

---

53 Falls, *Armageddon*. This is an unconvincing premise – not least because Falls neither explains his categorisation or his reasons. Nor does he refer to the British use of cavalry in Syria in 1941.
54 Niessel, *Cavalry*.
55 Niessel, *Cavalry* pp. 89-90.
56 General P.I. Batov as referenced in Piekalkiewicz *The Cavalry of World War II* (no citation given) p.222.

After a strenuous engagement a cavalry unit needs some time to restore its hordes to fighting trim."[57]

In his contribution to Liddell-Hart's book, Niessel applies this aphorism as an eternal truth when dealing with horses, and as a comment on their durability. The British certainly found that it took weeks to get their cavalry division back up to fitness, after the sea journey across the Mediterranean. However it is also worth noting that in an army as large as that of the Soviets', individual unit discipline may not have been consistent. The British 1st Cavalry Division found that paying regular attention to their horses' feet went a very long way towards maintaining the mobility of their cavalry units. Stanley Christopherson refers to this explicitly in his experiences in Palestine where the Sherwood Rangers, who regularly checked their horses found they "lasted out the journey very well [despite the heat] and have suffered hardly any ill effects."[58] The British had also encountered in Palestine in 1917-18 that horses could in fact, with good care, be pushed to considerable feats. The 4th Cavalry Division marched 70 miles in 34 hours, losing only 26 horses lame. This speaks of prodigious levels of conditioning for the horses, of excellent veterinary care and of rigorous individual discipline. It is more than possible that these elements of personal and unit discipline were not standard throughout the very large Red cavalry arm.

Despite the apparent contradiction, cavalry forces were clearly far from technologically backward and it should be noted that the make-up of cavalry divisions did evolve throughout the war – and that the ratio of mechanised units to horsed units within a Red Army cavalry division did increase, but never replaced them. In other words, the Soviets recognised the tactical and operational value of horses throughout the war, despite having ever better, and more, vehicles at their disposal as the war went on. Similarly the Germans had better tanks after their short-term and ill-advised scrapping of cavalry than before it, but still reintroduced them.

By 1944, although the Germans had cavalry divisions again, they had scrapped the mounted reconnaissance battalions. Similarly, both the British and Soviets developed new tactical doctrines for cavalry once they'd seen how they fared on operations. It is testament to the effectiveness of the British cavalry that the newly developed tactical doctrine – developed to fight a possible German invasion of Syria – was significantly more ambitious than their pre-1941 arrangement. Interestingly, the operational use of cavalry that the British developed as a result of Syria used very similar principles to those of the Soviets and had them operating in a far more "Soviet" way. The new proposals included larding the yeomanry with mortars, which had been conspicuous by their absence in Syria. The cavalry were also to be deployed in the rear of the enemy advance, using the terrain to their advantage and being resupplied by aircraft. The

---

57   Niessel, *Cavalry*, p.340.
58   James Holland (ed.), *An Englishman at War: The Wartime Diaries of Stanley Christopherson DSO, MC, TD: 1939-1945* (London: Bantam Press, 2014), p.26.

rationale for using aircraft was however to be a response to the versatility of cavalry rather than to their limitations, as with the Red Army.

One striking difference however, is that the Soviets always expected to use cavalry in their army, even though the Red Army was the cornerstone of their national defence. The British meanwhile deployed cavalry, against their own expectation, in a comparatively peripheral operation. Much to everyone's surprise their cavalry were highly useful and proved to be needed a great deal throughout the campaign. Their subsequent re-rolling of Bren-carrier crews as cavalry during the Syria campaign indicates just how much they had under-appreciated the capabilities of the cavalry in that environment. The extent to which cavalry played a meaningful part - and were needed - deserves more attention that it has received.

Pielalkiewicz was righting the historiographical wrongs of omission suffered by the cavalry of his chosen era. Anglesey, Badsey and Kenyon were righting the wrongs of misinterpretation suffered in theirs'. Given that Piekalkiewicz was writing about the war in only 1976, and it took until Badsey and Kenyon to do the same service for the cavalry of 1914-18, this is actually quite a quick turnaround. Nevertheless, it is an incomplete one even taking Niessel's work into consideration.

Piekalkiewicz, a Pole who himself fought against the Third Reich, approached *The Cavalry of World War II* as a general history of the war's horsed units. As with Anglesley's First World War volume, the broad and narrative nature of what he wrote precluded an analytical investigation into British cavalry during the Second World War. That gap still exists. However the information and source material that would cover it does too and offers a rich seam of hitherto untapped material. The war diaries of the units that served in Syria in 1941 are at the National Archives in Kew. Fragmentary personal memoirs and biographies appear as well; those of John Verney of the North Somerset Yeomanry[59], Bruce Hobbs of the Yorkshire Dragoons[60] and Len Flanakin[61] of the Warwickshire Yeomanry. There is also the most substantial, detailed and clearly structured source of all; in the regimental history of the Cheshire Yeomanry.[62] This particular account compiled by a Cheshire Yeomanry officer, John Verdin, who served with the Cheshire Yeomanry in peacetime during the 1930s and later in the Syria campaign.

Taken together, these sources create a tapestry that chronicles the exploits of British horsed cavalry in the Second World War. Taken alone, Verdin's regimental history of the Cheshire Yeomanry provides more detail than Piekalkiewicz, as well

---

59 See John Verney, *Going to the Wars* (Collins: London 1955).
60 See Tim Fitzgeorge-Parker, *No Secret so Close: The Biography of Bruce Hobbs* (London: Pelham, 1984).
61 Len Flanakin, *The Teddy Bear Lancers* (Warwick,: The Warwickshire Yeomanry Museum Trust, 2010).
62 Sir Richard Verdin, *The Cheshire [Earl of Chester's] Yeomanry 1898-1967: The Last Regiment to Fight on Horses* (Birkenhead: Willmer Brothers Limited, 1971). In fairness, Piekalkiewicz, does make reference to this text.

as a sense of evolution. Add all the available sources, including the various war diaries - and especially that of the Cheshire Yeomanry in 1941[63] and there is a broad base of evidence and further first-hand detail. Strikingly, there is then an analytical perspective of the use of cavalry in the wake of the Syrian campaign. A primary source. This analysis comes from the compilers of the 7th Australian Division[64] war diary, the parent formation for 3rd cavalry brigade in Operation "Exporter". This document provides both day-to-day recording of Operation Exporter and its build up, which included the minutes of the decision to include cavalry, and it also provides a post-operation reflection. Finally, there are the 7th Division war diary's appendices, such as that explaining the additional cavalry force that the Australians raised during the operation to augment the British cavalry they suddenly found so useful – a phenomenon echoed in the US army's ODA 595 in Afghanistan.

In brief, there is a rich seam of material on British horsed cavalry in action in 1941. But no modern investigative analysis of that material. Work such as Piekalkiewicz's show how widespread and effective the use of cavalry was in the Second World War; as does Niessel's chapter in Liddell-Hart's 1956 compilation *The Soviet Army*.[65] But the investigation that analyses the efficacy of British cavalry as a whole in Syria does not exist. This volume is intended to start building into that gap; specifically by investigating the role of British cavalry on Operation Exporter in Syria in 1941. By way of contextualisation, this volume also aims to identify some strengths of cavalry that have been hitherto under-analysed or ignored. This also makes it an investigation into the nature of specific units that contributed to this arm.

---

63 TNAWO 169/1396: Cheshire Yeomanry War Diary 1941.
64 Australian War Memorial (AWM) WO 52 1/5/14 Divisions: 7 Australian Division General Staff Branch (7 Aust Div GS Branch).
65 Henri Niessel, *Cavalry*.

1

Two-Legged Yeomanry

The T.A.'s cavalry in 1939 was still theoretically required to cover a capability gap in a British army that had been neglected for two decades. As Milne pointed out in 1927, treasury cuts meant that cavalry was still required, and the same driver meant the situation persisted in 1939. The composition of the mobile formations also dictated that cavalry be retained; and the force was accordingly mustered. By the end of October the cavalry arm had its full establishment of men and horses. It was not however fit to fight, even if required to do so. This put it on the same footing as a great deal of the T.A.[1]

The fighting effectiveness of the British army as a whole in 1939, was the reflection of its position in Britain's strategic intentions, and of the operational doctrine that had evolved in *FSR* since 1920. It would take around two years of training before they could match German units.[2] The T.A. and more specifically the cavalry were a microcosm of that – the cavalry because it would take until 1941 to be ready to fight and until 1942 to be assigned a suitable role in the war against the Germany. The cavalry is in fact further representative of the rest of the British Army because its manpower was over time able to develop and meet the standards of its foes during the second half of the war despite its composition and leadership at the start – an element that has been vilified in the relevant historiography since 1945.

Like much of the T.A., the composition of the yeomanry was in fact a significant strength. The lack of training each recruit had received was in contrast to the quality of the manpower in those units. Again, this is a microcosm of the T.A. in 1939 as a whole. The yeomanry, being part of the T.A., of course benefited from the influx of quality recruits. There was a clear enthusiasm to join the reserve forces, so the books of the RAF and Naval reserves were very soon full, and in the army units like the territorial artillery batteries or signals were also soon full. Memoirs of the yeomanry suggest that the yeomanry regiments attracted recruits in their own right, however

---

1 French, *Raising Churchill's Army.*
2 French, *Raising Churchill's Army*, p.64.

their regimental prestige was probably incidental, rather than decisive, in attracting recruits during the final count-down to war.

That said, the yeomanry profiles was high in their localities; yeomanry race meetings for instance were commonplace and attracted all strata of rural society. George Hay identifies this key "element of yeomanry identity"[3] as far back as the mid-19th century. Hay shows the closely intertwined trinity of strands in many rural lives, of yeomanry, racing and hunting right up to 1914. The accounts of junior officers joining the yeomanry in 1939 suggest that little of this had changed since the great war. Indeed, the new junior officers sent from urban environs to join the yeomanry in 1939 cite these predilections among their new colleagues as rather disagreeable, yet overriding, features of a rural clannishness and insularity that outsiders stumbled up against.[4]

"My brother officers [in the yeomanry immediately pre-war]" John Verney writes in his 1955 memoir of the war "were squires, farmers, land agents and the like, born and bred in the country and sharing a hundred tastes and acquaintances from childhood."[5] While conceding that his own more sophisticated interests sounded "priggish", Verney complains that "None of my brother officers had ever heard of Proust or of Picasso. Nor did this gap in their education trouble them unduly."[6] The officer's mess of the North Somerset Yeomanry (referred to by Verney in his memoirs under the pseudonym "Barsetshire Yeomanry") was clearly not a welcoming environment to sophisticated young men from London. Nor was this insularity peculiar to the North Somerset Yeomanry. Bruce Hobbs also noticed the tension between the two mindsets: "When we arrived [as an officer, at his second regiment, the Yorkshire Dragoons], the ante-room [of the officers' mess] was empty except for three subalterns who had recently arrived from the Inns of Court, an officer-producing territorial unit from London... They had been with the Yorkshire Dragoons for about a month, of which it appeared they had hated every minute. They told us 'This is a terrible crowd. You won't enjoy it at all. Unless you're hunting, shooting and fishing people, you've got no chance!'"[7] Hobbs actually dismissed their claims, citing his own experience as proof of their distorted perspective – but Hobbs was unlikely to experience any hostility, as he had been hunting since the age of six and was already a Grand National winning jockey.

Stanley Christopherson had also been warned of the attitude he could expect when he joined the Sherwood Rangers and was "slightly apprehensive as we had heard the regiment boasted three Masters of Fox Hounds and that the pre-war officers were

---

3 George Hay, *The Yeomanry Cavalry and Military Identities in Rural Britain*, 1815-1914 (London: Palgrave Macmillan, 2017).
4 In the 19th century some units, like the Royal West Kent Yeomanry even had their own pack of hounds. see Hay and *The Standard*, 20 January 1892.
5 Verney, *Going to the Wars*, p.15.
6 Verney, *Going to the Wars*, p.16.
7 Fitzgeorge-Parker, *No Secret So Close*, p.83.

extremely wealthy and insular."⁸ However, despite being a London professional, he reported that a mess which even featured Donny Player, the heir to the Player's Cigarette fortune and a true *aficionado* of horses, was very welcoming. But then again, he was socially acquainted with a number of his new brother officers already. Also, Christopherson's editor James Holland is quick to point out that his subject's generosity of spirit does obscure the fact that other officers in his own regiment were not made as comfortable on joining. "John Semken, who joined the Rangers from the Inns of Court a few months after [Christopherson], says they were warned beforehand that they would not be welcomed with open arms, and that some, [including Christopherson] had been received quite huffily by the Earl of Yarborough, who believed it was still up to him to choose the officers for "his" regiment. 'They worked for a living', says John Semken, 'and didn't keep horses or hunt twice a week. They hadn't been to Eton or Harrow, so they had nothing to talk about and were pretty roughly treated."⁹

The driving factors behind this maltreatment of outsiders may well be due to simple snobbery, but the lack of a rigorous education in some of the lesser public schools that more provincial yeomanry officers might have attended (as alluded to by Verney rather than Semken) may also have played a part. At least equally important though must be the close-knit nature of rural society in the run up to the war – just as it had been for a century before. Scrutiny of *The Times* for 1937 and 1938 shows how established and popular the yeomanry races were for example, and the trinity of races, yeomanry and hunting was evidently still secure. "It was because of these ties that regiments like the Wiltshire Yeomanry existed from 1794 through to 1920 and beyond without disbandment [in actual fact the Royal Wiltshire Yeomanry mobilised with 1st Cavalry Division in 1939], why so many families became attached through generations, and why local newspapers reported their exploits and encouraged participation."¹⁰ They even reported "cavalry charges" by the Cheshire Yeomanry during the Syria campaign.¹¹

In the yeomanry of 1938-39, Verney, Hobbs and Christopherson don't indicate a social change in the officer corps since the 19th century. However, Hobbs's account of changes in the enlisted soldiery does, and it concurs with Verdin's, the chronicler of the Cheshire Yeomanry. They both describe these men as keen young townsmen, and very different from previous generations. Hobbs identified them as mostly bank clerks and professional men "– all a terribly nice lot, but ..., who knew very little about horses. With the approach of war the Territorial Army had become popular, particularly the North Somerset Yeomanry".¹²

---

8   Holland, *An Englishman at War*, p.14.
9   Holland, *An Englishman at War*, p.16.
10 Hay, *The Yeomanry Cavalry and Military Identities in Rural Britain*, p.135.
11 *Manchester Evening Chronicle* 14 June 1941.
12 Fitzgeorge-Parker, *No Secret So Close*, p.69.

Up until the First World War, the old estates had supplied men and horses for the likes of the Cheshire yeomanry. The word "obligation"[13] is used in this analysis by Verdin – and was in fact set-out in a clause in the tenancy contracts for estate-workers. Farmers and their sons were clearly part of the yeomanry demographic too, and consequently there was obligation involved in their joining as well. But this phenomenon had clearly ceased with the coming of the 1914-18 war. Following this, it was men employed in the towns who proved to be the main source of recruits, and Verdin is unequivocal in his assertion that this was an improvement. As chronicler of the full history of his family regiment, he would be in a good position to judge, and as an officer who led these sharp young recruits into battle, he would be in a strong position to comment on their effectiveness.

Hobbs's own observation that the yeomanry of 1939 were "clerks and professional men" is telling. These men after all would have to be adequately literate, in a way that many conscripted infantry recruits clearly weren't. One regular officer who served with the T.A. observed ruefully after the Hore-Belisha recruiting drive of 1938, that the recruits 'were what the regulars would have given their eye-teeth for as peacetime recruits.'[14] Many of the new yeomen were clearly well-qualified in other fields as well. The memorialists provide an interesting set of examples for this. The memoirs of Len Flanakin of the Warwickshire Yeomanry and Clifford Wrigglesworth of the Yorkshire Dragoons, indicate that both men worked in the building trade in qualified roles. They were indicative of the higher calibre of raw material joining the ranks of the T.A. in 1938-9. Flanakin is self-deprecating about his motives for joining; he cites the regular get-togethers in the pub. However the fact is that he was already on a qualified man's salary, could afford a motorbike and went out dancing regularly. This shows that his life was already a full one before he joined. Wrigglesworth meanwhile worked in the building trade in Leeds. He expected war and despite having applied for the South African police, decided to enlist in Britain because he thought he ought to do his bit. He had volunteered for the Royal Navy and RAF but was only offered a regular engagement – which many were refused – but he didn't want it and he was told there were volunteer vacancies in cavalry of the line (in October 1939). This is how he entered the ranks of the 1st Cavalry Division. The yeomanry was clearly drawing high-calibre recruits.

However the various yeomen entered service, half of them still joined as raw recruits in April 1939 when the units' strengths were doubled. As detailed above, there was a rush on the T.A. including the horse-bound yeomanry, and therefore these regiments were free to pick and choose who they let in. The resultantly high-calibre of recruit meant that many went on to be commissioned in the subsequent war.[15]

13 Verdin, *The Cheshire Yeomanry*.
14 Brig. S. Bidwell, 'After the Wall Came Tumbling Down: A Historical Perspective', *Journal of the Royal United Services Institute*, 135 (1990), p.60.
15 Verdin *The Cheshire Yeomanry*, p.215. See also French, *Raising Churchill's Army*.

For the likes of Flanakin, who had joined in the Spring of 1939, there was at least a summer's worth of ordinary T.A. training to get through before the balloon went up. This consisted of weekly drill nights (a couple of hours training at the local T.A. centre) with the rest of the troop, then a training weekend once every two or three weeks with the rest of the regiment, often in a farmer's field. This pattern indeed still stands in today's army reserve. However, there were slight variations to this pattern depending on the soldier's role. If they were a new recruit, then the Cheshire Yeomanry for example had them reporting for riding training every Sunday between April and July. If the soldier was an officer, then they did not need to attend any drill night at all.

In the absence of the officers, drill nights were run by the N.C.O.s. It actually seems that the yeomanry as a whole was very much N.C.O dominated; Verdin (himself a yeomanry officer) reporting that the "real burden however fell on the S.S.M.s and P.S.I.s and most squadrons would have run equally as smoothly with their Squadron Leader abroad."[16] For interest, he also notes that "to be a junior officer in the Cheshire Yeomanry was not a great military strain though it could well be a constitutional one."[17] Alcohol consumption evidently took its toll – though it should be added that it took its toll on all the yeomanry, not just the officers. It should also be noted that the *modus operandi* worked as much as it needed to in peace-time. Verney reports a very similar life in the "Barsetshire" yeomanry, but specifically identifies the effective working relationship between the N.C.O.s and officers:

> The happy relationship between officers and sergeants was an endearing, in fact an essential feature of pre-war Yeomanry camps. Many of the N.C.O.s were successful businessmen who looked upon this brand of soldiering as a fortnight's escape from responsibility [i.e. annual summer camp], with free riding thrown in. Between them they could have bought up the impecunious squirearchy, from which the officers were mainly recruited, without feeling it. [The R.S.M.] …came from a very different social background. With the adjutant and quartermaster he was the third of the triumvirate of regulars, seconded from cavalry regiments, who ran the yeomanry. The son of a Northumberland miner, he had risen in the army the hard way.[18]

And it doesn't seem that the regulars who oversaw the training in the yeomanry regiments resented the free and easy life in these volunteer units – even though it was so at odds with their own regular army experience. Bruce Hobbs recalls the very same R.S.M that Verney identifies seeking him out on his first night when he enlisted as a trooper:

16   Verdin *The Cheshire Yeomanry*, p.196.
17   Verdin *The Cheshire Yeomanry*, p.196.
18   Verney, *Going to the Wars*, p.32.

"Trooper Hobbs", I heard a loud voice of authority.
 I answered "Sir!", jumped to my feet and gave him a sloppy civilian salute.
 "You don't salute me. I'm the regimental Sergeant-Major."
 "I'm sorry, sir" I said.
 "Come and have a drink."
 "I don't drink, sir.'"[Hobbs had just relinquished his professional jockey's license to join the army, and at over 6" had had to live on a wasting regime in order to remain at a competitive weight].
 "You're in the army now, boy. You do as you're told!"
 So RSM Bird and I went out for a drink in a local pub.

This example indicates a continuity with the interwar mindset. Verdin also records a loosening of regular army standards in the adjutant of the Cheshire Yeomary on the 1933 camp:

The second week saw a visit from the Inspector of Cavalry, Major-General Howard-Vyse. [Essentially this was an audit.] It did not go quite so smoothly as usual. After inspecting the first troop the General made a very minor criticism which the Adjutant strongly resented; and when a member of the Blakiston-Houston family is aroused[19], annoyance is invariably most forcibly expressed... the sound of lively altercation was to be heard that morning as General and Adjutant cantered across the polo ground. It [the sound of argument] reached... the second in command of "B" Squadron, which was waiting its turn to be inspected. With the remark, 'Boys this is where we make ourselves scarce," he proceeded to disperse the Squadron with considerable military skill, while he and his subalterns hid securely between two haystacks.[20]

Despite then some very un-military features, these regiments were on the books to be called up immediately to do the only role they were officially trained to do, should the need arise. And in September 1939 that is exactly what happened. Len Flanakin recalled:

On the 1st September 1939 I was at work when mobilisation orders came over the radio, so I packed up my tools and asked a workmate to take care of my

---

19 Another member of the Blakiston-Houston family to have become visibly exercised was the colonel of the 12th Lancers, who took his regimental officers to task in 1928 when they were being stripped of their horses and mechanised: 'We've been given this role and it's a very important role. And you're damn well going to do it. I won't have you bloody well bellyaching.' IWM, Dept of Sound recording, Accession nos. 000892/06: Col. G.J. Kidston-Montgomerie of Southannan, 8;000985/04: Col. T.B.A Evans-Lombe, 19-20 as cited in French, *Raising Churchill's Army*.
20 Verdin *The Cheshire Yeomanry*, p.203.

things and draw my week's wages for me ... We were to present ourselves at the Drill Hall in Shipston-on-Stour at 6 o'clock.[21]

"These were" Verdin recalls "days of fond farewells and acute depression."[22] Equally commonly reported though are the accounts of high-spirits, specifically when the men were all together. In fact Flanakin recalls being excited right from the start. Honing the enthusiasm of men like Flanakin, and focussing the minds of the soldiers was carried out by the N.C.O.s. One SSM Parker achieved this by ordering all his squadron together in one room to start sharpening their swords; one of the defining memories of the war for Verdin.

Thus the yeomanry mustered as per the pre-ordained routine – potentially one that hadn't been scrutinised by the War Office since 1920.[23] And now the troopers were in, more incomers to the yeomanry regiments were about to appear.

Four-Legged Yeomanry

Within a fortnight, the horses started arriving. Regimental horse parties collected them from nearby towns – often from the usual agents.[24] On mobilisation, the seriously overworked army administration had, on top of their other functions, set about purchasing the horses required for the mounted regiments, who needed over half their mounts supplied. The army purchasers were not in a position to be diplomatic; they could only offer £60 for an officer's charger and £40 for other horses.[25] This was despite a very arbitrarily interpreted government policy, whereby horses were taken under compulsory purchase, at a price arrived at by the War Office and without negotiation with the owners who were told "Owners who are dissatisfied with the prices tendered have a right to appeal to a county court judge"[26] – any record of which has so far proved impossible to find. There were also complaints raised in parliament

---

21 Flanakin, *The Teddy Bear Lancers*, p.3.
22 Verdin, *The Cheshire Yeomanry*, p.218.
23 Most yeomanries made it to their muster points by the 5/9/39 – except for the Lancashire Yeomanry who were entirely missing until a contrite phone call informed the authorities that they had mistaken the day and would be in tomorrow ... Verdin, *The Cheshire Yeomanry* p.222.
24 For example, the Cheshire Yeomanry had a working relationship with Grange and Mason of Nantwich, whom they used to supply horses for annual camps. The majority of men did not keep their own horses like Len Flanakin: "Not owning a horse I had to borrow one. If you could borrow a horse to take with you it meant you were paid for the use of the horse too." *Teddy Bear Lancers*, p.1.
25 Verdin, *The Cheshire Yeomanry*, p.222.
26 See Hore-Belisha's response when asked in Parliament 10/10/1939. See Hansard: HC Deb 10 October 1939 vol 352 cc146-8.

that "remount officers are buying for £60-odd horses which are often worth to farmers over 200 guineas".²⁷

Despite the feeble prices being offered, some excellent hunters found themselves entering the ranks of 1st Cavalry Division. Colonel Verdin, a subaltern at the time, surmises that the owners realised there would not be the time nor feed to keep horses for pleasure during the war, and sooner or later they would have to be, inevitably, destroyed.²⁸

It was however clearly a painful process for the horse owners – not least because in September at least, despite the future, oats and hay were plentiful and the hunting season had only just begun. The yeomanry could only have been all too aware of the anguish of the owners surrendering their horses to the war effort. It was apparent in the heartfelt notes attached to the head collars of the horses. S.S.M. Osmond of the Cheshire Yeomanry selected a horse that had the following:

> Rufus, 7 years old, can be handled in and out of stables by a child – never known to refuse a reasonable jump – be kind to him.

Actually the Cheshire Yeomanry did not in fact enjoy the same standard of horses given to it as the other yeomanry regiments. Officers mostly brought their own, some 40 other ranks did the same. Many of the others' mounts came from the usual contractors and riding schools which the Cheshire Yeomanry had used in the past for their summer training camps. Of these, most were too old to be of use as wartime chargers, and to deal with sea voyages.²⁹ The North Somerset Yeomanry, who had scoured all of Cornwall, also drew a mixed bag with "all sorts – thoroughbreds, show horses, well-bred hunters, hairy-legged cobs."³⁰

Indisputably, the best of any horses 1st Cavalry Division received came from the hunting fraternity, and Flanakin of the Warwickshires – whom it should be remembered was not an expert on horses – could still see that "on the whole these horses really were beauties having been requisitioned from the hunts and private owners."³¹ The Warwickshire Yeomanry allocated their horses by colour – each of the four troops in any squadron would receive accordingly black, bay, chestnut or grey horses: "and what a pretty sight they were when you saw them all in a line."³² The best horses, as indicated by the prices indicated above, went to the officers. The superior quality of the officers' chargers should not be seen as simply a class divide. The officers'

---

27 Commander Sir Archibald Southby to Mr Hore-Belisha. Hansard: HC Deb 10 October 1939 vol 352 cc146-8.
28 Verdin, *The Cheshire Yeomanry*, p.223.
29 Verdin, *The Cheshire Yeomanry*, p.223.
30 Fitzgeorge-Parker, *No Secret so Close*, p.71.
31 Flanakin, *The Teddy Bear Lancers*, p.4.
32 Flanakin, *The Teddy Bear Lancers*, p.4.

mounts had to be good quality beasts that would be less likely to bolt under pressure and keep going at the front on long marches etc.

Assembled as the division now were, the yeomanry were well short of operational standard. The Colonel of the North Somerset Yeomanry was given pause to reflect on this lack of training after he ordered a full regimental mounted parade in public soon after his regiment was fully embodied. Essentially relying on his men to execute perfectly complex individual drills, without significant practice, on horses they didn't know, under the pressure of public scrutiny.

The *Manual of Horsemastership, Equitation and Animal Transport 1937* does give some idea[33] of the contortions to be achieved by a skilled trooper boarding his horse, with no less than two paragraphs on section 4. *To mount ; 'Prepare to Mount'* on the page concerning mounting drill.

What it doesn't do is indicate that the Lee Enfield .303 rifle in its bucket will cut short any inaccurate movement of the right leg. Nor does it give any advice on how to keep a skittish horse still while this comparatively straightforward process is completed.

Hobbs however does align intention (as specified in *The Manual*) with reality, recalling that "There were horses [rearing] up trees, up lamp-posts, in the gardens of seaside villas... Soldiers falling off or hopping round with one foot in the stirrup, trying to get their rifles into the right position, hitting their horses over the heads..."[34] In short, the North Somerset Yeomanry[35] for one, suffered true public humiliation, the horses demonstrated that they were not yet inclined to acquiesce with military standards, and many of the soldiers showed emphatically that they still needed to get used to their horses, as well as develop confidence, a basic level of skill, and a bond with them.

Further trouble lay in store because the horses were also going to have to become used, not only to regimental mounting drill, but also to mounted sabre drill. This of course involved fast-moving polished strips of steel moving swiftly past their equine ears. One troop leader in the Warwickshire Yeomanry decided it was time the horses got used to sword drill ("Remember all these mounts were as green as we were."[36]) His impressively realistic instruction was simply to draw swords and then hold onto the horses at all costs; the swords did not need to remain in hand:

> The orders were followed by complete chaos. The first man to hit the ground was the Troop Leader himself, seeing his sword his horse gave a couple of quick

---

33 War Office, *The Manual of Horsemastership, Equitation and Animal Transport 1937* (London: HMSO, 1937), p.86
34 Fitzgeorge-Parker, *No Secret So Close*, p.73.
35 Although Hobbs served as an officer with the Yorkshire Dragoons, he was initially enrolled in the North Somerset Yeomanry as a trooper.
36 Flanakin, *The Teddy Bear Lancers*, p.4.

bucks and he was off, others soon followed him to the ground and there were loose horses everywhere.[37]

More usually the soldiers were simply "out exercising the horses, riding with no saddle just a bridle and blanket." Flanakin records that "I was riding one of our spare mounts and it did not take long to find out she had a 'mouth like iron' and a will of her own."[38] Eventually the troop sergeant suggested giving her a canter to take the tickle out of her toes; this resulted in her then taking the bit between her teeth and tearing off at full gallop, with her pilot praying that the blanket did not slip. Flanakin was clearly determined, because when he felt the horse start to tire and ease up, he then put her back into a faster pace and rode her around again. This was quite a brave response as he was no seasoned rider himself – but it was experiences like this that stayed with the soldiers for life:

> There is nothing to compare with a horse at stretch gallop, a throbbing live animal beneath you, much more exhilarating than a motorbike or fast car – but do it in comfort with saddle and stirrups![39]

Familiarisation of course was only part of the task, and the next step was actually acquiring deployable skills with the weapons. These were revisited from the very first moment the newly mobilised soldiers were embodied, and before even their horses arrived:

> Sword drill could be most unpleasant. The instructor was armed with a long bamboo pole with a boxing glove on the end which was jabbed with full force at one's body. While with sword in hand, the tyro was meant to parry the blow. Missing invariably meant a bloody nose or being knocked to the floor.[40]

More objectively, Hobbs observed with some amusement that "dismounted sword drill is one of the funniest spectacles to the uninitiated. The squad, well spread out, stand with their legs apart [as if riding] ... Now the recruit, sword in right hand, must imagine that he is mounted, facing an enemy who may jump from the ground, [or] assault from either side on the same level. He must be prepared to thrust, parry and punch..." [41]

Further individual skills training that winter included rifle drill, machine gun drill with the Hotchkiss guns (the more modern Brens having been taken off them to

---

37   Flanakin, *The Teddy Bear Lancers*, p.5.
38   Flanakin, *The Teddy Bear Lancers*, p.5.
39   Flanakin, *The Teddy Bear Lancers*, p.5.
40   Flanakin, *The Teddy Bear Lancers*, p.1.
41   Fitzgeorge-Parker, *No Secret So Close*, p.70.

fully equip the regulars) and signals training with the No.11 sets. Live firing on the ranges was also included for some units, but the most notable absence from the winter training programme was any troop training; i.e. going out training as a troop of cavalry practising troop tactics. In fact there were no manoeuvres with the horses for any of the regiments. This suggests, rather unsurprisingly, that the unit commanders and Brigadiers did not envision operational deployment of the horsemen any time soon – if at all. It is also a product of the lack of horse fodder issued to the division.

Further problems also arose to undermine standards of equine care, because the army administration had purchased horses for its cavalry, but it had not put thought into quartering them. The end of September was cold and wet, and the horses could not remain in open lines. Fortunately, the well-qualified recruits whom 1st Cavalry Division had taken on recently, included many joiners and builders; and they worked with the intensity and efficiency that had come to characterise the yeomanry since early 1939. Costs were further reduced by the "commandeering" of local standing timber.

With these yeomanry recruits now stabled in their makeshift autumn accommodation of 1939, the next wave were embodied. These were the reservists. Ex-regular cavalrymen, "these were cavalry men of the old school who really taught us how to soldier, but they were also very resentful at being drafted to a yeomanry unit." "I admit our feelings were not too warm at having to accept them either, but after a few weeks all was fine and a bond was formed and we became one solid unit."[42] Clearly the institutions that could corrupt the standards of proud regulars like Captain Blakiston-Houston could also soften the attitudes of hard-bitten Great War veterans.

The addition of the regular reservists – the natural choice of men to act as NCOs for the very youthful yeomanry – was clearly a beneficial move. As mentioned above, it was these men "who really taught [them] how to soldier." The NCOs and experienced enlisted men were clearly key in setting and driving the standards. Not the officers. Any new officers,[43] incidentally were added by centrally allocated drafts and, like Stanley Christopherson in the Sherwood Rangers, many found it harder to assimilate than the ex-regular reservists who joined the enlisted ranks.

Nevertheless, a division of horsed cavalry had been embodied, and they were at full strength by the end of October. In that sense they answered Britain's first problem in providing a quantity of theoretically trained soldiers quickly. Their role was in the army's doctrine and ORBAT, and this hastily assembled formation would now be sent to fulfil that role despite their lack of training – and at least the issue of professional standards was being solved by the arrival of the reservists.

---

42   Flanakin, *The Teddy Bear Lancers*, p.4.
43   David French cites the inexperience that all T.A. officers suffered from; they simply had not had the chance to command bodies of men regularly on live exercises. See French, *Training Churchill's Army*, p.54.

Yet they weren't sent to France. The BEF that was sent to France 1939-40 was a more modern force than the vast majority of the German army that was to be mustered against it. It was also a single component in the vast array of the French army - and it was the French who would cover any capability gaps. This they did do, and at times with mounted cavalry. The British cavalry meanwhile were earmarked for Palestine. They could relieve the regulars then garrisoned there and take over the occupation duties that had recently included fighting and crushing the Arab revolt. Palestine was therefore still a posting that required security duties, and this was deemed within the capabilities of the yeomanry as hastily assembled as they were.

"Not many days in November had gone by before rumour of the impending departure began to circulate."[44] This was confirmed by the arrival of various reservists, and also of the fact that replacements were being nominated for those disallowed from embarking overseas (soldiers under the age of 19, plus any earmarked to attend an Officer Cadet Training Unit – or O.C.T.U). Inevitably the destination of the new division was kept a secret. Equally inevitably, almost all the speculation on the destination was entirely accurate:

> It was ... difficult to imagine any possible destination other than Palestine.[45]

For those who doubted this, the penny dropped when a lecture on navigation by the stars was delivered, showing the constellations not as they appeared in southern England, but in Palestine.

There are various suggestions from contemporaries for why Palestine was chosen as a destination for 1st Cavalry Division. They range from "the War Office had to decide what to do with these two Cavalry Brigades and the other Yeomanries who had been reformed as cavalry in 1920 and still had their horses" (Verdin)[46] to Flanakin who specifically cites the usefulness of the horses on the terrain there. Ultimately the argument boiled down to:

1. Troops were needed there.
2. These had to be 1st Cavalry Division because:
   a. The First World War had shown them to be very effective there.
   b. The country was a good training ground for cavalry in north and mechanised units in the south, so the horsemen could be sent to police the north while they waited for vehicles to arrive, whereupon they could mechanise by training in the south.
   c. 1st Cavalry Division weren't any use anywhere else.

---

44 Verdin, *The Cheshire Yeomanry*, p.226.
45 Verdin, *The Cheshire Yeomanry*, p.227.
46 Verdin, *The Cheshire Yeomanry*, p.226.

All sources however agree that Britain was still suffering from the run-down of her army during the inter-war period,[47] as a reason for the slow mechanisation of the British cavalry. Verdin, Holland and Flanakin themselves are able to identify the usefulness of highly mobile troops in the political climate of 1940 Palestine, but Flanakin adds a further point that is echoed by James Holland:

> Apart from Syria and Lebanon which were French colonies [in early 1940, France had still not fallen], no other country was at war with Germany.

Italy had not yet entered the war. "But there were many [local Middle Eastern] politicians who would have sold out to the enemy at the drop of a hat had it not been for the presence of British troops".[48] Indeed the Iraqis were to go on to ally with the Germans despite a British presence. The importance of a garrison in the Middle East to protect Suez, Britain's arterial route to India, has been covered elsewhere – and this explains the deployment of 1st Cavalry Division (a full nine regiments). But the expensive deployment of their horses with them is far less obviously justified. Hobbs suggests it was the respect that the Arabs paid to mounted men, others that it was just sentimentality in the corridors of power where enough veterans of Allenby's campaign still served – the Liddell-Hart paradigm in action. Very few credit the operational capability that cavalry still possessed.

The minefield of problems and pitfalls that this logistical enterprise threw up are portrayed colourfully and effectively in the many reminiscences of January 1940, as detailed below. Together they map the cross-channel ferry to Dunkirk, the train journey across France to Marseilles, the holding camp there and then the sea-journey. Horses hitherto kept in generous stabling and open fields by hunting families were unlikely to take kindly to the journey.

Although fully mobilised, most of the yeomanry were simply not fit to fight in 1939. The majority of soldiers were half-trained and furthermore substantially unfamiliar with horses, half of whom had joined in April 1939 without previously having sat a horse. The majority of the division's horses meanwhile (despite the range in quality) were high-quality hunters surrendered sadly but willingly by the hunting fraternity. Despite their quality they were neither fully trained nor hardened for military purposes yet either. On top of this, although undoubtedly high-quality by any market-place inspection standard as the hunters were, these horses were all simply sold-as-seen and there was absolutely nothing the army could do to establish their true background and any underlying conditions. This was not going to make the future work of the division any easier (some mares were pregnant), or the financial cost any easier to justify to Churchill when he eventually got wind of the cavalry division's existence.

---

47 Particularly French, *Training Churchill's Army* and Harrison-Plaice, *Military Training in the British Army, 1940-1945*.
48 Flanakin, *The Teddy Bear Lancers*, p.8. See also Holland (ed.) *An Englishman at War*, p.18.

2

Embarkation

By the time the yeomanries moved out of the United Kingdom at the end of December, they had been in their respective concentration areas for some time, propping up the trade of the local hostelries. They had also been getting to know the other locals quite well and being men of the 1930s had honoured the consequent obligations invoked. December 1939 saw a great many marriages, hastily solemnised, between troopers who had been temporarily billeted in private homes and the sweethearts they encountered there. Precisely the same thing had happened during the Great War, though now the period of absence was to be even longer. For now the horse soldiers packed up their kit, saw to their animals and began a laborious process that would have been far simpler if the units had simply been raised as infantry.

Yet the yeomanry now embarked on a geographical and operational odyssey made all the more complicated by the fact that 7,800 horses were involved. The accounts of the journey reveal much about the yeomanry, not least their prodigious capacity for alcohol, and the fact that many of them knew only slightly more about horse transportation than the rest of the army did. Even a cursory glance at the *Manual of Horsemastership* reveals that few of its statutes were followed in the following weeks. This itself is indication of how little training time there had been opportunity for, even since April 1939. Fortunately there were just enough yeomen who did understand horses well – many of the recalled reservists for instance, and the crop of professional jockeys who had joined up in 1939.

A key flaw in the transportation process was that almost none of the officers would have had experience of anything approaching the scale of numbers involved, the range of horsemanship skills required or the length of time involved. As David French (2000) points out, those officers had not even gained practical experience of commanding significant numbers of men, let alone 8,000 mounted men on a journey across France and the Mediterranean. For that matter, the regular officers had no experience of this kind of undertaking either. The guidance came solely from the Whitehall planners and was to be executed by men who had very little experience or training.

The first hurdle was that of boxing (i.e. loading into boxcars) horses that were unused to travelling, and unused to each other. To give an indication of the impracticalities involved, even leaving the United Kingdom, one of the chargers, which being the mount of Donny Player of Player's cigarettes was an expensive animal, was badly bitten by its neighbour and fell with a severe head wound. The other chargers had to be moved into another truck altogether so that Player's charger could be laid on its side where it gave groans that were "terrible to hear."[1] Others kicked great holes in the wooden transport trucks. None of this was specifically allowed for in standing orders or the *Manual of Horsemastership*, and the delaying impact of this compounded with sundry other incidents to create a sheer mass of problem-solving which effectively meant that the process was never under complete control.

The usual format was for most of the regiment to form a dismounted party, and a smaller advance group to form a "horse party". These men were mainly those who had known horses well before the war (although Flanakin was in the Warwickshires' horse party) but were only a smallish contingent and were consequently under a lot of pressure as they handled the large number of horses by themselves. A more typical member of the horse party (in this case of the North Somerset Yeomanry) was Trooper Bruce Hobbs, the ex-jockey. "It was a hell of an operation" he recalled; there were mines in the English channel to evade, and then, even more treacherously, smooth decked transport trucks with no straw laid down for the horses, and upon which they kept slipping. Hobbs recalled that "our manpower consisted, not only of inexperienced yeomen, but all sorts of French dockers and assorted helpers... slapping, pulling, pushing, encouraging" the animals under floodlights for the entire night until all were loaded.'[2] The extra manpower made the loading possible, but the lack of expertise created a chaotic and poorly managed transition. The main focus of the British army's logistic infrastructure and expertise was the BEF in northern France - not a division of cavalry being entrained to move out to Palestine.

The next stage was to load the entire division onto 24 trains that would then travel across France to Marseille. As Major Johnson-Houghton of the Cheshire Yeomanry collapsed exhausted into his seat on the train, he looked out of the window, and saw one of the regiment's horses galloping alongside the moving train. It had somehow escaped its boxcar. Nor was this the most difficult situation to befall the division during the train journey. A Major Hutchinson similarly found himself compromised. He had climbed out at a rest-stop to inspect the damage done when the 17hh 'Hephalump' had kicked a hole through the side of a truck. As Major Hutchinson climbed onto the buffers in order to shove Hephalump's leg back inside, the train jolted into motion and departed, with Hutchinson balancing on the buffers for the next stage of the journey, gripping Hephamlump's leg for support. Meanwhile the weather was so cold that the men's water was freezing in their bottles, and the horse's urine on the floor of

---

1   Holland (ed.). *An Englishman at War*, p.16.
2   Fitzgeorge-Parker, *No Secret So Close*, p.75.

the box-cars was also freezing. When the cold and rather-shaken Johnson-Houghton reintegrated with his brother officers at the next stop, they all claimed that no-one had noticed he was gone.

More initiative however was displayed by Corporal Harrison of the Sherwood Rangers. He had, before the war, been stud groom to the Duke of Portland at Welbeck and had mustered in September 1939 with one of the Duke's hunters – a sort of mobilisation present from the Duke. This animal was easily recognisable because it had an enormous wart upon its nose. No doubt both horse and man were familiar with the practise at the time of giving stout to horses after a day's hunting and therefore used to the idea of administering alcohol to horses. This proclivity was demonstrated when Harrison, during the gruelling journey across France, identified signs of colic in the expensive horse, of which he was clearly very proud. Knowing that it should be removed immediately from the crowded wagon, he duly acted on this highest priority of horse-care and did so at the next stop. Unfortunately, he had overlooked the more military priority of informing his superiors, and the train departed, leaving Harrison and horse alone in a foreign land. Deciding that they both needed a pep up in morale, Harrison departed for the nearest town to purchase some Brandy – for both him and the horse. Recognising the needs of his horse over those of men, particularly those of Frenchmen, Harrison ensconced his horse in the waiting room, locking it in with a key obtained from the station-master. Returning shortly thereafter, Harrison then joined his horse in the waiting room, with several bottles of brandy. Both horse and man were now warm and content, so Harrison did not heed the protests of the civilian passengers trying to obtain entrance to the waiting room on this cold January day.

A more pressing problem to corporal Harrison was how to re-join his regiment. Fortunately, the solution came to him while he and his horse were in the waiting room. Knowing that H.R.H the Duke of Gloucester was the British liaison officer to the French army, Harrison decided to call in a favour. His reasoning was this: The Duke of Gloucester had been acquainted with the horse (and one assumes the groom) in the summer of 1939 at Welbeck. With such a striking wart on the horse's nose, the Duke would of course recall the animal. Harrison, steered by purpose, desperation and brandy, commandeered the station master's telephone and addressed the operator, thus beginning a long telephonic odyssey to get connected with the British army's chief liaison officer in France. All the operators encountered were at first incredulous, then simply rude; but Harrison had the bit between his teeth and was finally, miraculously, connected to the Duke of Gloucester. Starting with "You remember the horse with the wart on his nose when you visited Welbeck?", Harrison was able to win H.R.H to his cause. The next train to arrive at Harrison's station had a box for the horse and a carriage containing three Indian army veterinary officers. Both Harrison and "Wartnose" arrived at Marseilles with plenty of time to re-join the Sherwood Rangers.[3]

---

3   T.M. Lindsay, *The History of the Sherwood Rangers in the 1939-45 War* as cited in Verdin, *The Cheshire Yeomanry*, p.231.

Harrison and "Wart-Nose's" arrival at Marseilles, however, were overshadowed by the conditions of the camp there allocated to 1st Cavalry Division, at Château Renard. The main problem was the fact that Marseilles was experiencing an exceptionally cold winter. Worst of all, before the frost there had been a heavy fall of rain. The horse-lines were flooded, the men only had bell-tents to sleep in and the duckboards were unusable. The cold-snap descended so quickly that Hobbs recalled seeing "four big black Household Cavalry horses standing stark and stiff, frozen to death on the lines."[4] It was the first snow in Marseilles for 17 years. Flanakin recalls that "It was essential to take your boots into your bed too, because if you left them outside they would be frozen hard by morning." Disturbingly for the soldiers though, such was the limited access to unfrozen water, that the horses started fighting to get near any trickles that appeared. The phase of disorientating flux continued, and the snow and frost soon began to thaw – around noon on the 31st. This ushered in quantities of mud, to the point that a farrier's anvil disappeared from sight and the duckboards started floating. The fact that horses had been freezing in their lines and the camp area was then deluging into mud would have posed severe challenges to any outfit. But the way point in the journey of 1st Cavalry Division was singularly ill-equipped to handle the strain imposed upon it.

Nearly as destructive as the weather, at least according to the annals of the Cheshire Yeomanry, was the underpowered military administration. Verdin does point at the camp commandant, a second lieutenant, and the camp R.S.M, but also allows for the fact that the blame probably should be laid elsewhere. Indeed it should; putting an officer of the lowest-commissioned rank in as camp commandant for an entire division seems brutally unfair, especially when by his own admission he knew nothing about horses.[5] Special opprobrium does seems to have been reserved though for the R.S.M, who is portrayed as having claimed to know everything about horses and combined this with a very unpleasant approach – though this assertion should be tempered by the fact he was undoubtedly under heavy pressure. He did undoubtedly however, choose the wrong man to pick out and correct in public when he criticised the riding ability of a trooper of the North Somerset Yeomanry. He was Trooper Hobbs, winner of the 1938 Grand National. Rather admirably, Hobbs does not even mention this in his own memoirs.

Flanakin also recalls that the camp authorities failed to charm their guests. Not least because the transient yeomanry were ordered to strip their beds in the bell tents and return all their blankets a full 24 hours before loading could happen. This compounded the camp commandant's earlier error of reprimanding the entire regiment because of an isolated incident in just one of the squadrons. In a bid to keep warm, and riled by the attitude of the camp administration, a wide-ranging mass forage for firewood – or indeed anything flammable – took place. In return for the unwarranted reproach

---

4   Fitzgeorge-Parker, *No Secret So Close*, p.74.
5   Verdin, *The Cheshire Yeomanry*, p.234.

from the camp commandant, the men also added the camp's wooden duckboards to the woodpile and soon a merry blaze was going. The "everything must go" attitude was carried further Flanakin recalls, when his troop sergeant appeared armed with one-gallon drums of army issue rum – he insisted conspiratorially that they were not to be handed back in. The rum was in fact so plentiful that it was still flowing at 0200 on New Year's day when Flanakin returned from his stint on guard. In fact, even then there was so much that he was unable to finish his, and so decided to shave in the remaining quantity of his rum ration.

The 0400 reveille "was hilarious".[6] The entire complement of the Warwickshire Yeomanry were drunk and were endeavouring manfully to; get the horses off the lines, board them, and to do all this while riding one horse and leading others. A 15km ride to the docks did no one any favours and resulted in a significant number of tumbles. Given that these men were actually far from the eyes of authority in their own unit (the horse party travelled separately), and the unpleasantness of the Marseille experience, and the apparent absence of any effective army administration, this episode is not entirely surprising. It does not therefore necessarily indicate a critical lack of unit discipline across the yeomanry, or even in the Warwickshire Yeomanry. At least not by 1939 yeomanry standards. Regardless of this, men and horses were now loaded onto ships at the Marseilles docks and embarked for the Middle East on ships of the British India Line. Further cultural experiences are recorded by Hobbs, whose ship was crewed by sailors who made bread by kneading it with their feet and spitting into it. Despite this "we never got any tummy bugs, but two horses died."[7]

Interestingly, Hobbs identifies as the main calls for the veterinary resources on his boat, as not the newly mobilised horses, but those travelling out with the regular Household Cavalry. This was "chiefly because of the Household Cavalry horses ... were so soft from living indoors all the time that they were constantly sick with colic and every other sort of illness." If anything indicates the lack of priority given to cavalry in the British army – territorial or regular – it is the condition of the Household Cavalry's mounts. These horses were clearly only regarded as props for ceremonial duties, and not as remounts for operational mounted cavalry units, even though three such units did exist. Clearly then, these regular units were never envisioned for any mounted role in case of war that would require mounted reinforcements and remounts. Meantime, the problem with the hitherto civilian horses, on whom no background checks had been done, was shown when one of the North Somerset's mares foaled during the journey. This cannot have ended well for either the mare or the foal.

The journey across the sea was to account for other horses in the division too. In total, 140 horses, 1.6. percent of the total strength, perished on the journey.[8]

6   Flanakin, *The Teddy Bear Lancers*, p.7.
7   Fitzgeorge-Parker, *No Secret So Close*, p.76. Presumably the horses did not expire.
8   A further 722 were hospitalised on arrival at Haifa docks. See Dennis C. Bateman, *Syria: The Last British Cavalry Action* (Publisher and date unknown: Chester City Archives:

Christopherson recalled the Sherwood Rangers losing two, despite their unremitting care of the horses on the journey. He also noted that from his boat he could see the Yorkshire Dragoons dispose of the bodies of nine or ten:[9]

> We had to wait until dark until we could manhandle the two dead horses into slings, slit their bellies open to make them sink and let the cranes put them overboard. It was vital that enemy submarines should not find the trail of blood.[10]

Submarines were a real threat. The yeomanry may also have reflected bitterly on the lack of effective secrecy which surrounded their departure. As they set out, Lord Haw Haw broadcasted that the 4th Brigade of the 1st Cavalry Division were setting sail and would be the first convoy success for the Fuhrer. Despite this threat, on the morning of 9 January 1940, the convoy anchored off Haifa in Palestine. As if to make the newly arrived British feel truly welcomed to the Holy Land, it immediately began to pour with rain.

On disembarking in Palestine in January 1940, the 1st Cavalry Division was still very much a collection of quaint county institutions that had only ever been called upon to fight as entire units during the previous world-wide conflict – mounted on horses with even less military training and pedigree than the riders. These old-time entities were the Cheshire Yeomanry, Sherwood Rangers, Yorkshire Hussars, Yorkshire Dragoons, the Staffordshire Yeomanry, Royal Wiltshire Yeomanry, North Somerset Yeomanry and Warwickshire Yeomanry.[11] These units expanded the hitherto regular army-only presence of the Royal Scots Greys, The Royals and an incoming composite regiment from the Household Cavalry. The regulars were fully mounted, had higher quality equipment and both men and horses were clearly professionals, with the animals carefully sourced and bred from established dealers - though their condition in the winter of 1939 casts grave aspersions upon the standards of the household cavalry. The salient point which arises from an overview of the cavalry's performance during the Second World War, is that these previously amateur replacements adapted no less well than the rest of the army (Regular and Territorial) by 1942.

NCY 19/57).
9 Holland, *An Englishman at War*, p.23.
10 Fitzgeorge-Parker, *No Secret So Close*, p.76.
11 The component artillery was also formed from yeomanry personnel.

3

Palestine, Training and Official Scrutiny

The Middle East was and remains a melting pot of cultures, and has been the stopping off point for Phoenicians, Babylonians, Great Silk Roaders, Greeks, Romans, Crusaders, Seljuks, sundry Muslim civilisations, Venetian galley captains, Napoleonic warriors and more. This heritage is augmented by the fan-like spread of culinary heritage, and the linguistic and architectural diversity that serves the residual populations of Jews, Muslims and Christians; and their attendant trading partners from Egypt and the rest of North Africa, the ring of the Mediterranean and the hinterland of Asia. The result is a genuine cornucopia for all the senses. "My most vivid memories" recalls Flanakin "are the train loads of delicious oranges which came through, which we pilfered and the continual blast of 'South of the Border' coming from a nearby cafe."[1] The music presumably appealed to the western contingent of recently arrived European Jewish refugees, be-suited and respectable, or sitting out on their verandahs in silk pyjamas, as Verney recalls.[2] Like the yeomanry, the point of their presence in exotic Palestine was to avoid the European war. And the erratic bursts of rain no doubt brought all of the European newcomers down to earth.

The 1st Cavalry Division disembarked at Haifa, which had the most modern port in the world at that time and an established British garrison; it proved to be refreshingly easy to unload the brigades there after the tribulations of their journey. Now landed, they found themselves at a point of key strategic interest; Haifa was the terminal for a great oil pipeline running out of Kirkuk in Iraq. Protecting this pipeline was to cost yeomanry blood within eighteen months.

Verdin makes reference to the historical depth in which the yeomanry now found themselves. Returning veterans and recently-joined teenagers alike could cast their eyes out on where Allenby's army had fought, and also on the biblical hinterland beyond Haifa and Acre. Above them rose the magnificent Mount Carmel where Elijah had foiled the prophets of Baal, and running past Haifa, the Kishon river

---

1 Flanakin, *The Teddy Bear Lancers*, p.8.
2 Verney, *Going to the Wars*, p.48.

Palestine, Training and Official Scrutiny 53

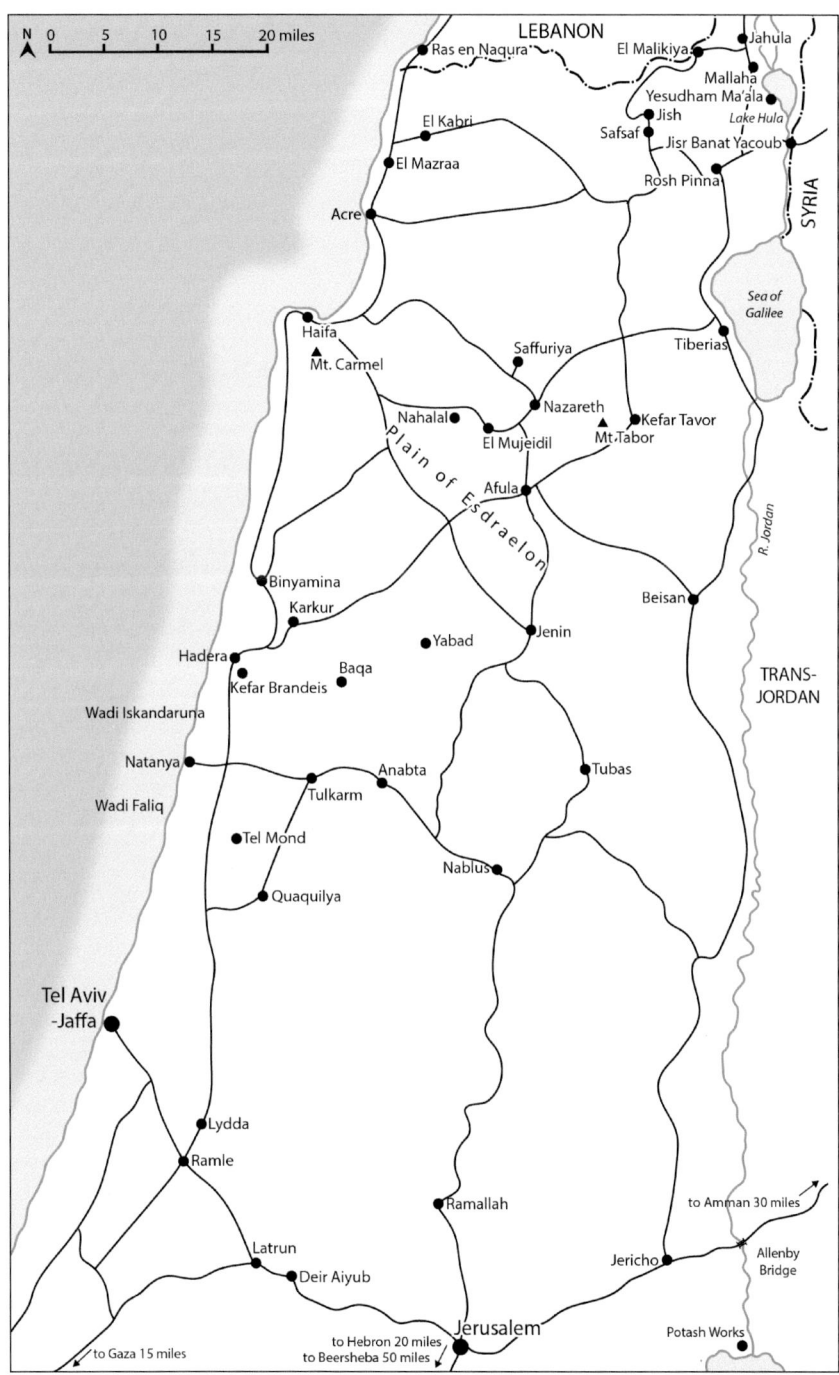

Syrian campaign, 1941

– where scriptures have it Elijah then slaughtered them. Clearly visible too were the plain of Sharon, and shell of the last Crusader stronghold at Athlit. Situated to the east of the Carmel range, if walking along it, the yeomen would be able to see the plain of Esdraelon; site of battles for time immemorial and foretold to be the site of the clash of armies at Armageddon.[3]

In early 1940 of course, there was time to absorb the ancient history and biblical significance as well as the diversity. "Apart from grooming and taking care of all the other horses' needs we did very little."[4] The reason the soldiers could do so little was the fact that their mounts were simply not in a condition to start training yet. This clearly was no hardship though and the horses themselves were evidently delighted by the plethora of oranges available, which they were fed with the skin on, and developed a real love for. There was normally at least one horse in each troop that would eat oranges directly off the tree, much to the delight of their riders.[5] Despite the chagrin of the orange-grove owners, the yeomen were enjoying a spell of peace and exotica that virtually no-one else in Britain could relate to. There was, it seems, a bit of a holiday atmosphere.

Taking advantage of the comparatively warm temperatures (and probably to the surprise of the locals), 1st Cavalry Division took to the sea. Firstly there was not much else to do with the horses so short of condition after Château Renard and their sea journey; and secondly the beach was right there – though the Cheshire Yeomanry could not sea-bathe as it was too rocky near them. This was not a privilege exclusively for the human members of 1st Cavalry Division either; the horses could not be worked hard out on the plains, but they could frolic in the waves with their masters and learn to swim. And slowly – no doubt greatly helped by the oranges and the waves – the horses began to regain their strength. A key link in the bond between man and horse was also being formed.[6] Nonetheless, some of the yeoman were clearly bored, as exemplified by Christopherson:

> At the moment [17/2/1940] we have done very little real training. None of the men, since the start of the war, have fired a single shot on the range.[7]

Although some yeomanry regiments had actually done some live firing, Christopherson captures the mood here of the yeomanry as they relaxed on the beach. But the situation was inevitable. They had simply been in transit since the start of the war, and now they were waiting for everyone to arrive in Palestine. Furthermore, their horses were still regaining strength.

---

3   Verdin, *The Cheshire Yeomanry*, p.239.
4   Flanakin, *The Teddy Bear Lancers*, p.8.
5   Fitzgeorge-Parker, *No Secret So Close*, p.85.
6   Flanakin, *The Teddy Bear Lancers*, p.11.
7   Holland (ed.) *An Englishman at War*, p.27.

The fact remains that it took time for the horses to regain condition after their journey. Where a force of men only would have proved more resilient, the animals needed to be nursed back into trim comparatively slowly, before they could even start training fully. Thus we see the limited strategic manoeuvrability of cavalry. Possibly the German 1st Cavalry Division's horses, or Allenby's walers, would not have required such a recovery period as they would have been as professionally conditioned as their human counterparts, and furthermore, selectively bred - although the Household Cavalry's mounts seemed alarmingly under-prepared. Britain's cavalry horse herd in 1939, like the rest of its army, was mainly a collection of all-sorts, with no prior guarantee of resilience.

Regardless of the weaknesses that came with this new garrisoning force, the strategic objective of maintaining a deterrent garrison had now been achieved. For now, the main effort was simply bringing in the rest of the division as the last draft reached Haifa in March, before then getting the horses into condition and ensconcing each regiment in its new quarters. These were widely spread out and with each regiment moving frequently. Probably this was due to the need to provide adequate coverage as a security force - but it also could be a result of the drain on local supplies of fodder. Under Major-General G. Clark M.C. the nine, now quite nomadic, regiments which made up the strength and so widely adorned the Palestinian territory, were almost exclusively yeomanry. The Household Cavalry's composite mounted regiment in 4th Brigade was the only regular formation, and the incumbent garrison of the Scots Greys and Royals were not officially on the divisional strength. The latter were soon to return home anyway.

The newly-arrived Division's pastimes included an extensive array of race meetings, such as the Palestine Grand National – in which Bruce Hobbs and the other ex-pro jockeys were inevitably involved. There was also football, hockey and rugby, (for the other ranks – the appendices to Verdin depict a range of results) hunting (with the Ramleh Vale Foxhounds) and duck-shooting for the officers – the Huleh marshes were world-famous for this. When the Cheshire Yeomanry had embarked from the U.K. they had foresightedly loaded 20,000 shotgun cartridges. These activities continued throughout the division's time in Palestine - even when standards were improved under Clark.

Clark presumably let these continue because, once the horses had recovered he was able to implement a thorough training regime that would eventually bring the yeomanry up to standard. A significant ingredient in the expediting of this was the diet available for the horses, upon whom the intensity of everyone's training depended. Bruce Hobbs, who had grown up around horses being trained for elite sport, was "horrified" to find a very rich diet for the horses; rather than oats they ate barley, tiffin (chopped straw chaff presumably for roughage) and a form of haylage called *dreis*. His concern was misplaced; the British cavalry had been feeding horses in hot climates for centuries, and they had long since learned that rich forage counteracted many of the ill effects of the heat. In the cooler weeks of February the rich food also helped with restoring strength and weight. Hobbs did in fact observe that the horses thrived in Palestine.⁸

Soon, however, they were to start a period of intensive troop training (starting 23rd February for a month). This started with 5th Brigade and would also see strict standards applied (and enforced) upon the officers. They had a good starting point; the horses in 5th Brigade were fit enough by then. In actual fact, their first move date was to be 15 March so they would have had plenty of time to recoup. The ensuing journey across country to Latrun (for initial training) proved the innate versatility and durability of the horses; this is where the Sherwood Rangers found that regularly checking horses' feet improved their staying power. Despite this, their feet were not in as good a state as they could have been, and it was still proving difficult to pick them out." ⁹ 6th Brigade meanwhile were carrying out troop training by mid-April. In each case of course, the work only started when the men of the Brigade could see, like Christopherson reporting on 19 February, that "the horses are gradually beginning to look better and are getting full of life."¹⁰

A key part of both the recovery and training regime for the horses was the divisional-standard practice of teaching all the warhorses to swim:

> There are two ways of swimming horses. Either you can swim alongside your horse, if you are a very good swimmer, giving light pulls on the reins if you wish the horse to come towards you and splashing water in its face if you wish it to go in the other direction; or, if you are doubtful of your own prowess in the water, you can drop behind the animal, seize its tail and allow yourself to be dragged across. This is a perfectly effective method and, although perhaps a little alarming in prospect, does not result in kicks in a vital place.¹¹

The Warwickshire Yeomanry carried out a great deal of swimming training when they were stationed at Lake Tiberias. This was mainly a function of the temperature that summer, which below sea level as they were, was 100° F. Because of the heat, reveille was at 0400 and the men and horses were worked until 1000, then two hours in the evening. Much of the rest of the day was spent swimming the horses – which also meant that there was little grooming to do. Flanakin recalls the delight in riding the horse until it was out of its depth, then sliding off and hanging onto its mane, or swimming with it. Verney preferred the option of swimming by holding onto the horse's tail – an exercise which required a great deal of faith. "The horses loved swimming and it was never any trouble to get them into the water. It also made life

---

8   Fitzgeorge-Parker, *No Secret So Close*, p.80.
9   Holland (ed.) *An Englishman at War*, p.26.
10 Holland (ed.) *An Englishman at War*, p.28.
11 Holland (ed.) *An Englishman at War*, pp.85-6.

[was] easier for us as a light brush down when they were dry made their coats shine like silk."[12]

For the North Somerset Yeomanry swimming training was done largely in the Sea of Galilee. Because of its size, and the fact that the far bank was always out of sight, it was a daunting venue to swim in. Invariably, new arrivals to the regiment were allotted one of the few horses that swam for pleasure, even if they could not see the far bank. Just as invariably, the young soldier would find himself in the middle of the Sea of Galilee, alone and out of his depth, with a horse that seemed like it was going to plough on until it just sank. The desperate young man would eventually have to let go of the horse's tail lest he be lost with it and return exhausted and demoralised, thinking that he had let a valuable horse swim to its death. Greeted on the home bank by his more experienced comrades in fits of hysterical laughter, he would then turn around to see the horse swimming back, having turned about of its own volition.[13]

The most common wastage of horses was in fact the regimental "casting" parades; a time-honoured necessity in regular and yeomanry regiments alike. Any horse that was deemed unfit for service or had reached the arbitrarily set limit of fifteen years old was "cast". In peace-time they might have been bought out for £60 if a buyer could be found. In Palestine they were passed to the farrier-major (a senior warrant officer) and shot. Like the regular R.S.M. in each regiment, these men – all of remarkable toughness, even by the standards of the 1930s army – had grown up in the service the hard way. Each would have been a farrier all of their military and civilian career, working harder and drinking harder than anyone.[14] Legend has it that the farrier tradition had them, even at the start of their careers as fourteen year-old apprentices, working at the forge from six, only stopping for a fifteen minute break, in which they were expected to see off at least three pints of strong ale.

Whether all the vestiges of this working life had survived until 1940, the aura about the farrier-majors certainly had; and with it came a grim sense of humour. One evening, after the North Somerset Yeomanry's farrier-major had had to shoot five horses, he then attended a sergeants' mess "smoker" to which all the officers were invited and which was a typically drunken affair, with most officers' drinks being spiked. The next morning, one very hung-over captain was woken by the unusually hospitable farrier-major with "Good morning, sir, I have brought your early morning tea."[15] Turning over, the officer was presented with a bucket full of horse guts.

---

12 Flanakin, *The Teddy Bear Lancers*, p.13.
13 Fitzgeorge-Parker, *No Secret So Close*, p.86.
14 Fitzgeorge-Parker, *No Secret So Close*, p.86.
15 Fitzgeorge-Parker, *No Secret So Close*, p.86.

Open lines

A degree of toughening was in prospect for the horses deemed fit enough to continue, as most now were. This was helped along by the highly necessary requirement of keeping all of the horses in "open lines", referred to in *The Manual of Horsemasterhip … 1937* as "picket lines":

> "Picketing will either be on an air-rope breast high ["breast-rope"], secured between wagon wheels [or presumably truck wheels...], or on a ground rope secured by means of picketing pegs, in which case heel pegs must be used [generally the division used a heel-rope anyway]... The rope... should be strong and well secured and kept taught … Single horses or kickers are best picketed by means of a shackle on the fore fetlock secured to a peg by a rope one foot to 18 inches in length."[16]

This is how horses would be bedded down at the end of the day when out on campaign. For the meantime, the individual units followed a nomadic garrisoning regime and as such often quartered their animals like this, as they moved from one place to the other, every couple of weeks. As it so happened, it proved to do the animals no harm, as least not in the main, and despite days out on the rocky ground or hard flinty tracks, they survived very well in these conditions. The soldiers, who checked them very regularly, made sure that their equine companions were always as comfortable as could be and would always dismount for the last ten or fifteen minutes of any day's route march (typically about 18 miles), to ensure that the horses were cool by the time they were bedded down. Many of the large midlands hunters, like Verney's "Caesar" who had hooves like soup-plates, would have especially appreciated this. It was not just because the climate was hot, even in March (although the animals were adapting well under army care), but because the hard, broken ground was better suited to smaller-footed animals:

> Unlike the nimble Arabs [ponies] ridden by the police, our horses stumbled painfully [Caesar in particular].[17]

There were further problems in store too, as the army came to count the cost of requisitioning horses in Britain, blindly bought without proof of prior condition and all of whom had "browsed peacefully in English pastures". "Many foaled after arrival in Palestine."[18]

---

16 *The Manual of Horsemasterhip …* , p.20.
17 Verney, *Going to the Wars*, p.57.
18 Verney, *Going to the Wars*, p.57.

One such mare, was that of the North Somerset Yeomanry's intelligence officer. Despite her condition (heavily pregnant in this case), she was now an army horse and therefore "stood out in the sun" ceaselessly tossing her head and stamping against the flies, like all the other horses.

> They were shackled to prevent kicks, but accidents happened. One day I heard a sharp 'crack' and, turning, saw Amos's mare standing on three legs, the fourth dangling. Caesar, aiming at a fly with one of his soup plates, must have caught her hind leg. The bone below the hock stuck out broken. She made no sound and was not apparently in pain [presumably temporarily inured against the pain by the shock] but waited quietly for what she perhaps knew was the only end. We half-dragged, half-carried her away from the lines. I shot her with my revolver. What had been a precious living creature, in fact two living creatures, became instantly a carcass, loaded on a lorry and deposited in some dry wadi to be devoured in a night by the jackals.[19]

The problem of unwanted pregnancies was further exacerbated by the arrival of the Free French cavalry's stallions. They were part of the exodus of French troops fleeing from Vichy authority, which culminated at the beginning of July in a squadron of Spahis under Major de Courcelles arriving, apologising profusely for the delay. Having fought their way through Vichy lines, they had stopped to clean themselves and their horses up before they crossed the border so that they might look the part when they presented themselves to the British forces. The effect of their brightly-coloured uniforms and striking Arab mounts served to add to the sense of drama at their arrival. A key striking visual was that their sabres, slung lengthways, very low, were of the slashing variety. So a traditional light cavalry sabre and not at all the straight-bladed tent-pegger carried by the British. They also had carbines rather than rifles, to which were attached extraordinarily long bayonets. The ratio of machine-guns to troops is not recorded. It seems a safe assumption that they used the French-built Hotchkiss light gun as well. On reaching the British their horse lines were kept separate from the British ones as all the Spahi mounts were stallions. As welcome as they were, taking them onto the strength was not without its problems, least of all when the Syria campaign later got under way. In the meantime, their mounts had to be kept under a firm eye. As recorded by Flanakin, these Spahis had fought their way out, and the absence of a major border incident recorded in any war diary of the yeomanry regiments suggests that the Vichy French had been unable to put up an effective blocking force at the border in time. Evidently, speed of movement had been key to this mini success, and this in turn foreshadows the comparative successes of the British cavalry the following May.

---

19   Verney, *Going to the Wars*, p.58.

The arrival of the Spahis further encouraged the delusion among high-command that the Vichy soldiery had no intention of putting up determined resistance against Allied forces. The Spahi defection was after all part of a larger cross-over; of Colonel Collet's 1000 impressive-looking Circassians. The optimistic high-command then failed to take due notice of the fact that 600 of these erstwhile Vichy cavalrymen then returned when they learned Collet had defected to the contemptible Gaullists at the cost of their pensions.[20]

There were other drawbacks involved in maintaining thousands of horses – and not just because of the new French stallions. One hot day in late March two squadrons of the Sherwood Rangers stopped for lunch during their transfer march from Latrun to Karkur. The horses were being watered in a nearby village by the horse party and the main body of men were eating lunch in a grove of gum trees, with a long trestle table set up for them in the shade as they relaxed. A sudden thundering roar however only gave them seconds to leap out of the way as their 200 stampeding horses came crashing through the grove. Two jumped the table, the rest just charged through. "Some of them crashed headlong into two army trucks which were parked in the lane, others hit the telegraph poles which fell like nine-pins... When the dust had cleared [there was] an incredible scene of destruction – injured men, dead horses and a tangle of equipment lay everywhere and, far away, a moving trail of dust showed the horses

Horse lines at Sidney Smith Barracks, Acre March 1940.

20 Smith p.191. It should be pointed out that Collet himself had warned his new masters that Dentz and his officers would fight with determination.

Walls of Acre, March 1940.

were still racing madly on… [It happened again in the night] one horse crashed into the cook-house and sent it up in flames. The poor cook had both his legs broken.[21] "…no one knows what caused these stampedes. Some think that there may be a mad horse which is the ring-leader. But the fact is that at some indefinable signal a hundred horses will move as one, and nothing will stop them."[22]

This was demonstrated in equally dramatic fashion to the Cheshire Yeomanry when a horse party from A sqn was taking the horses out for a walk before their breakfast. Without warning the leading horses suddenly turned around and cut loose, with the rest following suit immediately:

> To those in the horse lines at the time it was an awe-inspiring sight as they approached full gallop. Expecting their destination to be the horse lines where their feed awaited them, orders were given to close the gate. There was no attempt [on the part of the horses] to stop, however. On they thundered through

---

21 Holland (ed.) *An Englishman at War*, p.34.
22 Countess of Ranfurly, *To War with Whitaker: The Wartime Diaries of the Countess of Ranfurly 1939-1945* (London: Heinemann, 1994).

the main street of the barracks to the southern end. There they were confronted by the barbed-wire fence surrounding the internees camp [around seven feet tall]. In the lead was the grey charger Jubilee[23]... Eye witnesses are all unanimous that he cleared the fence without touching it. The same cannot be said of the others. Some attempted to jump, others just galloped straight into it. By the time that all had passed nothing remained standing and the ground was strewn with tangled wire both barbed and otherwise... [they charged on through the other side of the camp, Jubilee again unscathed]. After crossing the second fence the horses divided. Some turned left towards Haifa road but most galloped straight on into the ancient town of Acre...and raced towards the cliffs of the sea beyond. The first four horses never hesitated. Straight over they went to be killed instantaneously on the rocks below. The remainder checked, turned left and were eventually scattered far and wide."[24]

The ensuing courts of enquiry were completely unable to establish the causes of the stampedes. However, measures were taken in hand; the Cheshires decreed that when leading horses, they should always be in bridles and bits rather than merely headcollars, as these had given the soldiers absolutely no chance of holding on to them when stampede broke. In the Sherwood Rangers, the decision was that C Squadrons's horses should be kept separate from the rest of the regiment. Managing horses was proving a complex and expensive business, but it is noticeable that thereafter there are no more stampedes recorded, as the division tightened up its standards.

In other areas the division was also confronting the realities of soldiering; even in a backwater like Palestine. Shortly after the arrival of the division in the Middle East, the formation had been surprisingly joined by the indomitable Lady Yarborough and a number of other officers' wives. Christopherson recalls in his June diary that "six of the officers have got their wives here; they managed to bring them out by the back door. They have all taken houses in the Jewish village across the field, which has been most convenient for them... [they were also still allowed to dine in the mess twice a week] In a way it is rather hard on the men when they see that officers have their wives out."[25] These women had been inspired to travel to Palestine by Lady Yarborough, the colonel's wife. One of them, Hermione, Countess Ranfurly, documented this experience in *To War with Whitaker*. This literary legacy aside, the outcome cannot have been positive for everyone else, as intimated by Christopherson. The whole episode was was deeply inappropriate. Christopherson's editor Holland notes that the wives had obtained the destination of the division from the War Office (not that it was difficult to guess), and taken it upon themselves to make the journey. John Semken added that a blind eye was bound to be turned, because "they weren't hoi-polloi, so

---

23 Recently bought off the Royal Scots Greys.
24 Verdin, *The Cheshire Yeomanry*, p.251.
25 Holland (ed.), *An Englishman at War*, p.36.

those rules did not apply!" This attitude clearly had permeated further though, as in December 1940, the Yorkshire Dragoons eventually decided that they really ought to send their officers' wives back home. These anecdotes are useful on two counts; they show that the people in question clearly didn't see Palestine as a serious danger, more as a colonial posting. Secondly, the watered-down official reaction shows significant double-standards in relation to class. The eventually repatriation of the officers' wives does show that standards were eventually being tightened and peace-time soldiering, as the division had evidently thus perceived it so far, could clearly seen to be over.

It was now the second half of 1940, and there was to be realistic training for all. This was the year that saw the fall of France and the Battle of Britain. Consequently, from the very first regimental exercise in 1st Cavalry Division, all movement was carried out with full tactical awareness, as they would on campaign, with a properly posted lead section, lead troop and flank guards. They moved cautiously and well-spaced out; this was of course of singularly high importance in the age of aircraft. The machine-gun troop meanwhile was primed and ever-ready to gallop to any patrol that came under enemy fire, and this reaction time had to be a key part of regimental training. As was fitting in a division preparing for the possibility of war, these practices were observed even on standard movements from one barracks to another. "The regiment was preceded as always by ... 'points'. They carried drawn swords with which presumably to prod lurking enemy tanks. You can see the same cavalry formation any day of the week when the Life Guards ride down The Mall." Verney is presumably so dismissive of this practice, because unlike the Cheshire Yeomanry and other members of the division, he was never personally required to lead a troop on horseback through enemy territory. Ultimately the pervading air of cynicism surrounding 1st Cavalry Division that persists to this day is unsurprising if even officers on the division's own strength at the time scoffed at its role. Yet this tactical awareness instilled a defining characteristic of measured advance and caution in all those who found themselves in the position of men like those of the Cheshire Yeomanry who found themselves isolated and under fire on the Litani during operation Exporter. Fitzgeorge-Parker in fact is overtly critical of the culture pervading the rest of the mainly mechanised British "cavalry" at the time who never had the same experience:

> With the notable exception of the Greys [Fitzgeorge-Parker's own regiment], the Royals and Household cavalry, many other cavalry regiments, who had been mechanised for some time before the war, suffered badly because they believed that "dash" was the chief characteristic of a cavalryman [meaning a member of the Royal Armoured Corps – which was formed by the mechanisation of the old cavalry regiments in the 1920s and 1930s], even when it was patently foolhardy. They had never experienced the naked feeling of the leading section and troop of a horsed cavalry squadron, who used to advance led by one man with a drawn sword to deal with... [any ambush]. He was covered from just behind, round every corner and over every rise, by a man with a drawn rifle; he in turn was covered by the leading section who were covered further back by the remainder

of the troop and so on to the squadron and regiment on longer [tactical] bounds. So they moved like a caterpillar, covered at every stage and ready to deploy immediately into attack or defence at the first sign of danger. This conception of tactics, which is surely the right one, was to pay handsome dividends and save many lives in the years to come.[26]

In other words, it was horsed cavalry who learned the true value of caution, before they acquired any false sense of security in Britain's under-protected the Second World War tanks. It is also pointed out that being in charge of a horse and navigating it across tricky ground prepared the average soldier for promotion far better than simply driving a vehicle, taking orders and driving directions from someone else. When navigating distance, the officers in a horsed cavalry regiment had to be as good a judge of pace "as the best flat-race jockey". "The march table worked out at exactly six miles to the hour;... Trot fifteen minutes, walk ten, trot fifteen, dismount and walk ten, halt ten, in each hour." This thoroughness was to be instilled across the division in the following months. Even in Palestine, away from the European war as it was, there were operational pressures that required this level of caution.

Security Operations

The security situation in Palestine was complex and toxic. The vaguely written Balfour Declaration of 1917 that had sought to win Jewish support hinted much while delivering little, yet simultaneously inciting suspicion, fear and hatred. Since then, Britain's confused involvement in Palestine had been enacted both with confusion and unwillingness. Arab and Jewish populations each claimed the land, the post-Great War British authorities were under-resourced and their role poorly conceptualised. During Britain's tenure of Palestine from the end of the First World War to 1948, the colonial secretary changed 17 times.

Recent bloodshed included a full-scale Arab revolt that required up to 50,000 soldiers, police and paramilitaries to crush, and had resulted in thousands of deaths. The suppression of the Arab revolt had exacerbated lingering rancour and not just against the British. As the British had used Jewish militias in the suppression of the Arabs, they had now further hardened the schism between the two competing populations. However, Britain was soon to be facing swathes of hatred from the Jewish population too. This was the result of the 1939 white paper. The document laid the way for an independent, binational state in ten years-time – during which period Jewish immigration would be limited and so would the transfer of land from Arabs to Jews.

---

26 Fitzgeorge-Parker, *No Secret So Close*, pp.78-9. This system of tactical movement for reconnaissance troops is very similar to the Green snake/Red snake system of the author's own yeomanry days on CVRTs.

By the time the Second World War began, Britain's position in Palestine was therefore under ferocious scrutiny from its Jewish population.[27] With David Ben-Gurion reflecting bitterly that it effectively rescinded the Balfour declaration. His view was mirrored in strikes and demonstrations – some of which were put down violently. Bernard Montgomery (the great 'Monty' of the war) truculently observed that Jew and Arab would continue to kill each other. Britain, Tom Segev writes in *One Palestine, Complete*, was 'stuck in a dead end and [they] knew it'.[28] The one saving grace was that Britain was at war with rabidly anti-semitic Nazi Germany.

The complexity of the situation was entirely lost on most of the yeomanry. In a 2000 year long struggle characterised by symbols and persecution, it was the firmly established economic advantages of the Jewish population caught the eye of the newly arrived British soldiers. Their sympathy for example was exercised by a highly divergent rate of pay comparison between Arabs and Jews. Then there was the fact that the yeomanry were naturally drawn to Arabs rather than Jews who mainly spoke German (or German sounding languages). But fundamentally, the British authorities simply didn't want to be there, and most of the British soldiers themselves felt no empathy for the deeply painful turbulence in which they now lived and worked.

The mutual resentment between the occupying forces of Palestine, and its denizens was illustrated at a party that the Jewish mayor of a small town gave for the officers of the North Somerset Yeomanry. Almost all the British present could not speak either German nor Hebrew. The mayor opened proceedings with a long-speech in Hebrew – which was translated a line at a time by the one guest who understood – and it was exclusively an attack on the British policy in Palestine. The civilian guests applauded each point, while the officers became more and more embarrassed. When the dancing started (astoundingly the party had got that far), the boorish comment of one yeomanry officer 'Bloody Jews' was presumably lost in translation.[29]

The rancour though did also spill out into violence; and this is where the yeomanry could earn their crust in the meantime. Thus the Sherwood Rangers found themselves living up to this (a little to their surprise) when they were called to Sarafand to deal with the rioting. "Things looked rather bad at one time" recalled Christopherson[30] in particular when some police found themselves cut off by a dangerous looking crowd. The Rangers duly drew swords and conducted the division's first mounted action of the war by charging the rioters, who promptly melted away. "We did not do much damage to any person and suffered not many injuries ourselves, except for a few broken heads and limbs caused through some stones and bricks. Fortunately no

---

27 Despite this, four months after the outbreak of war, the Jewish agency presented the British with a list of 134,000 Jews who wished to fight for the British forces. Tom Segev, *One Palestine Complete: Jews and Arabs Under the British Mandate* (London: Abacus, 2002), p.450.
28 Segev, *One Palestine Complete*, p.442.
29 Verney, *Going to the Wars*, p.54.
30 Holland (ed.), *An Englishman at War*, p.32.

horses were damaged at all." The attention given to this incident is misplaced. That it is even regarded as a noteworthy event in the evolution of cavalry is also misplaced thinking. The "action" was hardly typical of real cavalry operations, didn't involve casualties, and was to be followed by far more daunting cavalry actions that actually involved well-conceived tactics. The mention given to this charge though (not just by Holland) is symptomatic of the patchy historiography about the division. The Rangers for example – the regiment involved in this episode – were fairly soon de-horsed and never went near combat as mounted cavalry. Thus this incident in their history receives more attention that it deserves; because it stands out. Meanwhile, small patrols from the Yorkshire Dragoons and Cheshire Yeomanry, acting as cavalry in June and July 1941, came under heavy fire and have received much less attention on paper.

Despite the fact that this was one of few disruptions to the division's training routine, it does show one reason that the division had been deployed; as military aid to the civil power. The fact that so much time could be devoted to training (rather than security duties) however, does invoke the thoughts of Verney on this role, that "we [were there to force] unwanted help on the already adequate Palestine Police."[31] This then suggests that the key reason for deploying the yeomanry *en masse* to the Middle East might actually have been primarily for deterrence. It should be noted that until high summer 1940 there was no war on in the Holy Land – and certainly not with France. Therefore, having a horsed division actually made rather good sense, if their role was primarily to be a police unit. The deterrent role to Italy would be addressed simply by having a critical mass of men in the area. In the meantime, mounted patrols proved effective for daytime patrolling of the streets, although the men were lorried for night-time patrols (in the case of the Rangers at least).

Individuals and Camels

There was meanwhile more strenuous war work being done by individual members of the division. In the interests of recording the work of the lesser known extremities of Britain's military capability during the war, it should be known that Lieutenant Rogers of the Cheshire Yeomanry for example was detached to join the Camel Corps fighting the Italians in British Somaliland. He was only there in time to take part in the fighting retreat and evacuation to Aden. Although it came down to the wire, the camels were successfully loaded throughout the night to escape by boat just in time. Having thus campaigned through the summer of 1940, he was therefore back in time to also take part in the Syrian campaign, this time on horseback. Lt Rogers it should be noted, was therefore the only officer in the entire British army to fight on both camel and horse in the Second World War. Other officers and soldiers were in time to be seconded to take part in the battles for Greece or Crete. Some returned to

---

31 Verney, *Going to the Wars*, p.69.

the division having just faced the panzers and were particularly contemptuous of the division's odds.

The remainder of 1st Division were also coming into contact with camels though – they were still a frequent enough sight in 1940s Palestine. For the Warwickshire Yeomanry, the first sighting of a camel train came just after they had begun a new phase of controlled exercising for the horses, as they were so recently landed. The carefully controlled ride in question was reduced to pandemonium however when the strange and powerful smelling new apparition hove in sight. As with all things though – even shell-fire later on – the horses learnt to simply accept these strange experiences as a matter of course. Of note is the fact that the Cheshire Yeomanry record it taking six months for the horses' natural aversion to camels to wear off, whereas in the previous war, when there had been more regular exposure, it had taken much less time. Not that the delay seemed to matter.

There was a clear sense of being a distant and irrelevant footnote to the tribulations on the continent. "The war against Hitler seemed far away as, early every morning, we exercised our horses among the tall silvery trees of the eucalyptus forest grown to drain what had been a malarial swamp; or splashed them in the sea", such was Verney's impression.

Despite Verney's cynicism however, there was a general improvement throughout the division. Older officers were being moved on to desk jobs, or sent home, training was both regular and more intensive than anything experienced to date, and there was a more plentiful supply of live ammunition. No doubt, the overall improvement of the division was inevitable as they were, for the first time in two decades, together and training full-time as a large formation. Money was also being spent on ensuring that there was always a full complement of horses for each regiment, and local remounts were being purchased to ensure the roster was full.

The development of the personnel involved was also being attended to. Apart from the detachment of the odd officer to elsewhere in Middle East Command for experience, there were non-commissioned soldiers, who already had experience, being nominated for commissions and other soldiers being selected for officer training and dispatched to an Officer Cadet Training Unit. These O.C.T.U.s popped up throughout the full geographical expanse of the British army during the war, and typically took outstanding soldiers or N.C.Os, trained them for six intensive months in a specialist discipline, before commissioning them as second lieutenants. There were O.C.T.Us for infantry, artillery, signals, armour (meaning tanks) – everything in fact, including horsed cavalry. The cavalry school and O.C.T.U. had been set up in Palestine at Karkur, predominantly by the Royal Scots Greys, who supplied most of the instructors. They took on around 20 cadets on each course, and condensed the eighteen-month course that had been run at the peace-time cavalry school at Weedon. The Middle East was widely adorned with O.C.T.U.s, so it would have been strange for the cavalry not to follow suit, it was after all accepted that they needed to continue training and development like everyone else. Ultimately, as the continued investment in remounts for them also showed, the policy was not yet for them to simply wither on the branch.

The cadets in question were generally speaking effective but young sergeants, or very promising troopers. On the course they learnt "every branch of horsemanship and horsemastership." "For the first two months we never put a saddle on our horses but rode them in just blankets and surcingles. This taught us balance in the most amazing way." These are the words of Bruce Hobbs, who in 1938 had won the Grand National. "As a lifetime professional I could do plenty of things to and with a horse, but now I learnt to shoe, rasp and extract teeth, deal with all sorts of minor ailments..." Furthermore, the cadet became "a very proficient swordsman... The dummy course, mounted and galloping, was something else...[it] included a large padded knob like a hard boxing-glove which would spring at your head just as you stabbed the dummy on the ground and as you were jumping an obstacle. You had to learn to parry this new attacker by punching it with the hilt of your sword – or pay the consequences!"[32]

Hobbs's account of officer training reveals some key points. One is that officer education in late 1940 was still training 1st Cavalry Division cadets to become staggeringly proficient with swords. And, as an established mounted cavalry school, the investment was clearly being made in order to recycle personnel back into a division that was originally dispatched to Palestine for de-horsing. Furthermore as the other pages of Hobbs's biography show, many of the troopers being commissioned were what would be described as "gentlemen troopers" and that there probably wasn't a huge diversification of the officers' social demographic even on a wartime footing.

Very senior N.C.O.s, like a Regimental Sergeant Major did not have to go through the Karkur course. As it so happened, many of the senior N.C.O.s had been commissioned during the course of the Great War a generation earlier, then simply resigned their commissions and returned to the ranks during peacetime.[33] Now they were being called upon to be officers again. In more normal times a senior N.C.O. being commissioned would go to another regiment. It would not be easy for the R.S.M. for example – hitherto the second-most respected man in the regiment – to suddenly go from the top of one food chain to the bottom of another, as a junior officer. However, this was war and, more unusually, this was a cavalry division. It meant that the S.N.C.O.s being commissioned each had a working lifetime of equine expertise that the regiments could ill-afford to lose. This being the case, newly-commissioned officers of this ilk were retained in their regiments and given extra roles in horse management on top of their normal duties. This augmented the newly increased training standards of the Division's officers well. The leadership spine was certainly being developed.

---

32 Fitzgeorge-Parker, *No Secret So Close*, pp.81-2.
33 As the British army had fought so hard to down-size after 1918 and downgrade its capability from being the most effective in Europe, it had simultaneously reduced nearly all its "Temporary Gentlemen" who had been commissioned from the ranks during the war.

1940 was a transformative year for the division as a whole – they had only just come together by January and then had had to learn soldiering, and soldiering as entire brigades, from scratch. The brigade officers meanwhile had had to learn to fight alongside other brigades in a division. Over the course of the year they got their horses fit for rigorous training, and they began to conduct this training on a war footing. Even despite the sense of being in a Middle Eastern bubble, this became increasingly conscientious. A key example of this is the leadership audit evidently being carried out by Major-General Clark. After a T.E.W.T. (Tactical Exercise Without Troops – essentially a map exercise or war-game) towards the end of May, it became apparent that the charming Brigadier Wily of 6th brigade was not a suitable brigade commander. He was shortly returned home and replaced by the newly-promoted Brigadier J. Chrystal – this was to be of profound relevance to the Cheshire Yeomanry in particular.

In short, the division was self-auditing and professionalising. There were undoubtedly egregious lapses, such as the episode of the wives and a still rampant class divide. However, there were also clear signs of an evolution in the leadership of the division. It cannot have escaped attention that there was a very serious war on the other side of the Mediterranean, with Britain fighting for its very existence. The other knock-on effect of this fighting across the sea was to sharpen the attention of the Palestine garrison even further, and as Hitler's forces bore down on Paris in early June 1940, defeat for the allies seemed inevitable. Furthermore, America had not entered the war, and the Soviet Union was still nominally in alliance with Hitler's Germany. At a minute past twelve on the morning of the 11 June, 1940, Mussolini nailed his colours to the mast of his Fascist ally and declared war. The entire Mediterranean was now very much under threat. As Verdin records, the effect was virtually immediate; yeomanry were placed on one hour's notice to move, and a detachment was dispatched to Haifa to protect against a surprise attack by enemy paratroopers. Very soon, other detachments were being moved out of barracks (if they were lucky enough to be in them) into open lines at key strategic points.[34]

This immediate rise in threat level was an opportunity for Brigadier Chrystal to stamp his personality upon 6th Brigade. He had come with the reputation of being "fierce but fair" and had until the war been commander of the Trans-Jordan Frontier Force. This was essentially a gendarmerie cavalry and armoured car force equipped like a British unit, tasked with continually policing the frontier. They had done this throughout the troublesome inter-war period, including a very intense Arab revolt.[35] Chrystal therefore had a great deal of operational experience to draw on,

---

34 Not the case with the Rangers apparently, nor with the North Somerset Yeomanry; one of whom, on watching his comrades out on divisional exercises, referred to them as "Hitler's secret weapon". See Verney, *Going to the Wars*, p.69.
35 Montgomery had commanded a brigade during this campaign and on its conclusion in 1939 remarked, "I shall be sorry to leave Palestine in many ways, as I have enjoyed the

not to mention a full realisation of the demands of war on mounted units. In short, a professional was being brought in. One of his first acts was a round of casting parades, whereby the horses that had not yet achieved an appropriate condition were removed from the strength. It was in fairness May, and those that still hadn't adjusted to the climate, were clearly not of a suitable physical disposition.

Major-General Clark and his Brigade commanders, were from the middle of June subjecting their men to a major exercise, as either a regiment, brigade or division, every week. During the first divisional exercise (the week of the 20 June), conducted on the Plain of Esdraelon, the Cheshire Yeomanry were forbidden from starting before 1600 hrs, yet were situated 25-30 miles from their objective. They therefore had to ride through the night, along narrow tracks through the hills in order to reach the battle against 5th brigade the following morning. They reached it at 01.30 and the battle started immediately, finishing at midday. Parts of the division launched into a charge with drawn swords, and this resulted in one man getting stabbed in the arm, and a horse breaking its leg and having to be destroyed. As soon as the umpires declared the exercise over, it was straight into a conference for the divisional officers and senior regimental officers. The feedback was rigorous, with the Cheshire Yeomanry for example applauded for their approach march, but criticised for not making full use of the surprise they could have achieved. The subsequent march back home was in hot weather and the horses certainly struggled, especially as they simply weren't fit enough at this stage – though in fairness they had just fought a battle after marching 25 miles and were now being asked to do the same march again. The main problem turned out to be the proliferation of sore backs among the horses, caused by the tired riders rolling about in the badly-fitted saddles, and the rucking of saddle blankets. According to Verdin, this was a source of shame to every single officer, and it never happened again; every trooper thereafter learned to assiduously smooth out the blanket on his horse's back, and every horse was sized again to ensure that the saddle fitted properly.

The marching distance had gone up from 18 miles a day, and the fact that illness was no longer an excuse to avoid exercise is indicative of the heightened bar set by General Clark and his officers. New blood throughout the levels of command, and the added sting of imminently having to fight off the Italians, was bringing out a hitherto unseen vigour in this most unlikely of divisions. And it was also being trimmed down. On Tuesday, 2 July 1940, the Sherwood Rangers were paraded and informed that they were to lose their horses (future role unclear) with immediate effect. It turned out they were to become coastal artillery. In September, the Warwickshire Yeomanry were told they were to be de-horsed, though in actual fact they kept theirs until shortly after Christmas. No yeomanry unit could have been surprised at the news that they were to

war out here". See John Bierman and Colin Smith, *Alamein: War Without Hate* (London: Penguin Group, 2002). pp.223-230.

lose their horses. But this did not stop the process from being an emotional one, not least because of the confusion it engendered in some cases.

The Rangers' de-horsing for example was clearly driven by the war-footing the division was now on. The fact that their role was unclear at first is surprising but it shows was that the authorities didn't want them to be mounted anymore and would decide later what to do with them. Holland's interpretation[36] is that horses were incompatible with front-line duty. However this is clearly not the view of all of those in authority; if it was they would have immediately de-horsed every unit. It suggests that they simply saw a need for fewer horsed units – though even this was not a standard view. The units that remained mounted meanwhile were being very intensively trained. For example, cadres for all of the division's machine-gun troops together were being held, and the resulting high-standard of the Vickers gun teams was impressive. The Cheshire Yeomanry also had one squadron de-horsed and converted to lorries, so that when the general mechanisation occurred, they would have a ready-made pool of instructors. Nevertheless, the process of mechanisation, or rather de-horsing was beginning. Christopherson recounts some of the emotions on 3 July 1940:

> We spent the whole of today packing. The horses went off to Remounts [the remount depot] at Nathaniya under Stephen, one man to two horses. It was very sad seeing them all going away. I shall miss "Bob" terribly. I didn't ride over myself but left Gardener to take my horses. Donny player was perfectly miserable when he saw the squadron leave ... He broke down, poor chap, as the last horse left camp.[37]

It did not escape the attention of the rest of the division, that the regiment boasting three M.F.H.s and Donny Player was relinquishing its horses.[38] Like buzzards, officers from the other yeomanry regiments descended upon the Sherwood Rangers before Player's moment of high emotion and bought up some of the best-bred animals in the army. While some regiments were being re-roled and de-horsed, the fact was that the remaining cavalry units were upping their level of training on horses, commissioning highly skilled cavalrymen and upgrading their bloodstock. Holland's interpretation[39] is that horses were incompatible with frontline duty – but this is the product of only focussing on one regiment. In other units the capability upgrade focussed very much around preparing horses and riders for front-line duty. Whatever the rest of the army (and some politicians) thought of them, the remainder of 1st Cavalry Division was getting ready to fight as cavalry and doing so with determination.

---

36 Holland (ed.), *An Englishman at War*, p. 44.
37 Holland (ed.), *An Englishman at War*, p. 44.
38 Verdin, *The Cheshire Yeomanry*, p.262.
39 Holland (ed.), *An Englishman at War*, p. 44.

This determination and rigour was at odds with the prime minister's attitude to maintaining a cavalry division. This became known in some quarters of the division in September, when they received a minute from Churchill dated 8.9.40. The North Somerset Yeomanry were finishing their own tiring part in a divisional exercise at Musmus Pass, ironically with far less combat power than Davidson's 2nd Lancers 20 years earlier. The exercise, which had ended in a charge where one soldier was stabbed in the arm and one horse had to be shot after breaking its leg, had been carried out under the watchful eye of Major-General Clark M.C. whom Verney described (without specifically naming) as "very smooth", "charismatic" and "sublimely egotistical"[40]. No doubt Clark was impressed by the ever more polished standard of his (ever-shrinking) division, and maybe the vigour of its charging. While an admirable endorsement of the level of scrutiny that the division was ever under, Clark's presence also explains the presence of a visiting staff officer Verney saw reading a wire from no less than Churchill. That document was also copied to the Foreign Secretary, the C.I.G.S and Clark. It read as follows:

> It has been heart-breaking to me to watch these splendid units fooled away for a whole year. It is an insult to the Scots Greys and Household Cavalry to tether them to horses at the present time. There might be something to be said for a few battalions of [mounted] infantry or cavalrymen mounted on ponies for the rocky hills of Palestine, but these historic Regular Regiments have a right to play a man's part in the war.

Whilst there is no mention of the historic, but not regular, yeomanry regiments in this passage, the underlying attitude requires no further explanation. All that is worth adding is that, while Churchill regarded the use of fine soldiers as cavalrymen anachronistic and emasculating, it can be assumed that he meant any units, and not just regular ones. This telegrammatic outburst was prompted because Churchill was at the time acutely concerned about the ratio of non-combatant troops to front-line troops. On scrutinising the ORBAT for the Middle East, the mention of 1st Cavalry Division must have stood out just as the *Manual of Horsemastership, etc 1937* stands out in the age of publications on RADAR.

The issue was not to be forgotten about either. He mentioned it again in a minute on 6 January 1941, before going into some depth on the issue six days later after he presumably received an unsatisfactory reply:

> The mechanisation of the 1st Cavalry Division in Palestine is a distressing story. These troops have been carried out with their horses and maintained at great expense in the Middle East since the early months of the war. Several months ago it was decided by the War Office that they should be mechanised. I gladly

---

40   Verney, *Going to the Wars*, pp.72-3.

approved. Now I learn, as a result of one of my own enquiries, that nothing has been done about this, that the whole division is to be carried back home again - presumably without their horses - and that this is not to begin until June 1...[41]

Churchill then went on to list various options for re-reoling: Bren Carriers, captured Italian tanks etc.

Like many a chief executive before and since, he had found that what was to his mind a simple and evidently necessary action, had been disobediently ignored – the phrase "Now I learn, as a result of one of my own enquiries" seems particularly loaded. Churchill's interpretation in the document seemed to be that; the division was pointless, and that its re-roling was tardy, even though he had specifically signed off for this to come about those "several months ago". Moreover, it seemed an easy fix to undertake. Churchill in this missive went on to provide a list of options which further suggested that he perceived such an unnecessary delay in re-roling, if not actual full mechanisation, to be reprehensible.

What exercised Churchill during this exchange more than anything was that, despite a plethora of seemingly obvious and cheap options; a) nothing had happened b) the only future action planned so far was to ship the entire formation back home – an undertaking he viewed as pointlessly time-consuming and expensive, and contrary to all obvious logic and sense of initiative. While the anger he demonstrated is certainly justifiable, given this interpretation, the stridently black and white view of the situation in his mind was misplaced.

What Churchill had not factored in was that the yeomanry had been expecting to become fully mechanised since 1920, and but for limited funds and training time this would have been achieved by 1939. As it so happened, the latest incarnation of the "When will we re-role?" conversation had been being muttered in the Cairo bars since December 1940. And, just like Churchill, the mutterers regarded the prospect of shipping the whole division across the Mediterranean to re-role as ludicrous and unlikely to happen.[42] The matter of equipping the cavalry with any new hardware (they didn't even have the army-standard Bren-gun anymore) was however a complicated prospect. The idea of being able to send anywhere like sufficient armour or trucks out to the Middle East seemed a short-term impossibility, with the lack of production and dangerously threatened supply route.

The other complicating factor – and presumably the reason that Churchill's memos on the irrelevant horse-soldiers then got shifted to the bottom of the in-tray – is that by the time of these later memos (early 1941), the Greek campaign was attracting both attention and resources. All able-bodied men were required to defend Middle Eastern Command, and if some of those were cavalry, then at least they were only

---

41 Winston Churchill, *The Second World War*, Vol. 3, (Boston: Houghton Mifflin, 1950), pp 639-40 as cited in Verdin, *The Cheshire Yeomanry*, p.278.
42 Verdin, *The Cheshire Yeomanry*, p.279.

defending Palestine, where there was less of an immediate threat. Meanwhile the rest of the Mediterranean theatre was being stripped down to man and equip the Greek expeditionary force. Furthermore British forces manning treaty bases in sovereign Iraq had now suddenly came under siege following an Axis-inspired coup.

Nonetheless, Churchill was listened to... to an extent. The yeomanry would not be shipped home to re-role. Their de-horsing was in fact to happen out in Palestine; but it was to be done piecemeal. Evidently the captured Italian tanks weren't such a sensible option. No doubt this would not have impressed Churchill either; but at least he had quickly become pre-occupied with other matters.

In the interests of brevity, the subsequent de-horsing of the division was governed as much by seniority of regiment as it was by operational considerations, and this involved moving regiments around between brigades, in order to re-role an entire brigade at a time. This did mean that the Sherwood Rangers were re-assigned no less than three times within a year, but at least the prime minister could not identify them as cavalry anymore. Elsewhere, the remaining horsed regiments were reorganised into 5th Cavalry Brigade. It now consisted of the Cheshire Yeomanry, the Yorkshire Dragoons, and the North Somerset Yeomanry. The Staffordshire Yeomanry were also training under Chrystal. Between these units there were individual mechanised squadrons, but the simple fact was that there was no equipment to merit replacing this brigade's horses with. They would therefore remain as mounted (and now quite well-trained) cavalry, and furthermore, their individual mechanised squadrons were in fact *re-horsed*. Churchill was undoubtedly not appraised of this development. The now fully-trained motorised yeomen re-converting to mounted cavalry were certainly not impressed.[43]

It was at this stage, despite the cavalry's training becoming ever better under Chrystal, that they were in fact to be further de-powered. Their manpower was to be cut by one troop per squadron, and all mechanised training in each of the three affected regiments was to immediately cease (though there did remain a limited Motor Transport capability with each regimental headquarters). In one squadron the decision as to which troop was to be axed and redistributed was decided by a horse-race between the officers concerned.

The wider world's opinions of Britain's cavalry may have varied, but they don't seem to have diverged much from one common theme. This theme is represented at one end, by officers returning to the division after facing the Wehrmacht's Panzers in Greece. Falling back on Verney again as a ready source of cynicism, an example is cited of an officer returning to be told of the North Somerset Yeomanry's defence plans for northern Palestine. The officer merely quipped, "C'est magnifique, mais ... c'est bloody silly."[44] At the other, more severe end of the cynicism spectrum, there was

---

43 Verdin, *The Cheshire Yeomanry*, p.265.
44 Verdin, *The Cheshire Yeomanry*, p.85.

Churchill. A scrutiny of his missives to G.O.C Middle East does much to explain the confusion surrounding units such as the Sherwood rangers.

Conclusion

1940 was the year the British army was humbled on the continent, before the rest of the defensive capability that Chamberlain had built came up to scratch and prevailed against the Luftwaffe. It was also the year that the yeomanry had to start contemplating the dangers their homeland faced. "We were no longer a light-hearted band of solicitors, squires, farmers, butchers and businessmen playing at soldiers but a cavalry Regiment on active service overseas preparing itself – for what?"[45] The most likely answer to that was war with Italy. For now Palestine was no longer a strategic backwater for the yeomanry to deploy to until they became a useful mechanised division. Palestine was now close to centre stage (Suez and the war for it), and itself a key route in for an enemy like the newly declared Mussolini. But even when war with Fascist Italy became a reality mid-year, what shape 1st Cavalry Division's participation in any forthcoming campaign would look like was unclear.

Despite their undoubted improvements throughout 1940-41, the division's capability and role were being eroded. Furthermore, neither their superiors nor the yeomen themselves seemed to seriously harbour ambitions of carrying their swords, or their machine guns, on horseback against the axis powers, despite the unforgiving exercises that so often involved both. However much depleted they were by a process that had begun in 1920, they were still more capable of fighting than they had ever been since that year. The division had been scaled back to a brigade, the individual units had had their strength reduced by a quarter; but their individual discipline and sub-unit training was immeasurably better than it been for twenty years. Despite the cutbacks, they understood what it took to cover vast expanses of ground, even at night. They knew just how much work it took to ensure that men and horses were maintained in fighting trim at all times. They fully understood the details of tactical movement, and their long night marches could be done quietly. They may not have been as well-equipped as even Allenby's cavalry, but as a highly mobile, stealthy and now resilient force, they could offer any brigadier a forward screen of eyes and ears that no other unit in Palestine could deliver. Though the stripping of resources to fight in Greece meant that this comparison to any remaining units was not a very high bar.

Churchill may have fumed about the maintaining of the division. He may have excoriated those he believed responsible for not consigning them to the history books. But the cards had now been shuffled and the survivors of the administrative rehash were successfully concealed from him, still on the strength and capable, such as they were. Nor were their military superiors likely to bow to political pressure and fully

---

45 Verdin, *The Cheshire Yeomanry*, p.49.

re-role them any time soon. Better an operational, highly mobile cavalry force, than an armoured formation in training with no armour.

"The transportation of a cavalry division, complete with horses, across three thousand miles of land and water costs a lot of public money. 'They'.. would surely see that the money was not wasted."[46] Maybe it was Churchill's own point about finance that had made Middle East Command continue with 5th Cavalry Brigade, in pursuit of finally claiming their money's worth of work out of them. Maybe they simply didn't have a choice. The fact was that Iraq was looking increasingly threatening, and nobody admitted knowing whether France's colony Syria would declare for the Free French General De Gaulle, or the Vichy French General Dentz. The pressure was increasing; the substitutes' bench looked likely to be called upon. Now was not the time for an entire brigade to be taken off the strength.

46   Verdin, *The Cheshire Yeomanry*, p.50.

4

Coming to Scratch

In April 1941 the German forces were simultaneously pushing across North Africa and down through Greece. On the 4 April, Lieutenant-Generals Neame and O'Connor were captured in the Western Desert. On the 13th Yugoslavia fell. Rumours started to circulate that there were German agents in Syria. Further trouble was fermenting in Iraq. Palestine, Britain's easternmost (and last) bulwark protecting Suez, was now facing threats from two sides. It did not help that no one in Whitehall knew to which side the French colonial forces in Syria would turn.

This might have been guessed at. In 1940, with operation "Catapult", the Royal Navy had attacked a harboured French fleet when Admiral Somerville shelled it in Mers-el-Kebir before it could be handed over to the Germans, killing 1,297 French sailors and wounding about 350. It could have been safely assumed that this was rather a polarising event. There was also reasonable evidence by May 1941 that all the French soldiers, who were planning to defect, had by now already done so. As if this was not enough, French forces had shown themselves more than willing to resist British forces when they had ferociously fought off the Dakar raid. Immediately after this, the French had bombed Gibraltar in revenge. Furthermore, fighting at sea during the Dakar operation had yielded the captured Vichy French submarine *Ajax*. With it was an instruction from Admiral Darlan that the fleet use a specific radio code that could be read by all the Axis powers. France was now actively sharing resources with Germany and Italy. Clearly Vichy France was not neutral and the Vichy French were sharing all reports on the position of British ships with their Axis overlords. This had gone very much against Churchill's anticipated pattern of events. With the Dakar raid for example he had predicted that the governor of Dakar – the raid here took place after Mers-el-Kebir – would want to 'fire a few shots' 'for honour's sake', but then stop and accept De Gualle's invitation to dinner that evening.[1] Churchill was wrong, but his subordinates in the Middle East took a more pragmatic approach.

---

1   Charles De Gaulle, *The Call to Honour* (London: Collins, 1955), p.121 as cited in Smith, *England's Last War with France,* p.141.

As a response to the heightened state of alert, the yeomanry were assigned sections of northern Palestinian border to guard. Given the lack of meaningful anti-tank artillery and the almost total absence of mortars, in retrospect there was not much that could have realistically been expected of this defending force. Nonetheless they had soon developed a tactical doctrine that it was hoped would mitigate their failings in equipment. A screen of vedettes (mounted outposts) were the defensive eyes and ears, and the first line of resistance. The fact that they were cavalry rather than infantry meant that a longer tactical bound between lines could be established. By way of anti-tank technology, each mounted soldier had the rather unimpressive armament of two Molotov cocktails tied to his horse's saddle. These converted beer-bottles[2] were the primary anti-tank weapon for the yeomanry – presumably because of their ready availability. Their other weapon was the archaic and sparingly-issued Boyes anti-tank rifle. Once any advancing enemy had been engaged, the vedettes would then fall back behind a line of concrete pillboxes, each containing an almost complete section. The men in these positions, using their rifles and Hotchkiss guns, would take on the enemy, the tanks hopefully having been knocked out by the petrol bombs and Boyes guns. Meanwhile the last two men from each section would hold on to the horses in any available dead ground to the rear. There was also the theoretical means to call in artillery fire – although this valuable resource was stretched by 1941.

As it so happened, this configuration was equally useful for implementing the cavalry's other role in Palestine. At this stage "security duties" primarily involved stopping locals from smuggling kerosene over the northern border. This situation allowed some officers to indulge their predilection for duck flighting, and it was not unknown to see a shotgun rather than a rifle carried in the saddle mounted rifle-bucket. This despite the increasing level of tension along the border. Letters from home meanwhile – heavily interrupted by German activity – did not contribute to higher morale either; they were all about the bombing at home and were full of envy for the soldiers idling along in Palestine. One sergeant-major received a letter from his wife, saying that she had had all her teeth out and was leaving him to marry a Pole. His laconic observation was "It will save me money in the long run."[3]

The unreliable news feed from home, however, was more than compensated for by the very active passage of "blue lights", or rumours throughout the division. This was partly facilitated by the fact that many of the staff officers at divisional H.Q. had been seconded from the yeomanry only a few months earlier. Countless theories consequently circulated back to their old friends, as regiment after regiment had been re-assigned or re-designated. Many commanding officers were now keen on pushing their regimental interests at H.Q.; not least because nobody wanted to be caught short

---

2   The petrol bombs were almost exclusively assembled from beer bottles – a readily available resource – and were mainly created by defaulters, that is soldiers on charges.

3   Verney, *Going to the Wars*, p.81.

by the re-roling process "or we'll be turned into bloody signallers',[4] which they deemed beneath them. Others merely concentrated on the job they had been given. This sense of intrigue was greatly stirred on 10th May, when most of the division, less the still horsed 5th brigade, vanished. Not only them, but division H.Q. also mysteriously disappeared from all contact with the Palestine bubble. 5th Brigade's new instruction was simply to report to O.C. Troops, Haifa for administration, but otherwise continue as before - which was defending their border and stockpiling petrol bombs. Added to these directions was one notable piece of advice dispensed over the telephone by a garrulous staff officer:"I should make those cocktails of yours nice and strong."[5]

Their destination, along with the entire headquarters of 1st Cavalry Division, was an organisation known as "Habforce". The new column was being sent into sovereign Iraq, because it's new ruler Rashid Ali had struck against the few British troops still allowed in the country by treaty right. The salient point to both London and Alexandria, was that there was German influence behind this (some German aircraft were used in the ensuing campaign). The British military presence meanwhile consisted of an airfield at Habbaniyah, and it had been under siege by the Iraqis since 2 May. Habforce was intended to either rescue the garrison or recapture the camp and airfield, while another force landed at Basra.

Forming this relief force was inevitably an exercise in overstretch. Since the end of March, the British forces in North Africa had already been suffering from the diversion of men and resources to Greece, and after defeat in Greece by the end of April, there was further diversion yet to then defend Crete. The island then fell at the end of May. This powerful threat through the centre of the Mediterranean focussed the attention of Wavell. In March 1941, Rommel set foot in North Africa and immediately began pushing back Allied forces. Soon all of Libya was gone, bar Tobruk. Wavell, C-i-C Middle East, was under pressure. Regarding the direct threat of German arms as the priority, Wavell at the start of May 1941 felt compelled to deal with Crete and Rommel before all else. Among other factors, he considered his resources too overstretched to take on any other significant operations, like relieving Iraq. It was true that reinforcements had arrived from India, but Wavell did not feel that these were sufficient to take on a very capable Iraqi foe.[6] He urged Turkish mediation instead. The *Daily Telegraph*'s Christopher Buckley later explained, the "patient and much-tried Commander-in-Chief was in the position of the father of a family whose budget cannot cover all the needs of his numerous offspring... Ever since the preceding June his command had been primarily an affair of making ends meet with totally insufficient resources, and in the months of April and May 1941 it

---

4   Verney, *Going to the Wars*, p.86.
5   Verney, *Going to the Wars*, p.86.
6   Smith, *England's Last War with France*, p.171.

seemed that all the bills were coming together."[7] Little wonder Wavell argued for a path that would not further dwindle his manpower.

A further reason to suggest mediation – other than simple overstretch – was that he believed it would be counter-productive to fight the Iraqis. He did not want to trigger further Arab uprisings amongst the Palestinians and Egyptians. The Palestinian Arabs for instance having only been finally subdued by open war in 1939. It was not merely an issue of taking on further unnecessary commitments; it was an issue of triggering a regional conflagration in a region already quivering under Hitler's Damoclean sword. Besides, Wavell had suspicions he was soon to be asked to further overstretch by entering Syria.[8] In the meantime he would resist, in all ways that he could, the pressing for an operational commitment in Iraq, and even after its commencement he continued to advocate against further commitment to it. This is nicely crystallised in an exchange of telegrams between Wavell himself, Churchill and the Chiefs of Staff in Churchill's own *The Second World War*:[9]

> Wavell: I have consistently warned you that no assistance could be given to Iraq from Palestine in present circumstances and have always advised that commitment in Iraq should be avoided.
>
> Churchill: A commitment in Iraq was inevitable. We had to establish a base at Basra and control that port to safeguard Persian oil…. no question of accepting the Turkish offer of mediation. We can make no concessions…. Essential to do all in our power to save Habbaniya and to control the pipeline to the Mediterranean.
>
> Wavell: Your message takes little account of realities. You must face facts. I feel it is my duty to warn you in the gravest possible terms that I consider the prolongation of fighting in Iraq will seriously endanger the defence of Palestine and Egypt. The political repercussions may result in what I have spent nearly two years trying to avoid, namely serious internal trouble in our bases.
>
> Churchill to Chiefs of Staff: I am deeply disturbed at General Wavell's attitude. He seems to have been taken as much by surprise on his eastern as he was on his western flank… he gives me the impression of being tired out.
>
> Chiefs of Staff to Wavell: Settlement by negotiation cannot be entertained… Realities of the situation are that Rashid Ali has all along been hand-in-glove with Axis powers and was merely waiting until they could support him before exposing his hand.

---

7 This likely though undoubtedly sympathetic analysis has the benefit of being presented after censorship was over. From Christopher Buckley, *Five Ventures* (London: HMSO, 1946), p.45 as cited in Smith, *England's Last War with France* p.172.
8 Both these views, that Wavell feared an Arab uprising, and that he suspected he was about to be ordered to become embroiled in Syria/Lebanon, are identified by Smith, p. 172.
9 In this case the edited exchange is quoted from that employed by Smith, p.172.

Thus overruled, Wavell continued with juggling his ever-growing collection of 'hungry mouths'. Despite the pressures, the Chiefs of Staff's final message in the above quoted chain does present a very clear logic.

Logical or not, with the concurrent planning and resourcing of Operation "Battleaxe" to stop Rommel in North Africa, there were few reserve troops available with which Wavell, C-i-C Middle East, could secure the position in Iraq and stop it becoming a strategic platform for future German attacks. If these ever materialised, Wavell would be under extreme threat from both sides. Thus it came to pass that most of 1st Cavalry Division went to war in June 1941. But they did it as lorried infantry with Habforce. They went on to: reach Habbaniyah after the garrison had successfully repelled its attackers; then support the assault on Fallujah; take Baghdad and secure the pipelines running oil through the Middle East to Haifa and Tripoli. As it transpired they were then ultimately to swing round into Syria, while their still mounted former comrades in 5th brigade fought up from the south on their own separate mission.

The pipelines that Habforce had to secure each had pumping stations along the way and were designated by the letter of their final destination, then by a number showing how far along the pipeline they were; thus the Warwickshire Yeomanry first went into action securing H2 (the second pumping station on the way to Haifa). The Warwickshire Yeomanry approached in their lorries, then dismounted and fought through with Hotchkiss guns, rifles and bayonets, supported by two 1920 vintage Roll Royce armoured cars of an RAF ground squadron, a troop of artillery and Colonel Glubb Pasha's Guides. The fighting lasted all day and two Warwickshire yeomen were killed, with five wounded, before H2 was secured. Given the short turnaround from cavalry to lorried infantry, plus the light weaponry available to them, this suggests a respectable unit performance.

T.A. units such as the Warwickshire Yeomanry, newly de-horsed as they were, were cavalry. They had been trained to reconnoitre the enemy and to screen and flank their own forces, fighting small concentrations of enemy as part of this. It should be no surprise then, that the former members of 1st Cavalry Division were predominantly used to provide flank guard and secure pumping stations in an operation that was dominated by the 8,000-mile march required of its soldiers. At least though, they were doing it in vehicles. The rest of the yeomanry would not have to wait long before being committed to war – and this was quickly becoming obvious to everyone.

Cavalry in Waiting

May 1941 was a month of almost intolerable pressure on Middle East Command. By the end of the month, the threat was now the Germans island-hopping their way across the Mediterranean from Crete, while simultaneously pushing through the Western desert into Egypt with Rommel's Afrika Korps. The Suez canal, and Britain's route to India now seemed dangerously close to falling. Adding to the sense of alarm, must have been the pricking of Churchill's sense of revenge. On the night of 10-11 May,

1,483 Londoners were killed by the Luftwaffe, and the House of Commons's debating chamber reduced to smoking ruins. Britain was on the back foot and the momentum had to shift. "Battleaxe" was of course anticipated to restore British momentum – but any success here could not be undone by setbacks elsewhere; such as an Axis invasion from Syria. As Darlan's message onboard the *Ajax* had shown, there was already close cooperation between the Vichy and Axis forces. On May 14th, a Habbaniyah-based British Bleinheim, saw Junkers 90s flying out of Palmyra.[10] With such a flagrant breach of neutrality now documented, the British responded by strafing the Palmyra airfield later that day. This day of air activity was a microcosm of London's rationale to assault Vichy-controlled Syria; there was clear evidence of flagrant German collusion over an area in strategically alarming proximity to Allied territory. It would have to be dealt with. The decision made by Churchill and De Gualle to advance into Syria was presumably made easier for them by their belief that it genuinely would be a case of facing only perfunctory Vichy resistance.

It was undoubtedly easier for Churchill in London, than it was for Wavell in Alexandria, to decide that Syria had to be neutralised. Clearly, a Vichy French or German invasion launched from Syria would sweep through Palestine – defended by not much more than 5th (and at that point 6th) Cavalry Brigade and their horses, with no aircraft or armour – and take the Suez canal from the blindside. Yet it was obvious to Wavell that he couldn't divert forces from his west to protect his East; he had been strictly enjoined to launch Operation Battleaxe against Rommel that summer. The problem was that this was absorbing an awful lot of resources, and it wasn't as if the other distractions (like Crete) were trifling sideshows. Wavell was, quite literally, beset from all sides, each one clamouring loudly, as analogised by Buckley in the *Telegraph*. Nor did it strengthen Wavell's position that he had actually been wrong about Iraq – the campaign had been a success. Wavell called it a "bold and correct decision, which I really felt I ought to have taken myself."[11] Churchill clearly felt he should have done so too.

Wavell had further angered Churchill by delaying Battleaxe; but there was only so much Wavell could do. Churchill, at a distance in London and already short of patience with Wavell, was meanwhile being subjected to pressure from De Gaulle, the leader of the Free French government in exile. This pressure, plus the fear of what could materialise out of Syria imminently, combined to make Churchill promptly order Operation "Exporter" – the invasion of Syria.

---

10   They were the fruit of the Paris Protocols, implemented, but not signed, since the 6 May 1941. The force was really only a gesture. It consisted of 21 frontline aircraft, and a logistic train of 13 transport planes, three massive Junkers 90s, plus a Storch spotter and courier. Not all of these were intended to remain in Iraq.
11   John Connell *Wavell: Supreme Commander* (London: Collins, 1969) p.446.

Exporter is Ordered

Wavell's main objection was that he didn't have anything to launch Exporter with. His reserve force had just been launched into Iraq. He'd had to plunder even 1st Cavalry Division's manpower for this. Furthermore, absolutely nothing could be stripped out of North Africa, and a massive operation had just cost him 15,000 men in Crete. An invasion of Syria would mean resorting to the use of, among other things, horse-soldiers – the very same that Churchill had expressly ordered to be long gone by now. Futhermore, as Battleaxe would coincide with Exporter, there would be a serious overstretch of air support. In effect, Exporter wouldn't have much at all, and nor would it have much armour. All it would have of the latter would be the armoured cars and Bren carriers of the Australian 8th Division plus elements stripped from 6th Division.[12] From the outset of Exporter, Wavell had to use 1,0000 Australian infantry siphoned off from his desert force and away from Battleaxe for Exporter. Wavell's air chief, Longmore, meanwhile was understandably adamant that what he was being asked to deliver could not be delivered. He was immediately sacked by Churchill. This is one of the occasions that we see the effect on history of personalities. Churchill had had enough of complaints from the Middle East, not least from Wavell, and clearly there was an element of ignoring the latest round of excuses – the prime minister was already angry at the delay to Battleaxe, and especially so after he had laboured to send out a convoy of tanks to facilitate it in the Tiger Convoy.[13] As he saw it, the Middle East had to be shored up, and to Churchill's mind there was a very clear case to do it immediately, before the Axis approaches from the western desert and across the Mediterranean became even more threatening. Mussolini for instance was now planning a paratrooper assault on Cyprus – only 100 miles from Syria. The Vichy French could even launch an attack now.

Churchill was bullish, firstly because he considered that Battleaxe was bound to be a success; after all he had just sent out the hardware to do it. Secondly, he did believe that the Vichy French would rather not fight against what Churchill viewed as their natural ally. Thirdly, though only possibly, he may have wanted to force Wavell out by placing an obscene amount of pressure on him. Maybe Churchill felt stung by the failures in Greece and Crete. Equally, he could actually have believed that the situation was not as desperate as Wavell and Longmore made out, the men who after all had presided over the failures in Greece and Crete. Just as he had with the mechanisation of 1st Cavalry Division, Churchill could simply have been guilty of

---

12   The eventual integration of Habforce into the operation would therefore significantly increase the armoured component – by the grand total of two companies of obsolete 1920 Rolls Royce armoured cars of the RAF.

13   Unfortunately, the tanks that he sent still needed to be adapted for desert warfare. Furthermore some had sustained rust damage in transit from the seawater. Then the crews needed to be trained. All this could be overcome, but it would take time. Time was one resource Churchill was not prepared to give away at this stage.

seeing the situation in stark black and white; fight now or lose. The result though of his analysis, was the sending of the horse soldiers he so abhorred, against an enemy who were now willing to fight much more ferociously than he had anticipated.

Wavell's own planning systems are criticised by Gavin Long,[14] specifically from the point of view of Laverack who was tasked with leading 7th Division. He considered that Wavell's staff planners were approaching the problem with "undue optimism"[15] themselves; declaring "the success of the operation largely depends on lack of resistance" at least at first, and that then the French would fall back "into the Lebanon, thereby leaving the rest of the country open to invasion."[16] Besides being a rather obvious conception, this was a rather vague one. How would the sudden change in terrain affect the operational approach for example? Would the routes in or operational doctrine need to alter as the topography changed? Crucially, the hinterland of mountainous Lebanon is significantly easier to defend than the flatter entry points below the Litani.

The criticism of Wavell and his staff was possibly further stirred by frustration that, even on the 28 May – only one week before the operation was originally due to commence – Laverack had not yet been told exactly which units would be available to him. The 7th Division Report on Operation Exporter states that in the operations conference in Cairo on 21 May Laverack was informed that despite the order to "form part of an op to occupy Syria and deny it to the Germans." "It was not possible to obtain precise infm as to the order of battle," and that the division would be augmented by "A composite reg of two sqns [Todcol]. AA units, a sqn of armoured cars (the Royals) [who didn't even take part in Exporter in the end]. [17] Furthermore only a limited number of intelligence handbooks had been distributed and the only maps available were 1 to 200,000 scale; maps for detailed planning of warfare in mountain country really needed to be 1 to 25,000 or at least 1 to 50,000. The obstacles in front of Laverack themselves are indications of the overstretch that Wavell was suffering. The objectively fairer criticism of the senior British planners, is that they were being conceptually vague, and that this gave way to optimism. Precisely the same frustration that Wavell felt regarding his superiors. What they were precise on however was the exact nature of the terrain involved in the impending operation:

> Southern Lebanon is a country locally suited to the defence. Along the coast lies a narrow strip of flat land, seldom more than a few hundred yards wide, which carries the main north-south rd. This is dominated throughout its length by the LEBANON range… at several points the spurs of this range run out to

---

14 Gavin Long *Second World War 1939-1945* Vol II – Greece, Crete and Syria (Canberra: Australian War Memorial, 1953).
15 Cited in Long, p.337.
16 Cited in Long , p.337.
17 AWM 52 1/5/14-0110 7: 7 Australian Division General Staff Branch.

the coast itself and the r[oa]d has had to be cut through. North of Tyr the rd crosses the LITANI river, whose swift current makes it a formidable and easily defended obstacle."

"The mountain country that lies east of the coast rd is rugged and barren, its boulder-strewn hillsides and narrow rocky gorges, offering a tremendous natural barrier to military movement… and off the rds the country is impassable for wheeled or tracked vehs of any kind."[18]

A development that further perturbed Laverack was that the Vichy French seemed to be expecting an imminent attack. Clearly all available resources were going to have to be factored in. From the yeomanry's point of view this factoring in happened at the Exporter force conference on 4 June. The initial attitude to the prospect of using horsed cavalry is unsurprisingly skeptical:

"7. Use of horsed cav.

Forage will be a difficulty and it is desired to examine the proposal of the bdes for the use of horsed cav and sec if practicable for Q to produce the necessary fodder at the required places."[19]

Enthusiasm was lukewarm at the May conference, when the "Preliminary order of battle [Issued for 7 Div on 21st May]" were "issued by HGQ ME …[and] included 5 and 6 Cav Bdes, but Maj-Gen Laverack indicated that he thought this allotment of horsed cav excessive." However, it was then accepted that "5 cav bde had been patrolling Syrian-Palestine border for some time and contacted various French officials on the Syrian side. Supplied much useful information relating to the rds and tracks in the extreme south."[20] None of the scant resources available however, could afford to be overlooked, and concession is first visible at the 4 June conference "In regard to the use of horsed cav" "O [presumably G.O.C.] thought that it would be possible to carry out the preliminary recces in the op suggested by the two bde comds. It was originally intended by Bde comnds to use horsed cav in a restricted role north of the frontier, but views changed later and it was decided by them to try to have horsed cav operating, if possible, up to the third objective."[21] The initial plan in fact was to have "horsed sqn Cheshire Yeo to move along french [sic] frontier rd from south to north, taking the frontier posts en route". This itself was a comparative volte-face from the Ops conference on 21 May.

---

18 AWM 52: 1/5/14-0110 7 Australian Division General Staff Branch (7 Aust Div GS Branch).
19 AWM 52: 1/5/14-0110 7: Appendix A, Notes for Div conference 0900 Hrs 4 June 41.
20 AWM 52: 1/5/14-0110 7 Australian Division General Staff Branch (7 Aust Div GS Branch).
21 AWM52 1/5/14/11: June 1941, Exporter Force.

The fact that the conceptualisation of how they might be used changed throughout the course of the 4 June meeting alone indicates the stark need to fill the flanking and the brigade reconnaissance capability gap, as identified by Milne in 1927. A gap that got bigger the longer the Exporter planners had looked at it. At this stage, the rest of 5th Cavalry Brigade was allotted responsibility for watching the Palestine border and told to take an interest in the portion of the river Jordan between lakes Hula and Tiberias.[22] By the end of the meeting, the assets listed on 7th Division's strength duly included:

"ADDITIONAL TPS UNDER COMMAND
CAVALRY   Cheshire yeo   (Horsed)
          Greys   )
          Staffs Yeo   )[23]   Composite Mech Regt

As the last card in the deck, the remnants of the yeomanry division were going to war. Being cavalry, some were going to flank as well as scout ahead of the two columns launched into Syria from the south; one column being 21st Infantry Brigade advancing up the coastal plain to Beirut, and the second column being 25th Infantry Brigade advancing up the central route into Lebanon and Syria, past the Ante-Lebanon mountains towards Rayak. A link would also have to be maintained between these two elements. A third column would approach Quoneitra and Damascus.[24] Quoneitra was where the Yorkshire Dragoons were to fight their only recorded action as cavalry, but it seems from the scant records that they were not deployed as the original advance screen for this column, as the Cheshire Yeomanry were for theirs. The North Somerset Yeomanry would be used to move up behind these twin assaults. These yeomen would be simply maintaining the allied hold over the ground fought over by 21st Brigade and 25th brigade; essentially a patrolling role, with a few key positions held along the way; thus ensuring that wounded and prisoners could be passed back into Palestine, and supplies could be brought up towards the fighting echelons. Reinforcements were less likely to be seen on the journey north. Correspondingly, the Yorkshire Dragoons and the North Somerset Yeomanry found themselves pressed into action as infantry on occasion. Neither the Yorkshire Dragoons nor the North Somerset Yeomanry ever appear on 7th Division's order of Battle during Exporter. When they are finally listed in the operational strength it is on the Corps Order of Battle. This suggests that by the time the need for their extra boots and hooves was accepted, their value as a theatre asset, rather than brigade or divisional asset had been realised.

22   AWM 52 1/5/14: Divisions 7 Australian Division General Staff Branch (7 Aust Div GS Branch).
23   AWM 52: 1/5/14-0110: Order of battle: Appendix "A" to operation order no.7 dated 5 June 41 under "additional" troops under command.
24   Verdin *The Cheshire Yeomanry*, p.290.

Further fighting power was added to General Maitland-Wilson's force for "Exporter" in the form of Todcol. This was essentially The Royal Scots Greys, who had been attached at various points to different brigades within 1st Cavalry Division over the past year, and who were in theory still mounted. As regulars they had always seemed to march under a different star from the rest of the cavalry in Palestine and had originally been destined to fight in Greece as Todcol – the fighting column under Lt. Col Todd, the Greys' colonel. For "Exporter" Todcol was to be resuscitated and deployed as a "strategic reserve" for the operation, augmented with a squadron of the Staffordshire yeomanry. Given that the combat role of horses was now viewed strictly as one of screening and reconnaissance, it no surprise that an actual fighting column, which as an operational reserve would have to deploy and redeploy quickly, was mounted in 15 cwt trucks.[25] In short, their way of waging war was to be the same as those yeomen who had embarked with Habforce. Todforce (an all arms group) was to gain and maintain touch with the enemy, harass their retreat and discover their line of resistance. This actually came to be a short lived task. On 14 June Todforce became Monforce, and the Royal Scots Greys substituted out of this formation to remain in Merdjayoun responsible for internal security.[26]

If the deployment of yeomanry in 1941, particularly as an advance guard, seems desperate, then that is because Maitland-Wilson and Laverack were. They would have been less desperate if Churchill wasn't forcing the launch of Battleaxe on their boss as soon as he was. The upshot was that Maitland-Wilson's force was to consist of no tanks and only three armoured cars, the reconnaissance regiment of 6th Division, mounted in Bren carriers, plus a motorised cavalry "brigade" (lorried infantry), a horsed cavalry brigade, and two infantry brigades of 7th Australian Division detached from Tobruk. Naval support would see the use of naval bombardment to shell coastal targets while a detachment of commandos landed behind the enemy to secure a crossing across the Litani. The main columns meanwhile would also be augmented by two brigades of Free French added under Gentilhomme, specifically the Eastern-most column, otherwise consisting of the 5th Indian Brigade. This was the new force that Henry Maitland-Wilson, newly back from Greece, was given. Further support, it was hoped, could be provided by the forces currently fighting in Iraq. It is also notable that there was by this stage an air capability designated for Operation Exporter. As minimal as it was (Golster Gladiator biplanes inclusive), it was something to augment the fighting power on the ground.

It was a gamble and was generally accepted that success or failure would be decided by whether Dentz's men chose to fight or not. In the event that they did decide to fight there was the "fall-back" hope that Turkey would decide to become involved. In the end this proved to be as realistic a hope as the one that the Vichy French would not fight. The dredging required to put together the forces for Exporter in itself clearly

---

25 Verdin *The Cheshire Yeomanry*, p.289.
26 AWM 52: 1/5/14-0110: 7 Australian Division General Staff Branch.

shows what the British were gambling in order to simply launch Exporter. This is borne out in microcosm by the idea to approach enemy positions with loudspeakers and white flags, stipulated in the warning orders for the yeomanry of 5th Cavalry Brigade.

This is one of a series of significant planning misconceptions that stand out at this stage, which were to have significant repercussions for the cavalry in particular. The first misconception was that the objectives for the three columns (Beirut, Rayak and Damascus) were on paper to be achieved after four days. In the event, it took five weeks of fighting for just one of those objectives to be reached (Damascus). This does lend weight to Laverack's charge of vague planning done by Wavell's staff. The second, was that the advance troops for the invading force (i.e. the Cheshire Yeomanry) were thought to be so unlikely to meet determined resistance, that in order to avoid antagonising the French defenders they were to be under orders to *not fire until they had been fired upon*. By way of contrast, 7th Division's Intelligence summary documented the following once the fighting had started:

> 3. <u>General</u>:
> The following extract from instns which were issued to all concerned by the local military comd at MERDJAYOUN were received amongst captured documents:-
>
> … I amplify my instns on the attitude to be maintained in the case of GAULLIST action already detailed verbally at the last conference:- FIRE WITHOUT WARNING on any body of individuals, no matter what their uniform may be, who try to parley…[27]

Before this realisation though, as the advance troops crossed the border they were to carry; the British Union flag, the Free French flag, and a white flag. Each of which would make a handy aiming point for the defenders. A further comparatively minor solecism was the informing of the advance troops that they need not take their helmets if they did not wish to. Clearly, the delusion that the Vichy French would not fight was hardwired into every level of Exporter's planning. The level of trust in these instructions is shown in the fact that every Cheshire yeoman went into action equipped with his helmet.[28]

The army they faced had a much clearer remit and much better equipment. Dentz's Vichy forces included three legionnaire artillery regiments and two armoured regiments (120 guns and 90 tanks) serving 40,000 odd men in total. This was a slight

---

27 AWM 52: 1/5/14-0110: 7 Australian Division General Staff Branch.
28 An interesting statistical indication of how truly hostile the Free French were to the British is that at the end of the campaign, when 37,736 Vichy troops had been captured, only 5,668 agreed to join the Free French. See Verdin, *The Cheshire Yeomanry*, p.291.

numerical advantage over the British forces poised to attack them, if Habforce is factored in. The British planning had by now been bolstered with the addition of some aircraft, which had finally been bequeathed them by the end of May:

> Before general conference on 28 May Lavarack was told that AA artillery, Infantry tanks and some other units mentioned in the order of battle would not be available until mid-June. He was asked whether the op ought to wait for these units. Lavarack replied no – it was imperative to begin ops asap and deny Syria to the Germans. D1 set for 5 June.
>
> Air cover- it was estimated that for 7 Aust Div Tac R [Tactical Reserve] there would be 10-12 Hurricanes and 8-10 Bleinheims. [29]

The Vichy French would still hold a slight superiority in these terms too. The quality of the Vichy troops was not insignificant either; they included some French Foreign Legion and plenty of experienced officers. They had also by now acquired experience of dealing with the troublesome tribesmen of the area, most notably in the Great Syrian Revolt of 1925-27, when at one point they lost an entire column of soldiers at al-Suwayda[30]. It was this experience that ensured the Vichy French forces in Syria in 1941 were well-endowed with cavalry units like the Spahis. The shape of the fighting over the coming weeks was inevitably dictated by the mountainous terrain. It heavily affected the tactics that were used, and it equally heavily affected the ability of the defending forces to hold out. Meanwhile, strategic support for the men and horses trepidatiously entering this terrain from British lines was the Royal Navy blockade against the Vichy French that stopped all their fuel, and provided naval gunfire support for 21st Brigade. This it was hoped would apply more general pressure on the defenders in the tactical battles.

Because the mountainous geography of southern Lebanon and Syria made the various axes of advance obvious, there seemed to be little lost by accepting the absence of any secrecy. Aeroplanes therefore started dropping leaflets on the French forces, and radio transmissions began to announce the impending end of the French Mandate of Syria and Lebanon at the hands of General Catroux with his Free French. Verdin opines that this helped the civilian population (who hated the Vichy administration) but further ossified the mindset of the Vichy military.[31] This assessment seems reasonable.

---

29 AWM 52: 1/5/14-0110: 'First conference at 5 cav bde 26 May' 7 Australian Division General Staff Branch.
30 Joyce Laverty Miller, The Syrian Revolt of 1925, *International Journal of Middle East Studies*, 1977, pp. 550–555 <doi:10.1017/S0020743800026118> (accessed 3 August 2022).
31 Verdin, *The Cheshire Yeomanry*, p.292.

Eyes on the Enemy

With such a clear declaration of intent, the presence of German aircraft was no surprise during the run-in to Exporter. On 12 May, two German aircraft appeared over the Cheshire Yeomanry's barracks, came under fire, and again at Haifa, before then being seen returning in the direction of Syria. Later that day the regiment was dispersed, so as to be less of a target for aircraft. The planes meanwhile continued to be seen almost every day until the launch of Exporter. The mounted yeomanry were now for the first time under enemy scrutiny.

On the 21 May, the Cheshire Yeomanry handed over the guard at Ras en Naqura to the North Somerset Yeomanry. From this point the Cheshire Yeomanry knew for sure that they were going to be involved. The next day Australians from 7th Division started to arrive and the Cheshiremen started to report to a brigade HQ that had moved nearer to Nazareth.

Nazareth it should be noted is only a day's walk along a ravine from southern Lebanon (where the wedding at Canaa was held and is very close to Bent Jbail of 2006 Israeli war fame). The countryside is hilly rather than mountainous, but difficult nonetheless, with a scree of small rocks underfoot across the entire area. The proximity of each small hill to the others makes it a particularly daunting prospect for any infantry assault – as the Israelis were to learn in 1980 and in 2006.

Ripples of anticipation spread when, on the 29th the first line reinforcements of transport for the Cheshires arrived – they now felt "ready for any eventuality".[32] On the 31st May C.O. Cheshire Yeomanry was informed by Brigade that his regiment were to be attached to 7th Division and that it would be the only cavalry regiment taking part. The speed with which all these developments took place, indicate how quickly Wavell's admonitions had been overruled.

Certain parts of this story are clear; not least the preparations of the Cheshire Yeomanry and their operations in Lebanon and Syria. The most important source for these is the work of Lt. Col Richard Verdin, who served throughout these events as a Captain and later became colonel of his regiment after the war. The value of this testimony, recording later (the regimental history was published 1971) at his leisure is immense. However, it is firmly from the perspective of the Cheshire Yeomanry, a unit who fondly clung to their claim of being the last British regiment to fight on horses. It is here that facts start to morph into opinion. As such it is understandable that the contributions of other yeomanry regiments might have been overlooked. Not because Verdin wished to deliberately ignore them, but because he wasn't aware that further research needed to be carried out. Then there is the issue of recording memorable conversations, such as the one where he recalls the Cheshire Yeomanry being told on the 29th May 1941 that they were to be the only cavalry regiment taking part in Exporter. This could either have been said to them in order to inspire on the eve

---

32 Verdin, *The Cheshire Yeomanry*, p.292.

of combat, or it could simply have been true at the time. Clearly, subsequent to this conversation, other cavalry regiments were involved, and took their horses. Equally clearly, their mounted role was not as substantial as that of the Cheshire Yeomanry. The historiography therefore is blurred.

The general confusion is due to the attitude to cavalry, and lingering surprise that they had to be used at all. As much as they were on the army list as guests who had outstayed their welcome, they were only in the reckoning for operations in Syria as family who had to be invited. When battle commenced, a great deal of the cavalry's fighting was done on isolated hillsides, away from the bigger battles and main columns, which in any case saw heavier fighting. Historiographical sidelining, both then and now is really inevitable. Nevertheless, at the time manpower was overstretched beyond any projection that Wavell felt comfortable with. As such the minutes of Exporter Force's planning conference on 4 June reveal a certain amount about the attitude to them. "It was originally intended by Bde comnds to use horsed cav in a restricted role" for example; but clearly "views changed later and it was decided by them to try to have horsed cav operating, if possible, up to the third objective."[33] The development of this conversation indicates quite clearly the dawning realisation that they simply lacked the resources to only deploy the yeomanry in a limited role. The horse soldiers would take full responsibility for the flank. This would also include "clearing up" widespread enemy positions as the main column advanced up their comparatively narrow axis. This would make use of the cavalry's undeniable mobility – in comparison to slow moving infantry or vehicles that could not scale steep hill sides covered in scree.

Incidentally, the reason that the Cheshire Yeomanry were the only cavalry regiment initially deployed on horses in a reconnaissance and screening role (the main use of cavalry in British army doctrine) is pretty clear. Only the Staffordshire and Cheshire Yeomanries had had the benefit of Brigadier Chrystal's rigorous training, and the Staffordshire Yeomanry were depleted by an entire squadron (one had been mechanised and attached to Todcol with the Royal Scots Greys) so the Cheshire unit were really the only possibility. This would also explain why a squadron of the Staffordshire Yeomanry were selected to be a part of the operational reserve along with the regulars – although the distinction in operational effectiveness between regulars and territorials was now very blurred and even Churchill had referred to them as "quasi-regular". Presumably, the reason the rest of the Staffordshire Yeomanry were left behind is that there weren't enough trucks. The front line of Maitland-Wilson's cavalry however, whose only vehicles were with Regimental HQ, were in a state of high-readiness from the final two days of May. On 6 June they moved to their concentration areas; B Squadron Cheshire Yeomanry to Safsaf, the rest of the regiment to El Kabri. Horses and men, in line with their rigorous training under Chrystal, carried:

1. Two blankets one each for horse and rider

---

33   AWM 52 1/5/14: 'Exporter Force' 7 Australian Division General Staff Branch.

2. Saddle wallets with rations
3. Rider's personal kit and spare underclothes in either wallet or haversack
4. Greatcoat on front arch of saddle
5. Ground sheet on rear arch
6. Grooming kit
7. Rifle bucket with mess tin attached
8. Two feed bags
9. Shoe case with two spare shoes and nails
10. Sword
11. Two ground pegs, ropes and shackles
12. Canvas water bucket
13. Hay net
14. Hopping on can (for making tea etc.)

In addition the rider carried on his person:

Bandolier with 90 rounds
Haversack
Gas mask (later stored in rifle bucket)

In all, about 7 stone of equipment including the saddle, so with an 11 stone rider about 18 stone. The horses in the Machine Gun sections and regimental machine gun troop were further encumbered with 3000 rounds of ammunition. In theory half of the Machine Gun troop's ammunition should have been carried by the "B" echelon, but Williams evidently saw that close coordination and resupply in the foothills was going to be highly challenging, and his main fighting asset couldn't afford to ever be caught short.

There were sufficient rations for all horses and men to go 48 hours without resupply. Thereafter, they would use their "B" echelon, or if unavailable, simply live off the land. Unlike the herculean 72 hour marches without water that Allenby's walers had undergone in the first war, the hills of southern Lebanon would provide ready access to water throughout the operation.

Fully aware of this, and eager to be used as they had been trained, the mood prevailing in the Cheshire Yeomanry on the eve of Exporter was now "that of trespassers about to partake in a picnic on forbidden ground rather than that of an invading force going to war." Only a few seemed frightened rather than excited.[34] It was Churchill's optimism rather than Wavell's pessimism that had filtered down to tactical level.

Deployment for Exporter began for the Cheshire Yeomanry with Operation Order No.1., dated 5 June 1941. It began by detailing the opposition they would face;

---

34 Verdin, *The Cheshire Yeomanry*, p.292.

"Chasseurs Libanais (Cavalry); 22. Regt. Tirailleurs Algerien (infantry) or Spahis (probably Moroccan) Cavalry."[35] [sic] These units were expected at Ramiet, Kh. Jereine, Aita Ech Chaab and Remeiche – a stretch of no more than ten miles. The nominated positions were to be in British possession by 04.30 hours, the Cheshire Yeomanry having been told to "clean up the posts". The official view, expressed in these orders, was that "It is not known whether the French will oppose our adv. And in the first place the opportunity for them to surrender is to be given. <u>Nothing, however, is to be permitted to deny our adv. And the max. force is to be applied immediately in the event of resistance.</u>" [original emphasis].[36] Despite the optimism of De Gaulle and Churchill evident in the ambiguity, the Cheshire Yeomanry took nothing for granted – and the emphatic underlining probably shows their skepticism. The same document also specifies that all ranks were to wear steel helmets, that respirators were to be carried at the ready and all vehicles, once in the assembly area, were to be camouflaged and lie silent. The anti-aircraft light machine guns were to be mounted and at the ready, and slit trenches were to be dug at all locations.

The Cheshire Yeomanry (less "B" Squadron) were to act as flank guard in the Lebanon mountains. Elsewhere "B" squadron, who were completely separate for Exporter, would flank guard in the hills to the west of 25th Brigade. The Yorkshire Dragoons and North Somerset Yeomanry were to be deployed further back, in a patrolling role combined with protecting the Palestine border. The Yorkshire Dragoons, their steel helmets loaded in trucks, wore Pith helmets and had evidently taken the official view with less cynicism.

In silent anti-aircraft formation, the 21st Brigade's flank guard would cross the frontier at Hanita, at 5 a.m. and then proceed east along the frontier road, clearing the villages of any enemy as it proceeded. On reaching Remeiche, they would turn north and cross the Litani. The Litani river (nahr- al- Litani) runs its entire course within the boundaries of modern Lebanon; rising near Baalbeck and thence flowing through the Bekaa valley to the Mediterranean, a little north of Tyre. A course of around 140km in total. As it nears the coast, the fast currents of its waters are often 20 metres wide and with steep, thickly wooded banks. As it progresses, it feeds "irrigation systems older than the Book of Genesis".[37]

Unsurprisingly, Dentz's forces were mainly grouped behind this vast natural defence (their forces in front would fight mainly delaying actions). The main force was to be grouped in the south-west behind the river, built around the 22ème Régiment Algérien. In prepared positions, with ample artillery support, their Hotchkiss guns were belt-fed, unlike the cavalry's magazine-fed light machine guns. The Yeomanry

---

35   The National Archives (TNA) WO 169/1396: 'Operation Order No.1., dated 5th June 1941' Cheshire Yeomanry War Diary.
36   TNA: WO 169/1396: 'Operation Order No.1., dated 5th June 1941' Cheshire Yeomanry War Diary.
37   Smith, *England's Last War with France*, p.201.

were going to have to find a way across, some way inland, from the main group of French forces.

Once across, further orders would be issued, but it was envisioned that the subsequent objective would be to cut the road leading from Nabatiye et Tahta to the coast in the Habbouch area. As the "B" echelon would stick to the coast road, Lt. Col Williams knew that his Cheshire Yeomanry would therefore be separate from their rations, forage and ammunition until after they had crossed the Litani and reached Habbouch. Time would be against them, and each trooper only had rations for 48 hours. The horses would survive on any grass available, and the plentiful local supply of water. The extent of work lined up for them, the ground they were being asked to cover, and the consequent threadbare nature of their supplies, clearly indicate the lack of opposition anticipated for them by higher command – though fortunately this was surmountable. Nothing, however, illustrates this delusion of the authorities better than the insistence that the yeomanry visibly carry white, French and British flags with them over the border. In order to meet any eventuality.

On the night of the 6 June, Lt.Col Williams, the commanding officer, and Major Johnson Houghton O.C. 'B' squadron, were given their specific orders by their newly arrived Brigadiers. By morning of the 7th, all the Cheshire Yeomanry officers knew that they were due to cross the frontier early on the morning of the 8th, and precisely what their tasks were. Excitement was growing in the ranks of the Cheshire Yeomanry. A frisson ran through each of the sabre troops as the order was issued to blacken all swords, stirrups and brasses – the same order given to generations of cavalrymen going into action at night. "This task especially gave infinite pleasure to those who had spent so many hours burnishing the same equipment a year previously."[38]

The North Somerset Yeomanry meanwhile had been in a state of nervous expectation too. Their war diary shows that the regiment was, just like the Cheshire Yeomanry, standing to from the 6th June. That day their 'A' squadron left camp and moved up country. At 1500 on the 7th they were informed that operations would begin that night. By 0145 hours on 8 June, the Regiment was in its own concentration area, and by 0520 "A" Squadron was reporting that it could hear "firing" coming from Labouna. At 0745 "C" squadron was dispatched to Labouna. At 1055, A squadron received its order to move to Aima Ash Chaab, a Christian village in Southern Lebanon. They too were going to war on horses.

---

38   Verdin, *The Cheshire Yeomanry*, p.290.

5

The Horse Soldiers Fight

This is an important moment in your history. I have just ended the regime of Mandate. France, by the voice of those of its sons who fight for its life and the freedom of all the world, declares you to be independent.

Eve of battle broadcast by Free French Général Georges Catroux

The Cheshire Yeomanry departed the start line quietly, with sabres blackened at 00.45 on 8 June. They had dulled anything that might possibly shine, such as buckles, stirrups and bits. Anything that might jingle was tied down tight. They moved spread out in extended order, and at 0500 crossed the border in full light. "C" squadron were at the front, followed by R.H.Q., then the machine gun troop, the rest of H.Q. squadron, and lastly "A" squadron. According to S.O.P., the lead man carried his sword so as to be ready to tackle anything immediately in front of him. He would thus buy a precious second or two for the next man in the section to use his rifle, in turn buying time for the rest of the section to dismount, cock, aim and fire their rifles. The machine gun troop were near the front of the regiment, with their 3,000 rounds per gun. The machine gun troop marched immediately next to R.H.Q., in order to be easily dispatched to wherever fighting broke out. By way of anti-armour capability, Boyes anti-tank rifles were issued, along with 200 rounds apiece. Between the sabres, rifles, Hotchkiss, Boyes and Vickers guns, the Cheshire Yeomanry were thus theoretically armed for every phase of battle likely to befall them.

This included dealing with the threat of aircraft. The Cheshire Yeomanry were spread out thinly, to avoid sustaining excessive casualties from one strafe. The Regimental Intelligence Officer estimated that even when down a squadron, the regiment still covered an area of five miles when in extended order. This was to make timely and efficient coordination in hill-country very difficult. A further obstacle to command and control was the inefficiency of the No.11. wireless sets. As the officers reflected afterwards, a regiment was actually too large a formation to be deployed in this way – they felt it should have been divided into discrete squadron sized, independent units.

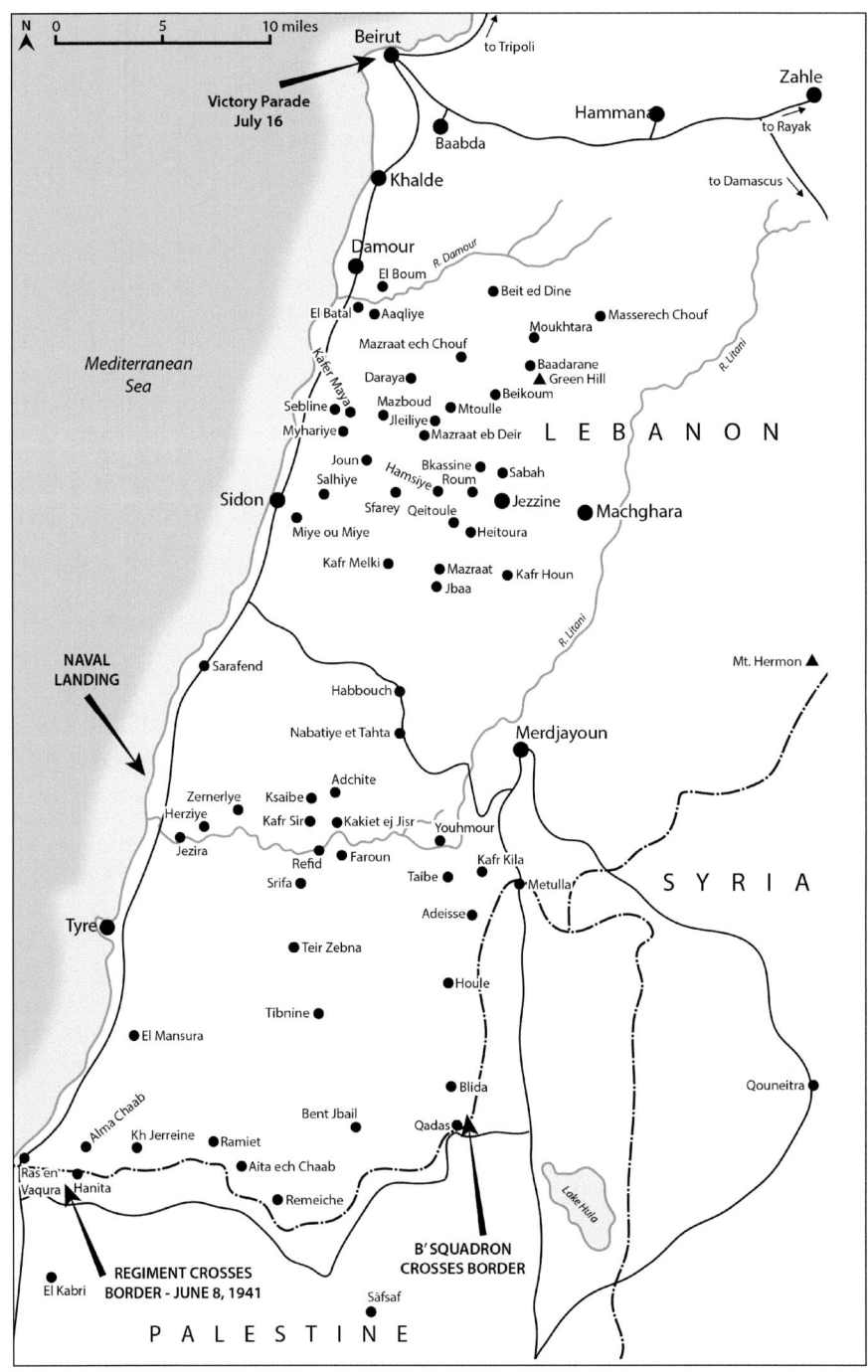

Syria 1941

This after all was exactly what "B" Squadron were providing for their brigade column. With the hilly terrain breaking line of sight for commanders, as well as the signal for the No.11. sets, command and control was naturally going to be difficult – especially when dispersed for protection from aircraft. Whether deployment in smaller groups for cavalry into British Army doctrine should have been standard is however a debatable point. The value of using a larger group did come to be of benefit later when it came to intimidating enemy observation posts.

For now, "C" squadron lead, with Lieutenant A.D. Paterson and Sergeant E. Burgess in command of the point troop. On reaching Alma Chaab, they deployed a section to quickly loop round to the rear, sever the telephone lines and cut off any enemy retreat, while the rest of the troop covered and observed before Alma Chaab was declared clear and the troop pressed on. As they were doing this, the H.Q. squadron came under fire at 05.30. It was long distance fire from the Australians responsible for taking the Alma Chaab extended area and, by way of indicating the liaison difficulties facing Exporter, this was not to be the only occasion of Australians mistakenly firing upon the Cheshire Yeomanry. This however should most certainly not be construed as a cavalier approach from the Australians. They were at war, advancing into enemy territory with constantly moving unit boundaries and therefore with regularly open flanks. An Australian artillery officer at Jezzine, Alwyn Clarke, later vividly recalled a moment when he countermanded a fire order that was just about to wipe out a Cheshire Yeomanry patrol from "B" squadron, someone had mistaken for Vichy Spahis.[1] Episodes like these amply demonstrate the confusion and panic experienced by the artillery as much as by the other arms. In the first instance at Alma Chaab though the only damage caused was to the regiment's time-keeping.

It was not just Australian eyes that had spotted "C" squadron, and the war diary also indicates that some Spahis later opened fire as well. It cannot have been terribly determined or effective though and Paterson's troop was therefore able to press on, only to find no enemy in Alma Chaab. They were soon to come under fire again from enemy Spahi cavalry, near Kh. Jerreine [sic] at 07.10. This contact with the enemy was only brief, and the Spahis soon obligingly ceased fire and abandoned the place at 07.38, leaving the Cheshire Yeomanry free to resume their advance, with a new troop rotated into the point position. It was an inconclusive engagement with an enemy that so far was unwilling to become bogged down in defence. In truth, the Spahis did little other than to slightly slow the British advance. It was becoming noticeable that the countryside seemed to contain very few enemy soldiers, determined or otherwise.

The approach was starting to seem eerily empty. Both the scant reporting in the war diary and the account of Verdin indicate this. As No.4 Troop under sergeant J.J. Burks advanced, they found all three of the villages that they entered to be empty. These British cavalry were now taking a slightly divergent course from the rest of their formation. While the main axis curled round to the West, the cavalry, being

---

1   See Chapter 6. See also Appendix III.

less road-bound, were to ride the contours of rough country north to the Litani. This was a role that only horsemen could do. It was also country that horsemen could easily defend, should the French have deployed Spahis for this role. However, none of the hilltops seemed to be occupied by Spahi machine gun teams. Burks, a former whipper-in for the Middleton, was "drawing a blank". Perhaps the flippant mood of trespassers, on the eve of Exporter had not been so far wrong.

The yeomanry were experiencing the positive side of attacking a strategic defence in depth. Dentz had decided that his defences, in true Clausewitzian style, could not defend everywhere at once, and had to be concentrated. It was also easy to anticipate where the key attacks were going to fall, because of the topography. Thus, the flank guards of still approaching columns were highly unlikely to meet committed resistance. In fact, the defenders may even have been under orders not to engage them fully. The yeomanry however could not count on this, and at this stage, Burks's troop were only too aware that rounds had already been fired in their direction, and that it would only take one machine gun burst to become the regiment's first casualty.

Williams halted the regiment to bivouac at 17.30. They had now been on the move for 17 hours and the tricky ground was taking its toll on both men and horses. Although they were evidently getting quicker as the day progressed at pressing on, after being shot at by distant enemies, there was still an obvious need to patrol carefully. Indeed this was vital in the likely presence of enemy, but it meant that progress was still both comparatively slow and nerve-jangling. The regiment had been able to cover over 30 miles, but the horses were getting bruised feet from the stones, and the soldiers were tiring from the extensive toing and froing both in the saddle and on foot as they covered their axis of advance.[2] Now they had halted, they would expect to dig in, tend to their horses and stand guard. Without firing a single shot, the true day to day toll of campaigning was being felt by the men and horses who plugged the army's mobile reconnaissance capability gap.

When 9 June dawned, Lt. Col Williams sent out two patrols from "A" squadron to investigate the Litani and ascertain whether the bridges were intact. By 07.30 they had passed through the villages adjacent to the river and had spoken to the locals. The villagers told them that 200 Spahis had passed through earlier. This was the first reliable bit of intelligence they had been able to glean on what faced them, and it was a nasty shock. The strength of the defending force, and the formidable prospect of crossing the river itself, was now making for an ominous build up. Taught with resolution, Lieutenant H.P. Rogers and 2nd Lieutenant D.F. Shaw now lead their respective troops out towards the Litani.

Rogers's 2. Troop had the regiment's first serious contact of the campaign. It was at a deep gorge with a 1000 ft cliff and a very fast current that ruled out crossing safely and reliably by swimming, even for the horses. Lieutenant Rogers (leader of 2 Troop) and his native guide had scouted ahead and found that the bridge they were reconnoitring

---

2   Verdin, *The Cheshire Yeomanry*, p.295.

was intact. Rogers and his guide had then linked up with the leading section of 2 troop under Corporal A. Salter. Further ahead still were the two "eyes men" of the patrol; Trooper F.E. Mellors (already over the bridge) and Trooper L. Rogers (nearly over it, and no relation). They were at that moment the foremost soldiers in Maitland-Wilson's invading force. Just as Lieutenant Rogers's horse set hoof on the bridge to join them, enemy machine gun fire erupted from the northern bank.

Their responses reveal a lot about men under fire for the first time; the reaction is often to get under cover immediately. In this instance the best immediate cover was the enemy-held northern side of the bridge, and Lt Rogers instantaneously galloped his horse through the hail of machine gun bullets over the bridge, towards the enemy but also into this cover. Cpl Salter however (acting entirely appropriately), returned to his section – thus having to turn back through the bullets – and Trooper Rodgers, thinking he should be with his section leader, re-crossed the bridge to the southern side, bypassing Lt Rogers, the troop leader, as he did so. This left Lt Rogers and Tpr Mellors on the northern side and very isolated. A moment later they were dramatically joined by Cpl W.H Spencer, machine gun bullets tearing the bridge and ground around him and his horse "Little Nell". Cpl Spencer, like Cpl Salter, was acting rigidly on standard operating procedure (SOP). In this case the Troop's arrangement was that the machine gun section leader should immediately join the troop leader when the troop came under fire. In this case all the SOP achieved was separating Cpl Spencer from his section.

2. Troop "A" Squadron approaching the Litani.

The rest of the troop had also come under fire from the machine gun position – in their case in a narrow defile as they approached the bridge from the south. Pinned down, it took the adept management of Sergeant O. Dearden to extricate the now dismounted troop and move it to a more suitable position. Given the heavy fire they were under it is reasonable to presume that the horses were extremely panicked, so Dearden's prompt handling is all the more commendable. Later on in the campaign this would have been less of a problem, as the horses eventually learned to ignore even shell-fire. In this instance though, the troop lost six horses to machine gun fire; some killed outright and some too badly wounded to be able to go on – these animals had to be shot by their masters.[3]

Lt Rogers's problem was how to inform Regimental HQ that the bridge was covered by the enemy. Finding this out had been his task, however he had no working radio, so he had to use a galloper. Trooper Mellors was sent. In order to avoid the machine gun fire, Mellors worked his way along the dead ground of the hillside until he reckoned he was out of range, before exposing himself to the view of the machine gunners by plunging into the fast-flowing Litani to swim it on his horse. He had little choice.

At this point Lt Rogers began to doubt whether a tired trooper, in tricky new country that Rogers himself had needed a guide to navigate earlier, could do the same without even a map. Ultimately he decided that Mellors was too likely to get lost and dispatched Cpl Spencer on Little Nell, with a second copy of the message, and a precious map. Spencer and Nell followed Mellors's route and they also swam the Litani. In the fierce current, Nell was not only separated from her rider, but also her saddle, the accompanying rifle bucket (and rifle), sword... and the map case. Finally her rider did escape the currents of the Litani, and when he hauled himself exhausted onto the river bank, there was Nell, standing still waiting for him and oblivious to the risk of machine gun fire. The War Diary records Cpl Spencer's arrival at RHQ nearly an hour later, still drenched to the skin. He was mentioned in dispatches, Mellors was awarded the Military Medal. Nell, predictably, went undecorated.

Rogers's 2 troop deployed at 09.30 before initiating the contact described. It was at 11.45 when the war diary records Cpl Spencer returning "soaking wet and riding bareback with a message from Mr Rogers [evidently he had overtaken the first messenger] that he has encountered heavy m.g fire from rocky ground N. of river Litani … and cannot move forwards or retreat … C.O. decides to advance with regiment to bridge … & relieve Mr Rogers."[4] The actions of 2. Troop, with Lt. Rogers, Cpl Spencer and "Little Nell" are further recounted soon after the event in the *Daily Express* of 17 June:

---

3   This is according to the regiment's chronicler Captain Verdin, who served in Exporter with 'B' Squadron. However, the unit war diary TNA WO 169/1396: 9 June 1941, The Cheshire Yeomanry 1941 states that some of the six dead horses actually drowned while swimming the Litani.
4   TNA WO 169/1396: 9 June 1941, Cheshire Yeomanry 1941.

British Scouts crossed the river and ran straight into a belt of artillery fire from a strong formation of Spahis who had dismounted and were hidden in the rocks. The British were pinned to the ground. One trooper jumped from his horse straight into the stream, lost his saddle and under machine gun fire galloped bareback to the rest of his squadron for help. They came on at full gallop. The Spahis withdrew.[5]

It is true that the help "came on at full gallop"; that help was in fact Lt. M.N. Mitchell's machine gun troop. They were however too late to deploy and deliver supporting fire. They therefore had to wait to reintegrate into the rest of the regiment when it arrived and with them execute Williams' ambitious order to cross the Litani by bridge and by swimming, before clearing the subsequent village. Forming as they did the rest of 21st Brigade's vanguard, when they reached the Litani, they had lost time to make up for and, rather bullishly, simply braced for an advance to contact, rode straight across the Litani, up the hill on the other side, and straight into the next village, thus establishing a bridgehead.

Rogers's 2. Troop meanwhile had now been very much under machine gun fire, losing six of their horses. Now Williams had to ensure that another sub-unit was rotated into point, and that the recovering troop was resupplied with ammunition and remounts; there was work still to be done and ground to be covered. Williams and Mitchell had now also seen how difficult it could be to deploy the machine gun troop in time. This once again must be a function of the difficulty of handling a regiment – too large a unit to be deployed as a single entity – in broken country while trying to mitigate for the threat of aircraft. Because of acting on all these considerations and events this meant moving quite slowly, despite the capabilities of the unit, there was actually very little ground being covered that day. Possibly because of this the next point troop, from "C" Sqn, only crossed the Litani at 1630 and was unable to press up in enough time to catch the retreating Spahi Machine Gun team. The preceding 200 strong Spahi battalion would now be long gone and have had plenty of time to redeploy effectively for the next phase of defence. Now that the Litani was crossed, both the Cheshire Yeomanry regiment under Lt Col Williams, and "B" Squadron under Major Johnson Houghton with 25th Brigade, could expect much stiffer resistance.

Despite this, the day ended when the Williams' men concentrated at Kakiet ej Jisr, bivouacking at 2200. Since 9.30 that morning the unit had covered only 5 frustrating miles as the crow might fly. That ground of course was broken by hills, hidden enemy machine guns, and the formidable Litani. A smaller unit would have been able to cover the ground faster, and they would still have found the undefended crossings over the Litani. The Vickers guns might possibly have been effectively brought to bear against the Spahis too. In spite of all this, the war diary records that spirits were high.

---

5   As cited in Verdin, *The Cheshire Yeomanry*, p.298.

The French cavalry could actually have dampened these spirits and made progress much slower, while inflicting many more casualties than they actually did. The appraisal at the time was that the Spahis should have been able to hold both the crossings that "A" squadron had reconnoitred until dark "with some ease".[6] They could alternatively have just destroyed the bridges. They had clearly become aware of "A" squadron's other patrol under Lt. Shaw at Faroun. This outflanked them and presented an immediate threat, which presumably they had not deployed to meet from the outset. The formation war diary observes the importance of flanking maneuvers, and how vulnerable the French were to flanking movements.[7] Equally they could simply have been under orders to use only delaying tactics. This would preserve their cavalry; a precious commodity for a commander in hilly southern Lebanon. More significantly, it would also keep the invading British force pushing up along what was a fairly obvious axis of advance. Fighting a determined up-front action at the border, risked not drawing Maitland-Wilson into a more decisive battle further up-country in a bottleneck with the columns too far separated to be mutually supporting. Given the importance of this premise to Dentz's plan of defence in depth, this alternative seems the more likely. The protracted negotiation that "B" squadron became embroiled in after one of their engagements would also support this.

Another factor to consider is that the French defenders did not need to put up much resistance to delay the Exporter force, who had to cover a formidable topography. The five miles of travel on 9 June clearly exemplifies this. The plunging terrain also made radio communications deeply problematic – a fact specifically identified in the war diary at the end of the 9 June entry. In essence, this meant that they would have to be given an area to clear within a certain time, then just get on with it, without referring to higher command until the communications started working again. A principle hardly in keeping with the British army's C3 system prior to Montgomery's reforms in 1942.

Brigadier Stevens's[8] orders for 10 June were for the Australian infantry of 2/27th to advance along the main road, having crossed the new pontoon over the Litani at 0500, while the Australian 6th Cavalry in trucks scouted ahead and the 2/16th cleared the hills immediately on the right. The Cheshire Yeomanry would form an outer

---

6 Verdin, *The Cheshire Yeomanry*, p.299.
7 AWM 52: 1/5/14-0110: 7 Australian Division General Staff Branch.
8 Brigadier Jack Stevens was the son of British emigres to Australia. He had started working in a cigar factory at the age of 12 before joining the Post Office. In the Great War he enlisted as a militia signaller in 1915, returning three years later as an officer. Stevens continued to serve as a militia signaller between the wars, before assuming command of an infantry battalion. During Exporter he commanded his Brigade during the battle of the Litani, for which he was decorated and in which he was wounded. He returned to command his Brigade for the battle of Damour. 'Stevens, Sir Jack Edwin Stawell (1896-1969)', *Australian Dictionary of Biography* <https://adb.anu.edu.au/biography/stevens-sir-jack-edwin-stawell-11763> (accessed 17 June 2019).

screen. It was only when bivouacking on the evening of 10 June that they heard of the main column's fight for the main Litani crossing which had "encountered the most determined resistance & had heavy casualties [the French were also able to blow the bridge]. The commando force who were landed from the sea [from the north side] lost 50% of their men. Their Colonel Pedder was killed."[9] The main column's initial assault had been a bloody failure. When it was finally pressed home, it required engineers building a pontoon bridge under shell-fire and in the face of an armoured car counter-attack. Dentz's men were fighting after all.

Precipitous slopes of the River Litani.

From the Yeomanry's point of view this did not alter things much. They still had to patrol the flank of the column's axis, and gather information about the ground, regardless of where they were and how quickly the main column was progressing. It was now 10 June and, as it was, they would now move west, rather than north upcountry, patrolling towards the eastern flank of the French defending the river. As they approached, they were to clear any enemy they encountered.

9 TNA WO 169/1396 Entry for 9 June 1941.

Troop horses watering on the Litani.

Lt. Shaw and his men lived this order when they entered the village of Adchite. They were the right flank troop, and therefore the troop most likely to come under fire from the north. Furthermore they were isolated and intent on rejoining the regiment at Ksaibe. Adchite was a sizeable operation for a troop, so they had been reinforced by two extra sections from Rogers's 2 troop. The extra muscle at first seemed unnecessary, as Shaw placed his Hotchkiss section in high ground overlooking the village, then sent in his rifle sections, who found the place apparently empty. Once down in the village, Shaw began writing out his message to R.H.Q, while the troop orderly rode over to him to take the note from his hand. Just as the troop orderly was reaching Shaw, a burst of waiting Spahi machine gun fire erupted, hitting the ground between them. As Shaw and the orderly dived out of the way, the machine gun section, under L-Cpl J.W. Townsend immediately returned fire at the Spahi position, the troop's rifle sections smartly following suit. Shaw meanwhile rode in haste to where Townsend's section was, because they were the highest placed topographically and could see the enemy position the clearest. As he returned to them, the only members of the troop not hotly engaged in the firefight were those on horse-holding duties – a tactical bound behind with one man to five horses. As Shaw reached the machine gun section, he could hear the handlers furiously imploring Townsend and the others with

"You selfish buggers, you've had your bloody turn, come and hold these long-faced bastards and let us have ten rounds apiece before that antiquated gun packs up."[10] Townsend ignored their admonitions. They were not the only ones to be frustrated – Lt. Mitchell's Machine Gun troop came galloping up, flat out and already too late. Before they could deploy the Vickers guns, the accurate shooting of Shaw's men (and presumably the Spahis' standing orders to delay rather than destroy) had forced the Spahis to disengage and retire at the gallop, pursued by a hail of yeomanry bullets "and a choice flow of cavalry language."[11] Arriving from R.H.Q. this was in fact a decent response time (slightly over a minute),[12] but the ancient Hotchkiss gunnery and accurate marksmanship had clearly done the job well enough. As soon as the whole troop had opened fire following the initial well-aimed burst at troop H.Q., the Spahis' shooting had suddenly become much less accurate, indicating the disruption caused by the counter fire of the British patrol.

The episode showed that the Spahis were now changing tactics. They had let the troop enter the village and waited until they had a good opportunity to take out the troop leader and his galloper. The fact that a galloper was needed also indicates the ineluctable radio problems; just as Mitchell's response time and the marksmanship of Shaw's men demonstrate the Cheshire Yeomanry's impressive level of troop training. Morale was clearly high too,[13] and this despite the dearth of effective equipment they had been issued with.

There were feelings that the regiment was too large a formation to handle effectively in the broken countryside, with no effective radio net to work from. However, this was war and daunting obstacles were being faced by everyone. The fact that the M.G. Troop had reached Shaw's troop within enough time should the Spahis have proved a more serious threat, is highly pertinent. But the size of the footprint that the regiment covered when in open order was also to have an effect on the operation as a whole. The sheer scale of the area they covered convinced the Spahi observers that here was a sizeable force (the Spahis did not habitually spread out, as they later found out to their cost). According to Verdin[14], it was the crossing of the Litani by an apparently large force – when in fact it was merely the right flank guard of 21st Bde – that persuaded Dentz to order a general retirement towards Beirut. Equally clearly, he was going to do this at some point anyway, but Verdin may well have grounds to claim that the

---

10 Verdin, *The Cheshire Yeomanry*, p.300. The wording seems incongruous, so it must be assumed that Verdin was paraphrasing.
11 See Verdin, *The Cheshire Yeomanry*, p.300
12 Given Verdin's time estimations, the M.G. Troop must have galloped flat out and along a decent track as allegedly, not more than two minutes firing, gave them enough time to cover the 2-2 1/2 miles between Kafr Sir and Adchite.
13 "Shaw's men had thoroughly enjoyed themselves." See Verdin, *The Cheshire Yeomanry*, p.300.
14 Verdin, *The Cheshire Yeomanry*, p.301.

yeomanry advance forced Dentz to play this card earlier than he would have chosen. After all, he was now outflanked.

The unit that had carried out the critical flanking manoeuvre was now to be pushed into a more forward role. 7th Division HQ reports on the 11th that while fighting began around Merjayoun, that Cheshire Yeomanry and "The Royals" (which regiment this is exactly being unclear), "which moved yesterday West from KAFR SIR towards QASMIYE are belived to be mopping up North of R LITANI towards Ed DOUER."

On 12 June it followed that the forward progress of the Cheshire Yeomanry, in the absence of reliable radio contact, indicated that Nabatiye was clear of enemy. This was a phase of the operation when the French were responding with machine guns and mortars. This therefore indicates that the Cheshire Yeomanry were the advance guard for their sector at this stage, and their role now included clearing out enemy forces.[15] It should be noted though that these bursts of fighting refer to "B" squadron Cheshire Yeomanry.

Brigadier Dunn's subsequent letter to his unit commanders shows a due level of appreciation to all involved:

> The forcing of the River Litani crossing was a feat of arms of which the Bde. Gp. can well be proud and I offer my congratulations to all ranks who took part in this operation.
>
> In the face of well organised and brave resistance the determination shown by all ranks in pressing forward revealed a true appreciation of our job. The continual pressure exerted on the enemy has enabled us to get over this most difficult obstacle and move on towards our ultimate objective.
>
> I am very grateful to all in the Bde. Gp. And am proud indeed to command it.[16]

Forwarded by Dunn's brigade staff on 13.6.41. the footnote from Lt. Col Williams, as delivered to squadron leaders in the Cheshire Yeomanry, read:

> Although the Cheshire Yeomanry did not take part in the attack on the left over the River Litani, the Brigadier has already congratulated us on the work done in the centre and I wish to add my congratulations on the way in which the Cheshire Yeomanry has worked throughout.
>
> Will you please convey this to all personnel of your Squadron.
> In the field
> 13.6.41"[17]

---

15   AWM52 1/4/1: I Corps docs: 10 July 41: 1 Australian Corps General Branch (1 Aust Corps 'G' Branch).
16   TNA WO 169/1396: Brigade letter to C.O.s: Cheshire Yeomanry 1941.
17   TNA: WO 169/1396: Brigade letter to C.O.s: Cheshire Yeomanry 1941.

There was a tangible thrill in the air after Shaw's troop had taken part in a textbook cavalry action, and the regiment's responsibilities in the field expanded. This presumably was all the more satisfying for those members of 2 troop who had been machine-gunned the previous day.

The elation however was soon to fall into frustration when the unit as a whole became spectators. Now closer to the coast, the yeomanry were to remain on hilltops while the brigade remained stationary on the coastal plain. The fact was that the entire attack had stagnated. Within only a few days of the campaign's start, the plan of a speedy three-pronged thrust against an apathetic enemy had turned into a hard-fought slog, with the only significant penetration achieved being the various crossings of the Litani, most notably by the commandos and Australians. On the right the Free-French were held and needed to be reinforced, in the centre (where "B" squadron were) the column had become embroiled still within sight of the border (advancing less than 10 miles in five days), and on the left the coastal advance was plainly about to come up against some severe tests.

The defenders meanwhile had a rather easier challenge to address. They had to decipher which of Wilson's columns presented the worst threat – not easy to do in the face of such uninspiring advances. Verdilhac had so far made little use of his eighty R35 tanks, and nothing yet looked threatening enough to merit their deployment. In the words of Colin Smith:

> The British, it seemed, had attacked Syria with an almost insultingly small and under-equipped little army.[18]

Clearly Churchill and De Gaulle would need more than the likes of Catroux's eve of battle broadcast. By this stage of the fighting, the three small thrusts had been halted, and all resources that could be deployed from Palestine had been (the rest of 5th Cavalry brigade were by now involved). Furthermore, the allied air support, while not being any bigger than the opposing Vichy formation, was now almost exclusively operating defensively to protect the naval part of the operation, being forced into a reactive role rather than a proactive one. This left the three landward thrusts painfully exposed.

The coastal column of this force was now attempting to break into Sidon; a siege operation. The Cheshire Yeomanry were consequently, albeit temporarily, to be dug-in infantry manning a fall-back position as little more than spectators. What they were about to see was to make grim viewing. While the regiment watched impotently, out at sea French air attacks were inflicting heavy damage on both *Janus* and *Jackal* on the 13th, and *Isis* and *Ilese* on the 15th. Yeomanry uselessness as spectators, as compared to their value when in role, was not lost on Brigadier Keith Dunn. Dunn's suggestion was that they be remounted (the horses by now with their "B" echelon) and used to

---

18   Smith, *England's Last War with France*, p.223.

approach Quoneitra [a town in modern-day south-western Syria, elsewhere referred to as Kuneitra] where the countryside required cavalry to flank any advancing force. Lt. General Laverack however refused, as he might need them himself when he came to advance, and his defence was already short of men.[19] Laverack had clearly not come round to recognising horsemen strengths.

Regardless of the military logic, the order was not appreciated by the British cavalrymen. Now stationary and bored while also shaken by what they could see, their irritation was further exacerbated when they were told not to fire at passing Vichy aircraft and give their position away. Despite this order the entire regiment, initiated by the fidgety Trooper "Talkie" Mitchell and his newly issued Tommy Gun, opened fire at one Vichy aircraft. The plane was brought down, although the coup de grace was probably delivered by the Australians' Bofors gun. Aside from this episode it was a lull, with the war diary reporting the morning of the 10 June for example as a "peaceful morning, tps well-hidden and bathing in the Litani."[20] There was also an insight into the troublesome waters of colonial politics. Lt Rogers and 1. Troop "A" squadron (not his own troop who we assume were being rested) were sent to garrison Tyre, on the Mediterranean coast south of Beirut. They were enthusiastically received and it is recorded that "All express hope for a future British administration – Rather awkward as the general idea is to hand it over to Free French and prove that we have no designs in Syria."[21] There is no ironic reference made to the Sykes-Picot agreement on record. More pressing issues appeared to be at hand though. The entry for 1530 on the same day records "large numbers of enemy cavalry are advancing from direction of Qasmiye". This information from the Australian Liaison officer proved inaccurate, and the cavalry turned out to be "a large herd of cattle". The yeoman could go back to their bathing.

On the night of 12 June, the regiment finally saddled up. They arrived that night at Sarafand, bivouacking in a fig and olive grove. As Major Dennis was directing "A" squadron under Major Langford-Brook to their area, they were fired on by what the war diary describes as a "windy Australian sentry." Major Langford-Brook's horse was killed instantly, Major Dennis's horse showed its class by hitting the ground instantaneously. "After this" the diary retells "the situation became a little obscure. Yeomen seized Tommy guns and fired but fortunately beyond the original casualty Major L.B's horse no one is hurt." [22] Verdin on the other hand was emphatic that after the initial challenge, the sentry who was described by the war diary as "windy", was under no illusion about the identity of the incomers, and "most unnecessarily fired". The implication therefore must be that he did so out of pure vindictiveness. [23] Verdin,

---

19 "Australia at War" as cited in Verdin, p.302.
20 TNA WO 169/1396: Entry for 12 June 1941.
21 TNA WO 169/1396: Entry for 12 June 1941.
22 TNA WO 169/1396: Entry for 12 June 1941.
23 Verdin, *The Cheshire Yeomanry*, p.303.

in his own subtle style, is generally scathing of Australian troops out of the front line – where he describes them as "nearly always superb".[24] He describes the Australians at rest as "liable to cause difficulties in base towns behind as had been demonstrated many times in Cairo in the 1914-18 war."[25] Allegedly for this reason, 3 troop "C" squadron Cheshire yeomanry were dispatched to take over. Apparently the situation had been further stirred by the appointing of two Free French officers to oversee administration. Whether the trouble was caused by the fact that they were French or "incompetent" is not clarified by Verdin. Nor is it weighed against the allegedly destabilising influence of the Australian soldiers. Nonetheless a marked change was reported in the town after the Cheshire Yeomanry took over. Verdin simply quotes Lieutenant Shaw's own letter, beginning with the greeting from the Headmaster of the American school in Sidon, expressing concern at the impact the Australian contingent had made and that the town had become like a volcano, with maybe only 24-48 hours before it exploded. Shaw addressed his troops and set them to work:

> For the first 48 hours the atmosphere in the town was quiet, tense – a probationary period. The men were billeted in the School, the horse lines were about one quarter to half a mile away in the middle of the town. For stable parades the men marched from the School along the main street. All the inhabitants stopped whatever they were doing to stare at the new lot of soldiers recently arrived. Dark beady eyes shone quizzically from within the meat shops and over the top of trays, laden with sticky sweet cakes, for which Sidon has a deserved reputation ... By night they carried out, in pairs, the curfew patrols. They were quiet, businesslike but understanding of those upon whom the curfew had been enforced. I did not insist on any "bull" but expected them to be as clean and tidy as conditions allowed. I was concerned only on how they carried out their task and with winning back the respect of Sidon for the Allied soldier. On the morning of the fourth day the stable party was swinging along the busy street for midday stables. It normally took about five minutes. This particular morning it took 45 minutes. Utter confusion reigned but the happiest of military confusion imaginable. The Troop had won the respect and hearts of the town. Every man in the stable party was seized and pushed into a shop and stuffed with the sticky cakes free of charge ... I was very proud of my troop. I had merely passed on a message from the Headmaster to them as best I could. The implementation of those orders was entirely in the hands of N.C.O's [sic] and men. I doubt if a regular unit could have succeeded as well as they did. It needed discipline but also an understanding. Here was our strength in the quality of our other ranks. It was warming then and I think worth recording now.[26]

---

24 Verdin, *The Cheshire Yeomanry*, p.303.
25 Verdin, *The Cheshire Yeomanry*, p.303.
26 Verdin, *The Cheshire Yeomanry*, p.304.

On top of their performance at Adchite, where they demonstrated such effective Hotchkiss gunnery and musketry, Shaw's troop do indeed come out of this episode well. The quality he indicates was a reflection of the riches that the yeomanry were able to choose their recruits from in April 1939; of whom a comparatively high proportion went on to be commissioned during the war years. There were however other pressing roles for the regiment to perform in the meantime.

Wilson's army was badly stretched and open to counter-attack. De Verdhilac (Dentz's deputy) knew the country he was defending well, and he planned his attack to hit three weak points at once: Kuneitra, Merjayoun, and the Deraa-Damascus road, using a by-passed garrison in the Jebel Druze to strike out, and hit the Indian brigade and Free French. Wilson's supply routes crossed tough terrain and were under-defended, so they were ripe for surprise attacks. The French counter-attack at Kuneitra on the 15th destroyed or captured an entire infantry battalion, 1st Battalion, The Royal Fusiliers. Among other problems, the Fusiliers under Lt.Col Orr, quickly found themselves relying on their Boyes guns to take on the 40mm armour of the Renault R35s.[27] Their bullets could not even penetrate the Renaults' armour.

While the attack at Kuneitra was getting under way, a similarly dangerous thrust was launched at Merjayoun, as the Vichy forces counter-attacked. They struck through the 6ème Chasseurs d'Afrique in R35s after the bulk of 25th Brigade had trekked 25 miles up the road to take the village of Jezzine in vicious fighting. Strategically this had been to protect the flank of 21st brigade at Sidon. Now the force at Merjayoun was in place, but weak. It had been made even weaker, because Lt.Col Monaghan, the new commander of Todforce had sent three rifle companies out on a reconnaissance in force. The remaining contingent consisted of 200 Scots Greys, who had been hastily re-roled as motorised infantry for Exporter. They were at least better supported by heavy weapons than Orr's Fusiliers at Kuneitra. However, when the Chasseurs surprised them on the 15th, the paltry defences started to give way. Unfortunately the news that tanks had broken through seems to have spread panic,[28] though this is understandable given the lack of allied tanks and comparative paucity of effective anti-tank guns available to the allied soldiers. The formation broke and order seems to have been lost as any available vehicle was commandeered by retreating, panicking soldiers, fleeing for Palestine. In fairness, there seems to have been considerable confusion, and the Greys did not break until they had run out of ammunition. Nonetheless, recalled one Scots Grey "we were cavalrymen doing an infantryman's job. We hadn't been trained for it, we didn't have much ammunition, and we didn't have much idea what was going on."[29] The French now were on the very brink of breakthrough and

---

27   Brigadier Lloyd had sent away all their effective anti-tank guns to support the Damascus operation. The only realistic anti-tank weapon, a captured Breda, was quickly rendered unserviceable when an internal spring broke.
28   Smith, *England's Last War with France*, p.232.
29   Interview with William Cross, Chelsea Hospital, June 2007 by Colin Smith as cited in Smith, *England's Last War with France*, p.233. The evident despondency compares

unprotected Palestine was only 10 miles distance. It would take truly heroic action at Merjayoun and Jezzine for this threat to be defeated, with Lt. Roden Cutler of the Australian artillery winning a Victoria Cross in the process.

The fight at Merjayoun meanwhile required stripping assets from the other columns and yet more responsibility was to be given to the cavalrymen. By now the 25th brigade, under Brigadier E.C.P. Plant, was at Jezzine and on the flank of the 21st Brigade. The precipitous countryside included several steep features as well as protected routes for the French defenders to resupply. "On the west the land fell away steeply, sometimes in sheer precipices into a deep gorge."[30] On the 15th, the 2/31st Australian Battalion had its lead companies on the high ground that overlooked Jezzine from the north, while the Cheshire Yeomanry held the road leading west across the countryside falling away from it. Meanwhile a detachment of French cavalry was caught under artillery and machine gun fire from the Australians and was annihilated. Ultimately though, the situation was being dictated by the aftermath of the French counter-attack at Merdjayoun. 21st Brigade had been halted, and Lavarack had ordered Stevens to set up an "aggressive defence" until Merdjayoun had been secured with "B" squadron fighting every inch with them.[31] I Corps staff documents record "on right flank cav patrols occupied MAZRAAT ED DAHR 129184 and JLEILYE 130185 and contacted enemy at EL MTOLLE 132186(,) after sharp engagement our cav still hold EL JLEILYE(.)"[32] On the 16th Wilson instructed Laverack to concentrate his efforts on Beirut. This would take time however, as the invading force rebalanced its assets in light of the new priority. The fightback at Merjayoun in particular had been heroic, but the fact was that the whole invasion had suffered a major setback.

In truth, the operational stagnation was indicative of the whole of Exporter. After the first week, when the Cheshire Yeomanry themselves had become so mired down, it had become clear that the invasion of Syria was going to fail without help.[33] Wavell began to send for reinforcements, and by 20 June they had begun to materialise. In the meantime, three sectors of the advance were either currently under attack from the French or had been defeated, while on the coast the advancing column was completely stationary, losses had been heavy across the whole of operation Exporter and the Free French were in low spirits.

The incoming reinforcements were Habforce. They were available because the battle for Iraq had already been won, and now they could be diverted into Syria,

---

strikingly with the fighting of the hastily-re-roled Warwickshire Yeomanry fighting in Habforce. They had a clearly defined objective, knew their roles, weren't taken by surprise (they were the attackers), and they were not against tanks.

30   Gavin Long *Second World War*, p.405.
31   Gavin Long *Second World War*, p.412.
32   AWM52 1/4/1: I Corps docs: 10 July 41: I Australian Corps General Branch (1 Aust Corps 'G' Branch).
33   Verdin, *The Cheshire Yeomanry*, p. 305.

"fresh" from their conquering of Baghdad and Fallujah. They were to move along the Euphrates towards Palmyra from Aleppo. Besides elements of the 10th Indian Division and other units, Habforce of course contained a great many former members of 1st Cavalry Division. Having been suddenly and mysteriously spirited away and re-roled, they now were serving on Exporter as lorried infantry and approaching from a completely different direction to 5th Cavalry Brigade. The Cheshire Yeomanry's parent formation, 21st Brigade was to receive no reinforcement. It was given orders for a limited advance north on the 25th. They could not come a moment too soon. In the fighting on 19-20 June, the 5th Indian Brigade, in fierce fighting at Mezze prevailed but in doing so had virtually ceased to exist, while the coinciding Free French assault on the 19th failed. But by the 22nd, following the loss of the Beirut road, Damascus had at last fallen. On the night of 23/24th, the French pulled out of Merdjayoun, thus collapsing the salient in between the main prongs of the allied advance.

Before this got under way, 21st Brigade's new commanding officer[34] personally asked the regiment to carry out a specific patrol for him on the 23rd. Interest was further piqued when it was said that only unmarried men should take part. It was an information-gathering patrol. It would reconnoitre the road between Damour and Beit ed Dine, to establish whether mechanised units were using it. The road was south of the main French defences (on the Damour river) and also the quickest link between any forces opposing the coastal and centre columns of the allied invasion. A key artery for transferring units between the French defences, it was also known that there were enemy piquets along the road.

Lt. Shaw led a detachment out at night with Cpl H. Leah, five troopers and a farrier.[35] Riding steadily they were able to reach the target area by first light with time to take up their position. From there, Shaw dismounted and crept up towards the ridge from which he could then see the road below. He could see a detachment of French Foreign Legion infantry with an armoured car – showing that there were mechanised units using the road. As the yeomanry patrol was well beyond where Vichy forces expected allied patrols to reach, these particular French troops were taking few precautions and had posted no sentry. The quick and quiet riding of the cavalry patrol had therefore been able to penetrate to a very great degree. As the information required by Dunn was immediately available, Shaw did not see the point of hanging around. Straight away Shaw withdrew and led his patrol back to R.H.Q. Now moving in daylight, the fact that this most dangerous of phases was completed without incident, in the vicinity of French Foreign Legion, is further testament to the penetrative capabilities of small cavalry detachments.

---

34 Brigadier K. Dunn, who was a stand-in for Stevens who had been wounded but would return for the battle of Damour.
35 Troopers H.V. Allsop, G. McConnell, J, Dunbar, A. Mullen and A. Norbury with Farrier F. Marland.

On receiving this information, Dunn realised that he needed further protection along this flank. He consequently detached a section of Mitchell's machine gun troop, Mitchell himself, and two sections of Australian infantry to take up a holding position that could both overlook and dominate with machine guns the Damour road. Mitchell and what the Regimental Intelligence Officer noted in his diary as the "Farmer's Union"[36] duly went as far as Aaqliye. Mitchell, who had by now been close to but never involved in any shooting on Exporter, was under orders to only fire at a target worth giving away his position for. The sedentary and un-threatening French Senegalese platoon they found therefore, were not "in season". The fact that they were within easy machine gun range and clearly visible made for a time of mixed emotions as Mitchell's patrol observed them for the next fortnight while artillery from both sides fired over their heads. Their only consolation was that the troop's other section was doing very little either. Thus two Vickers guns and six thousand rounds waited in frustration, having silently penetrated well beyond where the French forces expected enemy patrols. Despite this accomplishment, Mitchell and his team were bored.

Mitchell was dispiritingly clear on the prohibition placed on using his machine guns. However, rifle fire could, he rationed, be employed as it could be construed as that of isolated marksmen, rather than a formidable fighting sub-unit threatening a key artery. The fact that the platoon of Senegalese infantry under observation were out of rifle fire presented no problem to Mitchell, a Scot who had grown up deer-stalking. He therefore suggested to the Australian officer accompanying the two infantry sections, and therefore in overall charge of the position, that they engage in their own "stalk", to within sniping range of the Vichy infantry. The decision on when to carry out this stalk was easy. Each morning, a member of the Vichy Senegalese platoon would walk out in front of their position, partially disrobe, and squat for their morning natural function. The two allied officers, having observed this ritual for a week knew exactly when they had to be in position by, and were ready for a long but still reasonable shot by the time that no less than eight Senegalese soldiers appeared. This being war, and the propensity for vindictiveness rife, the two officers waited until the infantrymen had squatted, and presented them with clear targets. Both rifles were fired at once, and the infantrymen, caught at a moment of "considerable inconvenience"[37] ran for safety, pulling up their trousers as they went. Apparently the sight was too much for the two allied officers and "laughter prevented further accuracy". With the Senegalese unscathed but wiser, the allied troops watching them were significantly cheered by the incident. Whether the two officers escaped without censure is not recorded.

36 Troopers D.D. Owen, C. Pym, J. Hewitt and E.W. Williamson were all scions of well-known Cheshire farming families. See Verdin, *The Cheshire Yeomanry*, p.306.
37 Verdin, *The Cheshire Yeomanry*, p.307. Possibly that the fact both riflemen missed was down to an attack of conscience.

The regiment's next patrol was of more immediate military value, and it proved far more sobering. Taking place on 25 June it coincided with serious developments elsewhere. The 25th was the day that 21st Brigade as part of the coastal column was to resume its progress with a limited advance northwards. It was also the day after the rear elements of 25th Brigade, latterly reinforced by 6th Division had finally triumphed at the battle of Merdjayoun, despite a strong French counter-attack and were able to defend the pass back to Palestine. This followed a summary sent by Wavell on the 24th that the newly redeployed Habforce should take Palmyra en route to Homs, the Australians to clear up Merdjayoun and advance on Beirut, and that the 23rd Brigade was on its way from Egypt.

The Cheshire Yeomanry meanwhile sent out Lt Lockett. Shaw and Mitchell had demonstrated that penetration as far as the Damour-Beit ed Dine road was possible, with comparatively few enemy south of that line. Meanwhile the enemy were rumoured to be still holding positions even further south, following the battle of Marjayoun, close to 25th Brigade's sector. Lockett and 1 Troop "C" squadron, were to reconnoitre the village of Mazboud. They struck out at 0600, accompanied by an interpreter called Darwish, getting as far as Mazboud without incident or sighting of enemy forces. Two troopers stopped and asked a local whether the village was occupied. Taken together with their queries in the previous village, which had found the same answer, Lockett gave the all-clear signal and entered the village. Lockett was nervous, despite the reassurances of the locals. Darwish was clearly extremely anxious.

Lockett dismounted his troop, and they advanced on foot, behind the point section. Darwish and the locals had not lied; the village *was* clear. What nobody had told them though was that it was under observation from an adjacent hill, and the French unit there consisted of tanks and mortars. They opened fire as soon as the troop entered the centre of the village. In the initial salvo, the only casualty was Farrier J. Mills's horse – Mills was only missed because he was bending down to tie his bootlace when the shell exploded. It was a lucky escape for the others, who had no effective means of response and could not see the enemy. At any rate, they were a recce patrol and not a fighting patrol, so Lockett pulled them out immediately. Once in the dead ground immediately behind the village, 1. Troop mounted up and quickly shook out to gallop the next 300 yards across painfully exposed ground to a position where Lockett knew they would be safe. They got up to speed in the dead ground and galloped the 300 yards in open order. They needed to as they were in full view of the enemy. Nonetheless, the troop made it through the bursting shells and mortars – apart from Trooper J.P. Ewbank who had been hit so badly that his leg was partially severed. His horse was killed outright. Corporal D.P. Ralling was lightly wounded by the shrapnel.

Lockett saw Ewbank and his horse go down. He handed command over to Sergeant T.D.L. Bowden and went back for his injured trooper whom he was able to carry to the cover of a nearby wall. There Lockett handed over to the rear section of 1. Troop – who had been pinned down earlier and were now galloping by. Trooper R.G. Chesham was ordered to stay with the quickly fading Ewbank while the troop leader got back to the rest of his command. Chesham did not have long to wait. Soon

Ewbank had slipped into unconsciousness. The main artery in his leg cut, he was soon dead. The next morning, 1. Troop returned and buried him in an olive grove. The fact that Ewbank died without medical aid at hand was inevitable given that he was a recce soldier, operating in a group that used its mobility to get as far ahead of the main column, and away from its "B" echelon, as possible. In any case, it is very unlikely that he would have survived the wound.

The days following this incident were once again slow. And just as Shaw had been sent to garrison Tyre after the exertions of his troop, so Lockett and 1 troop were dispatched to garrison Sidon on the 29th. This was a period of divisional reorganisation as more troops were finally brought up from the south, and the Cheshire Yeomanry came to be used more frequently to report to Division. The location statement for Australian I Corps as at this time (1800 hrs 28th Jun 41) confirms:

> 4" cav mob vet sec N of Litani R 108481564
> While the Cheshire Yeomanry at Hassaniye 11331735, some 24 miles north of the Litani. And B Sqn even further north east at Jezzine …
> As at 1800 5 Jul 41
> We have NSY "to come under 5 Cav Bde" less one squadron which is part of 23 Inf bde gp; all part of 7 div.
> Units under 85 L of C area: TJFF cav regt (horsed) and mech regt, and Greys/ Staffs all in the Deraa area.
> Evacuation of horse casualties will be by Horse Ambs to 5 Mob Vet Sec ACRE."[38]

Elsewhere, progress was being made, and after heavy naval shelling the brigade moved forward, on the night of 29/30 June. Resistance was strong, with Dentz himself allegedly in the area galvanising his men, and the progress made was therefore only limited. The war diary for the 1 July starts with "No naval activity this morning. Bde. H.Q … m. gunning from enemy aircraft." No doubt because of the stern resistance, orders were received for the regiment to dominate ground further ahead. "A" squadron moved up, occupying positions at Sebline, Myhariye and Joun. Meanwhile news was filtering through of the newly started Russo-German war in the east, and even Captain Phillips-Brocklehurst writing in the war diary succumbed to speculation:

> News of Russo-German war still vague with astronomical figures of tanks, men and planes destroyed claimed by both sides.[39]

---

38   AWM52 1/4/1: I Corps docs: As at 1800 5 July 41, 1 Australian Corps General Branch (1 Aust Corps 'G' Branch).
39   TNA WO 169/1396: 1 July 1941, Cheshire Yeomanry 1941.

The R.I.O. recorded in his diary that "surely this means that the Germans cannot win."[40]

Closer at hand, Maitland-Wilson's forces in the south had been split. There were still strong enemy positions separating the columns that the Cheshire Yeomanry and its detached "B" squadron between them served. Furthermore, the coastal plain was proving a formidable obstacle. On the night of the 3rd, 21st Brigade tried a breakout inland through the hills, rather than up the coast. Jleiliye was captured but the strongest position, at Mtoulle on the flank of 25th Brigade, remained stubbornly defiant. When Lt. Brocklehurst toured the regiment's outpost on the 3 July, he found Mitchell and his machine gunners in "good order although they have suffered much from the strain of continual shelling and perpetual watch of guns & O.P. position at Dhar Aaqliya is very exposed… All men show signs of strain and perhaps the nastiest experience was on the night 29/30 when some of the young Australians going forward cracked up under gun and m.g. fire and came back blubbering aloud with Shell Shock. Mr Mitchell is a great support to his tps [troops] who have a great reliance in & affection for him."[41]

As part of the Mtoulle operation, a section of Mitchell's hard-worked machine gunners was moved to a position at El Batal, northwest of Aaqliye. This section however had been at R.H.Q. for three weeks, and as the second section, went up under the command of Sergeant A.J. Jarvis. In theory they were joining Mitchell and 1 section, but in fact they were several kilometres from them. They had to climb through the darkness up a precipitous hillside, leading the pack horses up the treacherous ground. Too treacherous to ride up, the ground precluded taking most of the troop's horses. As a result, time was against them if they were to be off the exposed hillside before dawn lit them up for enemy observers. They finally reached their objective and managed it while it was still dark. However they had been spotted. The darkness did not protect them from an accurate burst of mortar fire, as the men stood by their pack horses on the hard stony ground from which the bombs blew up off rather than into. The hind leg was blown off one horse, and two of the horses were blown clean off the hillside[42], while three of the Australians 50 yards away were killed outright. Despite the cost, the guns were in position and the required arcs of fire were covered. However, no enemy targets were to present themselves.

It was perhaps fortunate that the two injured horses were still serviceable. As the turn of the month into July saw the regiment regroup, a big part of the reorganisation involved replacing lost and lame horses. Unfortunately, the Advance Remount Depot

---

40 Verdin, *The Cheshire Yeomanry*, p.309.
41 TNA: WO 169/1396: 3 July 1941, Cheshire Yeomanry 1941.
42 Interestingly, both horses were recovered later, only mildly hurst and still "usable" – Verdin, *The Cheshire Yeomanry*, p.309. A theme is emerging here: despite heavy enemy fire, it is the larger targets (horses) that took the brunt of the casualties. The soldiers themselves suffered proportionally far less, except where like the Australian infantry they were not standing next to one of these four-legged bullet magnets.

was, despite its name, 50 miles behind. This did not hamstring the regiment's mobility altogether, as firstly there were captured local horses that could be pressed into service, and secondly, there was a Mobile Veterinary Section rather closer than the remount depot. The Location Statement for Aust I Corps as at 1800 hrs 28 Jun 41 shows 4 Cav Mob Vet Sec (evidently detached to support the Cheshire Yeomanry) North of the Litani. This however was not all that accessible as the Cheshire Yeomanry were at Hassaniye 11331735, some 24 miles north of the Litani. And "B" Sqn even further north east at Jezzine.

The I Corps ORBAT then gives the provision for moving injured horses in the Location Statement as at 1800 5 Jul 41: "Evacuation of horse casualties will be by Horse Ambs to 5 Mob Vet Sec ACRE."[43] This does not suggest that much thought had gone into the pre-operation planning about maintaining the horsed cavalry elements in the field. The result was that 21st Brigade's close reconnaissance capability for example, had its essential support not with the column but many miles south east. The planners of Exporter had never dealt with horses before and they had only added the full regiment to the Exporter force in the later stages of the planning. To further complicate matters by early July, Verdin indicates that relations seem to have been strained between R.H.Q. and the M.V.S. This though may have been a product of the distance between them and the difficulty in communicating.

The communications issue was becoming even more problematic as Wilson's army found itself getting channelled into three separate bottlenecks, divided by mountains, with enemy in between. The two great salients which Wilson's advance created first of all invited flanking enemy counter-attacks, such as at Merdjayoun. Even without these, they made movement between the three columns highly challenging. Without enough men available to form an effective divisional reserve in Todcol, now a largely spent force, the constant re-allocation of units between the columns was to be of ever more importance. As such, it is no surprise that Laverack turned his attention to his "laterals."[44] The laterals to which he was now forced to turn his attention, were the connecting tracks and roads between his main columns. They snaked not just through hilly, stony terrain, but through areas of enemy held territory. To make matters worse, there were not even very many laterals he could use, and one was constantly under shell-fire. These routes had to be firstly protected (hence Lt. Mitchell's constant redeployment on roadwatch), and secondly patrolled. The hard-pressed "B" Squadron, who saw so much action, were constantly involved in this too. The case for using cavalry to control these laterals was overwhelming – Laverack himself said that much of the terrain was impassable to even tracked vehicles. He must now have bitterly regretted his dismissiveness of horsed cavalry when planning Exporter.

---

43 AWM 1/4/1 Corps: As at 1800 5 Jul 41, I Australian Corps General Branch.
44 AWM 52 1/5/14 Divisions 7: Laverack's 7 Division report on Operation Exporter, Appendix A.

To make good his earlier planning error, Laverack now had access to a number of horse soldiers. Firstly there was the presence of the North Somerset Yeomanry, who from 22 June start to be referred to in any official records.[45] This despite being completely ignored throughout the war diary of their parent formation, I Australian Corps. The North Somerset Yeomanry were clearly not regarded as an operation level asset for Exporter in the same way that the Cheshire Yeomanry were. Secondly there were the Yorkshire Dragoons, who are rarely formally listed on strength at any point in either 7th Division's or I Corps war diary for the duration of Exporter.[46] There is, however, a reference to various patrols on the 16 June move to Queneitra, then again in a rear area role for 7th Division on 29 June:

> An OG of 5 Cav Bde made this bde responsible for maintaining law and order in the country as far north as the R LITANI.
> Of the Yorkshire Dragoons one sqn was in the area ROSH PINNA and one sqn QUNEITRA [sic].
> North Somerset Yeomanry – HQ Sqn and one sqn TYR, one sqn EL MALIKIYA and one sqn TIBNINE. This regt also had a sqn ready to move to MERDJAYOUN as soon as it was captured.

The fact that a patrol from the Yorkshire Dragoons is referred to on the flank of the Merdjayoun salient implies that they were entering the area of the centre column from one of the connecting laterals. Meanwhile the Free French column on the right had their own Circassian cavalry – who found themselves fighting Vichy Circassian cavalry, among others.[47]

Finally, there was the "Kelly Gang". This unit deserves its own brief treatment, not least because, like the British cavalry, their existence appears so incongruous, and their role became so important in the mountain warfare of Operation Exporter. It's

---

45 And only then because said records reported the creation of "The Kelly Gang" who requested 50 saddles from the North Somerset Yeomanry but were refused.
46 Elsewhere in Exporter, the erstwhile members of Clark's 1st Cavalry Division, having been assigned to Habforce for Iraq, were now assaulting from the top. There was particularly vicious fighting for these yeomen around Palmyra. The Warwickshire Yeomanry in one incident lost 22 men, killed or captured, when they were blindsided by a detachment of Vichy French Syrians under Fawzi el-Kawakji. The armoured cars they attacked the yeomanry from were flying white flags – in order to divert fire from their own aircraft. Understandably, the Warwickshire Yeomanry had misconstrued this and let their guard down.
    Interestingly, this northern thrust, including specially trained yeomen as it did, chose to use Glubb Pasha's Bedouin scouts as the flank protection force (a detachment of these it might be remembered had already fought alongside the Warwickshire Yeomanry at H2). Presumably the newly lorried infantry were too badly needed in a principle fighting role.
47 AWM 52 1/5/14: '29 June' Divisions 7 Australian Division General Staff Branch.

ad hoc creation, recorded in the 7 Div GS war diary[48] presents a capability entirely consistent with that of the yeomanry:

> When the 25 Aust Inf Bde entered SYRIA on 6 June 41 one of the greatest difficulties which presented itself was adequate flank protection to the inf moving along the BANAYS – MERDJAYOUN RD and in their ops in the KHIAM area. The rd ran along a narrow flat with a marshy valley on the WEST and a steep escarpment rising almost directly from the rd on the EAST. It was from these rugged hills that the inf feared an outflanking movement by enemy horse Cav or Inf. The use of tracked vehs was quite impossible.
>
> The solution of the problem came when the 33 Aust Inf Bn captured a number of horses in an attack on an enemy Cav unit in the BNERIO area. Brig. Berryman ordered that the horses be used to form a tp of horsed cavalry, the personnel to be drawn from "C" Sqn 6 Aust Div Cav Reg where losses in carriers and light tanks had left many of their personnel immobilised, and the HQ Sqn.[49]

Thus far, this document shows that more cavalry were required to meet this threat, let alone offer their own threat in return. The implication of course is that seeing the effectiveness of the Cheshire Yeomanry alerted the Australians who now had to improvise:

> The 6 Aus Div Cav Regt was enlisted chiefly from the country and contains many members of Light Horse Militia units and sons of Light Horsemen of the last War. It was fitting therefore that these men should make history when on 22 Jun 41 [;] they formed the first Aust Light Horse unit of this war ...
>
> A daring patrol was made into KEFR SHEBAA, a village where the enemy patrolled daily and from where the they could see the entire area over which our patrol was working. This patrol was particularly successful and valuable infm was gained including a location of enemy arty. A remarkable thing on these patrols was that the horses in spite of heavy shelling and MG fire showed no signs of panic."
>
> Patrolling in [DARAYA] provided even more difficulties than before. Water was scarce and often inaccessible. Increased enemy activity necessitated the choice of night bivouac areas providing cover from the air and shell fire. One section patrolled AIN El HOUR – CHEMARIN – EL JALIOH area. EL JALIOH was occupied by the LEBANESE who evacuated the village when the patrol approached.
>
> One cannot speak too highly of the personnel and their versatility. Coming from Tanks and Carriers after 18 months of training in mechanised warfare,

---

48 AWM 52 1/5/14: 'Appendix D' Australian Division General Staff Branch.
49 AWM 52 1/5/14: Appendix D, Australian Division General Staff Branch.

to adapt themselves to the totally different life of a horsed Cavalry-man was no mean feat. The long hours of riding in most difficult country, the nights broken by shelling coupled with the general hard-ships and the uncertainty of enemy night activity had made their task most trying. They have the satisfaction of knowing that they have played an important part in the successful SYRIAN campaign. Not only did they gather much valuable infm and stop infm getting through to the enemy but lived up to the regt's reputation of being able to adapt themselves to any conditions and circumstances."
13 July 41
John Abbott Lt-Col, 6 Aust Cav[50]

Put simply, as more ground came under allied control, more horsemen were needed. The efficacy of horsed units was also becoming more apparent, with the Cheshire Yeomanry being attached on 5 July to the divisional reserve. They could now scout, screen and flank for the whole division with a correspondingly wider geographical and operational remit.

Meantime, Dentz's forces were steadily being defeated and their counter-attack had failed. Palmyra fell to the Essex regiment and the yeomanry of Habforce on 3 July. By that week, French airpower was also in decline. This was the fourth week of operations and it concluded with 21 Vichy aircraft lost to six British. More were hastily being sent in from Morocco and elsewhere, and troopships were bringing ground troops (one troopship, the "Saint Didier" was sunk, and its accompanying "Oued Yquem" ordered back). But Syria was clearly now a losing battle for Dentz.

Like that of the 6th Division Cavalry Regiment, the remit of the Cheshire Yeomanry had now changed. Although now aligned to 7th Division rather than a particular brigade, in simple geographical terms they were to transfer to 25th Brigade, in the middle column, and to prioritise dominating important lateral roads in between two bridges. This was a role of high importance, because there were still hilltop enemy positions between the two columns. Brigadier Plant, who had admitted that he actually had little idea on how to use cavalry, was now clearly seeing some of the benefits. The fact that 25th Brigade's diary lists the regiment as coming on strength at 0800 6 July stands out. Only two hours earlier, two troops from "B" Squadron had been dispatched to support the advance of 2/25th Australian Battalion. And, as if to indicate the role in unit advances the regiment now played, the entry for 1600 on the same day records one of their patrols as being "held up at Hill 894".[51]

---

50   AWM 52 1/5/14: Appendix D, Australian Division General Staff Branch. See also, Hugh Cullimore and Stuart Bennington, *Hidden in the Archives: Australia's Second World War 'Kelly Gang'* <https://www.awm.gov.au/articles/blog/wwii-kelly-gang> (accessed 20 August 2021).
51   AWM52 8/2/25/7: 6 July, 25 Infantry Brigade: July-August 1941.

For the rifle sections and machine gun sections in the sabre troops carrying out these patrols, it meant setting up semi-permanent troop H.Q.s and patrolling out from these. With watchful French spotters around this required great care. The troop of Sergeant G.H. Bates at Daraya was able to use an olive grove as their troop H.Q. Each morning they went out on patrol to ascertain whether there had been any enemy movement during the night. The daylight movement inevitably meant being shelled and mortared. However, the troop H.Q. through careful positioning under the cover of the olive grove, was never directly hit, and the troop was able to avoid taking any casualties during this period.[52] This may equally have been because the French shells being fired at them were often duds; a section from 2 troop "A" Squadron emerged from their slit trench one morning to find an unexploded shell lying by the lip of the trench. As well-camouflaged as they were, the scale of traffic in and out of each position clearly attracted attention from very proficient French gunners and their spotters. None the less, the regiment was able to do plenty of valuable work for their new Brigadier, E.C.P. Plant, and he was quickly able to understand how versatile the mounted patrols could be. Verdin suggests that despite the lack of direct fire contacts, there was still a great deal of useful and dangerous work done well. He praised in particular Corporal Salter, who it will be remembered galloped into machine gun fire across the narrow Litani bridge at the start of the campaign.

Despite Verdin's low-key appraisal of this period of the campaign, the relevant war diary records some rather more dramatic episodes.[53] The fighting that the regiment was now to be involved in is a reflection of the fact that the central column was extremely hard-pressed and busy throughout the campaign. The column had after all seen the fierce fighting at Merdjayoun. Now the enemy were pulling back and this had to be exploited. Once all elements of the regiment were to be combined in one column, they were also to find themselves working closely with the Durham Light Infantry in particular. As if to emphasise the scale of the task still facing the central column of Wilson's force, the way north was to venture into the teeth of "pronounced air activity".[54]

This all came together on the 10 July and the isolated nature of each of Wilson's column's is shown by Brigadier Plant's deploying of one troop of Cheshire Yeomanry on his rear right flank, as the column progressed. The entire right flank of 25th Brigade's column was under threat, and in the hill country painfully vulnerable to ambush. Meanwhile, there was massing enemy reported in the vicinity on hills north of Mazraa Ed Chouf, and the Cheshire Yeomanry, operating as the Brigade's screen were reporting sniper activity north of Mazraa Ed Chouf. Due to the terrain, the regiment by the end of 10 July had been unable to make contact with the D.L.I., its immediate source of reinforcements.

---

52 Verdin, *The Cheshire Yeomanry*, p.310.
53 Some of these are recounted in Chapter 6.
54 AWM52 8/2/25/7: 25 Infantry Brigade: July-August 1941.

Therefore, the regiment had to be able to take on direct fighting tasks itself. A key part of the regiment's fighting power was however to go where the threat loomed largest, and so once again Mitchell's machine gun troop was kept busy. By this stage they were essentially there to stop the Australian 2/27th Battalion being hit by a flank attack, and as such dispatched under orders from the Australian C.O. at El Boum. Mitchell's men found themselves arriving in darkness at the foot of a steep hill that had to be surmounted there and then. The hill being too precipitous to be climbed in the darkness by horses, the decision was made to manhandle the guns up the rocky side of the hill. The 2 sections, their Vickers guns, and their 3000 rounds eventually, exhaustedly, arrived at the top of the hill. They were able to complete the whole journey in the relative safety of darkness, and now waited for dawn so that they could sight the guns. As they peered through the gloom, awaiting enough light to identify their arcs of fire and lay the guns, a message arrived to inform the troop that the threat was now passed; they were to redeploy. With bitter frustration, Mitchell, Jarvis and the rest of the machine gun troop, wearily descended the stone-strewn slope, back to their horses.

R.H.Q was keenly aware of what the troop had just endured. They themselves had had comparatively little to do for the past month; in stark comparison with the machine gun troop. It was therefore the men of Headquarters squadron who rode the weary machine gun troop's horses back down the line, while the exhausted machine gunners sat in the trucks of R.H.Q. down to the "garden and groves of the Emir Schaab."[55]

There was no feel of the campaign winding down elsewhere. Despite the High Command's hopes for an armistice with Dentz, the situation on the ground was very far from looking resolved. North of Merdjayoun and east of Jezzine, 25th Brigade's left flank and rear, seemed like a particularly vulnerable point. It did not ease Plant's concerns that all he had been able to hitherto deploy by way of cover on this part of the flank was a platoon of pioneers on the high ground at Machgara. Clearly very flighty, they reported that they felt like they were going to be attacked at "any time".[56] The handily mobile yeomanry were employed in the subsequent locating and screening task. "C" squadron in particular were to find themselves busily involved in trying to find the hidden menace. One of the troops, 4. Troop, under Sergeant Burks found the hidden enemy when they came under machine gun fire while out on patrol. Having only just dismounted to carry out a forward foray on foot, their horse-holders were still just metres behind. Now old hands at reacting to enemy fire, the dismounted troop held its ground, while the horse-holders retired to a safer position. According to S.O.P. one man could be expected to move while holding four horses. The troop's eccentric, Trooper Caradoc Jones, however, was holding five, theoretically enough for a horse-holder to control only when stationary. As machine gun bullets descended around the troop, Jones also held his ground, as did his five horses. Sergeant Burks,

---

55 Verdin, *The Cheshire Yeomanry*, p.312.
56 Verdin, *The Cheshire Yeomanry*, p.311.

the former whipper-in, was used to getting through a day's work with difficult horses thrown into the mix. But he was still surprised to see Jones's solve the difficulties of flighty horses by standing still under fire, holding his five horses. Burks was still surprised when Jones later explained exactly why he had remained so vulnerable under machine gun fire. Jones had been concerned. In the way that only a cavalry soldier at war might understand, he was fiercely attached to his horse, "Vixen". It was an attachment no-one else in the regiment shared. "Vixen" was highly-strung, restless, disobedient and a serial kicker of other horses, having managed to kick every other horse in the troop at some point. As the bullets had descended, and the other horse-holders retreated, Jones had realised that the price of safety, with the others, was to risk moving while precariously controlling five horses. He might well lose grip on the high-spirited "Vixen". The strength of his bond dictated the tenacity of his grip. Incredulous at Jones's testimony, Burks (himself an evidently stoic character) was in truth a little disappointed. In fact, "everyone else was sorry that she had not escaped."[57]

No. 4. Troop, complete with "Vixen", duly returned to S.H.Q. and were able to feedback. No-one felt reassured. Major Hutchinson, O.C. of "C" squadron and the man who had once travelled through France balancing on a train buffer with Hephalump's hoof for support, sent out another patrol. This one was led by Lieutenant Paterson and was tasked – directly from Brigade – with gleaning as much information about precise enemy dispositions as possible. The Brigade had to know if it was being encircled.

The nature of the Cheshire Yeomanry's deployment and principle function is discernible from, among other things, the frequency with which they are mentioned in 25th Brigade's war diary. By this stage of the campaign, troop and squadron tasks by the Cheshire Yeomanry are being listed, every three or four entries for any one day. The principle "fighting" units of infantry are generally mentioned around once a day, and usually identified by battalion task, rather than company task, and almost never by platoon task. This reporting shows the brigade commander's dependence on this very mobile and versatile asset. The versatile mobility of the yeomanry was what enabled them to cover ground on the march – where vehicles could not go; and to cover ground in defence or fighting formation. Mostly of course, the frequency of reference in the war diary indicates that as a mobile brigade asset, the yeomanry were much-used recce troops. This example from July captures this nicely:

7 Aust DIV op INSTN No. 18

Area of rd Rharife – Mtolle not yet cleared of enemy. Ches Yeo (less MG Tp under comd 21 Aust inf Bde) came under 25 Aust inf Bde night 5/6 July and used to clear this area. On stand by to place a troop along each of three roads

---

57 Verdin, *The Cheshire Yeomanry*, p.312.

running towards coast. Ches Yeo to deny their use to the enemy. Extra tps to be allocated if necessary.[58]

The same document also shows the deployment (as a divisional asset) of the rest of 5th Cavalry brigade from the end of June.

On the 9 July, Brigadier Plant needed a particularly important reconnaissance to be carried out. The information gleaned by Sergeant Burks' patrol had to be followed up on; more detail was needed. Enemy forces this close had to be kept under close observation and their strength and capabilities could not be left to guesswork. Lt. Paterson was consequently sent, and the "flighty" Australian pioneers at Machgara were only too pleased to see yeomanry again. The yeomanry themselves immediately appreciated why when their ration party on the first night was shelled heavily. The rations were being personally brought up by the squadron second in command, Captain Charlton. Presumably this killed two birds with one stone and allowed S.H.Q to get a detailed appraisal of the situation quickly. He was lucky to survive, as indeed were the rest of the group. Only one soldier, Trooper W.E. Morris was lightly wounded, the rest miraculously escaped unharmed – despite Trooper G.H.L Walters having his shirt blown off his back.

The enemy gunners may well have been firing blind and simply got lucky on a routine shoot. At any rate, the position was not abandoned, and Paterson's troop remained. From their position, Paterson decided to proceed with a small mounted patrol. They were in excellent country for cavalry – they could move easily and do so under cover or in dead ground – and thanks to the shelling they now knew the rough location of at least one enemy battery. Paterson decided to locate this battery with a flanking movement. After having patrolled some way, the land suddenly gave way to a clear view of the French battery, a mere half-mile away. It was a mountain battery, with its own horses positioned close by. An appraisal by Paterson, lead him to conclude that the ground would allow cavalry to get even closer to the battery without being seen, and carry out an attack.

This information went straight back to "C" squadron. Paterson's information was quickly recycled into a set of orders. The squadron was to attack and capture the battery then clear the area of any other enemy. The squadron moved into its forming up area, and on 12 July shortly after midnight was saddling up the full complement of horses and checking weapons. Just then a dispatch rider arrived from R.H.Q. An armistice had been signed – Dentz had given in following the capitulation of Beirut to 7th Division. The Cheshire squadron were not to fight the last mounted action of the British Army.

---

58 AWM 52: 1/5/14-0110 7: 7 Aust DIV op INSTN No 18, Australian Division General Staff Branch (7 Aust Div GS Branch).

6

The 5th Cavalry Brigade

Fighting up the middle – "B" Squadron, Cheshire Yeomanry and the Battle for Merdjayoun

"B" Squadron started Exporter early. Major Johnson-Houghton had hooves across the frontier early on the night of the 7th, the night prior to the planned invasion. They were carrying out a pre-mission reconnaissance. It allowed them to choose their line of approach to Blida, and to see conditions first-hand. It took advantage of the fact that Brigadier Plant had given them their orders early. Most importantly though, it gave them time to realise that the bright early-night moon disappeared from sight before 0300. Major Johnson-Houghton therefore realised that his squadron would have to cross into Lebanon on or soon after midnight, if it were to avoid navigating the difficult countryside in complete darkness. Permission for the whole squadron to do this however was refused. This is presumably because as flank guard, rather than advance guard, they had to leave in accordance with the march time-table of the rest of the brigade. Leave too early, and 25th Brigade's flank would be exposed.

The order did come as a relief to one man in the Squadron. For him the prospect of the total darkness of pre-dawn was worth any amount of treacherous footing in the gloom. Captain R.B. Verdin had agreed to carry the squadron's obligatory white flag, and it made him feel very conspicuous. The order was for the bearer to carry it visibly across the border, alongside the French and British flags, so that the half-hearted Vichy defenders might surrender immediately. Verdin, who also found the small white flag he had been issued with disconcertingly small and un-noticeable, duly crossed the frontier near Qadas with an entire bedsheet tied to his sword. If he was going to be spotted with a white flag, it was at least going to be an obvious one.

His fears however were not universally held – as evidenced by the sense of embarking on a forbidden picnic, that prevailed with the rest of the regiment at this stage. Within "B" squadron even, there were still hopes that the French would indeed fold early. In anticipation of this, the Pontiac that Captain Verdin and the squadron leader shared as support vehicle was duly loaded with "personal conveniences"; such as camp beds, spare clothes and shot guns, should the chance for sporting diversions arise in Syria. Driving the Pontiac was Yeomanry stalwart Trooper W.A. "Push" Wright, himself the son of another regimental stalwart. "Push" Wright was Verdin's batman and the orders he received were to start along the track to Blida at 0400 and drive until he met the rest of the squadron.

The main squadron formation crossed, as per march timetable, at 0200 with Lance-Sergeant Brown's section of 4. Troop leading. This section aimed directly for a position north of Blida and positioned themselves as the cut-off group, while the rest of the troop moved in. As Lance-Sergeant Brown would have now been all too excruciatingly aware, it is difficult to move horses across stony ground in silence. Noise travels far at night, and the feeling of being exposed and alone must have been particularly acute. It was therefore a surprise that the enemy they found in the village were taken unawares.

The fact that the French were taken by surprise must have been at least partly due to the careful entry of the troop. The final approach to the destination was understandably carried out on foot, given the noise the horses were making, closing in from the north and east. The three men who actually entered the village were Captain Verdin, Lieutenant G.B. Dawson, and their interpreter, simply recorded as Baadi.[1] Verdin, as per orders, carried the white flag high above his head, and still tied to his sword, Dawson the Union flag, and Baadi the French flag, and thus equipped tiptoed towards their enemy. Despite moving extremely carefully, the three of them still managed to almost walk into the first French sentry. Fortunately he was asleep. Baadi, whose view of war certainly did not include carrying flags at the walk into enemy positions, was keen to slit the sentry's throat as he slept. Fortunately for the Frenchman, Verdin was able to prevail upon Baadi; whose first significant act of the war was therefore a few steps later, as the three men trepidatiously entered the village and Baadi bellowed out a call to surrender. The result was an explosion of action as the night darkness disappeared in gunfire, tracer and confusion. The flag party dived for the nearest cover – though this proved merely to be a pile of straw – while their comrades laid on the covering fire. Lying behind a pile of straw in the middle of an enemy position, with all of 4. Troop firing into the position, and all of Lieutenant J.W. Cunningham's 3. Troop adding their supporting fire, the flag party were thus acquainted with battle. Cunningham, a decisive figure who had ordered his troop to open fire as soon as bullets started flying at 4. Troop, now got himself as close to the action as could be. It was night, 4 Troop's officers were separated and pinned down, and someone needed to take control of the firefight. Cunningham therefore ordered Trooper H. Brentall to engage a French machine gun position in a house with the Boyes gun, then pressed onwards himself, only to find himself moments later face to face with a French officer (the Commandant it later transpired). Cunningham instantaneously drew his revolver

---

1   Verdin, *The Cheshire Yeomanry*, p.316.

and fired all six rounds. In the chaos, darkness and adrenaline of this first contact, every one of Cunningham's rounds missed the Frenchman "to the fury of his squadron leader and the disappointment of his batman, Trooper A. Williams, both of whom were standing right behind him at the time."[2] Whether Cunningham heeded these sentiments while in the middle of his first firefight is unlikely. The salient fact was that the yeomanry were pressing hard, and there was a considerable weight of well-directed fire now being concentrated on the surprised defenders of Blida.

Within a few minutes the firing had died down to an uneasy pause as French and British eyed each other through the murk. An early burst of machine gun fire from one of the yeomanry Hotchkiss sections had set a straw stack on fire, and there was now a degree of illumination. Enough for Verdin and Baadi to stand up nervously and resume their passage forward, their flags as visible as they could be made to be. Fortunately, the impromptu truce remained long enough for them to approach the ruffled French commandant.

Continuing with the sense of unreality engendered by the carrying of flags into battle, there now followed protracted negotiations. "B" squadron, who despite being in parley, did not yet have the village fully under their control, and now had to engage in some diplomacy. Clearly the Commandant was still incandescent about Lt. Cunningham's attempt on his life, and possibly about being surprised so easily. The French officer insisted that while his garrison were prepared to surrender, they also wished to retain their weapons. Major Johnson-Houghton refused; however the clock was ticking and the fact was the French still held the village. The importance of negotiating however became ever-more pressing when dawn rose at 0400 mid-parley. The pink-grey light revealed roof-top machine guns covering all the approaches into the village. If diplomacy failed, there was going to have to be a very bloody assault.

Just as Johnson-Houghton was taking all this in, Verdin, to his horror, looked up to see "Push" Wright's Pontiac bumping along the track to Blida. French machine guns covered the Pontiac every rock-strewn inch of the way as Wright and his co-driver Trooper C.W. Thorley approached in blissful ignorance.[3] Whether or not spurred on by the now all too obvious vulnerability of any approach to the village, Johnson-Houghton reached a compromise; the French would surrender with their weapons. But all ammunition was to be removed. This important amendment finally brought down the curtains on an idiosyncratic first instalment in "B" squadron's war story.

Despite the attitude of Wright and Thorley, most of "B" squadron had clearly been ready for a contact as they crossed the border, whatever their earlier feelings. The alacrity with which Cunningham's troop had opened fire, coupled with the fact that within moments he, closely followed by his squadron leader, were pressing into

---

2   Verdin, *The Cheshire Yeomanry*, p.317.
3   His advance down this road was despite the recommendation of the field ambulance unit who urged him to wait until Blida was confirmed as clear. Wright had ignored these admonitions; he had his orders.

the middle of the enemy position testify to this. The heightened awareness of the squadron can only have made the advance of the flag party an even more excruciating experience. Particularly so the advance under white flag after the initial burst of firing. What was important was that – delay aside – Blida was secure, the squadron had proved proficient under fire, and no casualties had been taken.

The squadron however was on a tight schedule – perhaps even more so for being flank guard rather than advance guard. In the latter capacity a delay for them was easily identified by all the units behind who would then simply wait or send up support. In flank guard role, in such broken territory, the main column would simply be pressing on with its flank unknowingly exposed. Major Johnson-Houghton now spurred his squadron forwards. The fact they moved with such haste meant that they almost caught a detachment of Spahis unaware at Adeisse; the surprised Spahis (around 40 according to the war diary) were seen galloping full-pelt out of the village, just as the yeomanry arrived from the south. Adeisse was in fact their third village since quitting Blida. The capacity for putting on a burst of speed like this, as a unit, was of course a key advantage held by horsed cavalry in country where even tracked vehicles would struggle – and would do so noisily while creating more dust. The *Chester Chronicle* 2014 obituary of Trumpeter Dougie Hall (retired) states that Hall sounded the charge as "B" squadron approached a village on the Litani.[4] This was probably when the squadron were advancing at speed towards the river in a bid to catch up with the rest of the Brigade, rather than immediately after they had crossed.

Now they would have to make use of their general mobility capability, if not their cross-country speed. The central brigade column needed to find a way over the Litani and casting around for a suitable crossing point meant using every available unit capable of reconnaissance. Fortunately, "B" squadron could cross easily and look from the other side. Captain Verdin joined Lt Cunningham's troop in swimming the river when they couldn't find a bridge. As Rogers's troop with 21st Brigade was finding at this time, any crossing was a very likely ambush point. Nonetheless they were fortunate; there was no ambush waiting for "B" Squadron on the Litani. Lt Cunningham's troop, accompanied by Captain Verdin, found this after they had crossed by swimming the river.

Their technique was certainly robust: first a section swam across with their horses, they then scaled the steep side before securing the high-ground. Then the rest of the troop were committed to the crossing. Each man had to allow for being carried a little downstream by the fierce current and therefore to ensure that his packhorse, if he was leading one as well as his own mount, was upstream of him in order to control it. Exhausted, wet, but intact and ready to fight through if necessary, B Squadron's lead elements had now crossed the Litani ahead of 25th Brigade.

---

4   Cheshire Live, Last Post sounds for bugler Dougie, *Chester Chronicle* (2014) <https://www.cheshire-live.co.uk/news/british-army-veteran-who-led-7183656> (accessed 25 August 2021).

The horses' training in swimming now having paid its dividend, the troop used a goat trail to ascend the north bank. The horses managed this well – with no casualties – and on completion of this draining task, the patrol then cleared the village of Nabbatiye-et-Tahta. Verdin sent back a dismounted two-man dispatch team of Lance Corporal G. Shickell and Trooper L. Greatorix to re-swim the Litani and inform S.H.Q. The squadron's role was now to go firm and hold Adiesse as well as the newly found crossing at Chateau Beaufort, carrying out "active patrolling"[5] as they did so. With little to recommend this episode in the war diary – despite Trooper Hall sounding the charge on his bugle – this was still an object lesson in the versatility and manoeuvrability of cavalry. The 25th Brigade's desire to have a squadron of yeomanry was proving prescient.

With the rate of progress for the main column being slow, the squadron was not in fact to press any further until the 12 June. The war diary describes the establishing of standing patrols, and more alarmingly of Australian artillery mistakenly firing on the squadron at Kafr Kila. Verdin cites this as the reason that Johnson-Houghton then halted the squadron in some olive groves. "A" echelon had just completed this move and met in the groves with Captain Verdin when at 1430, Lt Dawson's 4. Troop was machine-gunned from an aeroplane at 100ft, in a defile. This attack was one of three that day.[6]

No. 4 Troop was patrolling along the Litani, traversing the main road for speed. It was therefore very much out in the open. The aircraft was able to surprise them at a vulnerable point – choosing to dive when they were at a bit of the road cut out of the hill, with a steep cliff blocking one side and a sheer drop to the river on the other. They were trapped. Corporal E. Laycock who led the point section undoubtedly saved them when he swiftly moved his section's horses into the side of the road, under the cliff. The rest of the troop immediately did the same and now could only be attacked from one side – the aircraft's machine gun fire hitting only thin air and rock as the pilot had to swerve before getting too close to the cliff. As the pilot then wheeled off to line up for another dive at the troop from a better angle, Lieutenant Dawson ordered the whole troop to dig in their spurs and gallop down the road. They were now moving horizontally along the cliff and at the gallop, so were a difficult target for the aircraft, flying straight towards it. They were soon off the road at the bottom and into cover, unscathed but shaken. Quick thinking of the junior commanders had proved vital.

The squadron was clearly very much at risk. S.H.Q was attacked again around an hour later, when most of Capt. Verdin's newly arrived patrol were still mounted and "B" echelon had just arrived in their vehicles. Two Vichy aircraft then came in on a strafing run. Lt Chalcraft put up sustained fire from the Hotchkiss gun mounted in one of the vehicles, while most of the rest of the squadron opened up – even those still

---

5   TNA WO 169/1936: Cheshire Yeomanry 1941.
6   Two other patrols were strafed. No. 3 Troop were able to seek cover amongst buildings at Taibe.

holding their horses engaged the aircraft with their rifles. Johnson-Houghton's entry in the war diary praises Chalcroft in particular who "stood manfully to his broken Hotchkiss and fired one belt into the Plane".[7] The *Manchester Evening Chronicle* in its 14 June 1941 was even more effusive; with an article entitled "Cavalry rout bombers". The only yeomanry casualty from this incident was the pack-horse of trooper Dryland, which "dropped dead from excitement",[8] a fate not unknown amongst livestock.[9] There was no hiding the fact though that they had been lucky – or the fact that they were in danger of being bogged down by repeated aerial counter-attacks. These attacks were now threatening the yeomens' ability to do their primary job.

No. 2 Troop "B" Squadron returning from patrol. They were attacked by a French aircraft shortly after this photograph was taken.

"B" squadron were stretched. They had main responsibility for covering the flank of 25th Brigade and were carrying out this function in the teeth of a French fightback. They were also pressing ahead, through difficult country that made communication and resupply difficult. As they did so they commandeered local Arab stallions to be used as pack horses in the machine gun sections. The yeomanry were not just losing horses to enemy action, but also to going lame on the rocky ground, and these

7   TNA: WO 196/1936: "B" Squadron 12 June: Cheshire Yeomanry 1941.
8   *Manchester Evening Chronicle*, 14 June 1941 as cited in Verdin, *The Cheshire Yeomanry*, p.321.
9   Elsewhere during this period, the brigade war diary reported the frequency of the strafing and that the Brigade Signals officer was killed on the 12th by air to ground fire. See AWM52 8/2/25/6: 12 June, May–June 1941.

casualties were having to be evacuated. The replacements, untrained as they were proved to be prone to "squealing" on the march – a quality which endeared them to no-one in a unit that had to advance unseen and unheard at night. The logistical problems thrown up by the horses were being caused by the very ground that made their use so invaluable.

The squadron's mobility was now a feature that 25th Brigade wanted to utilise beyond merely flank guard. Like Maitland-Wilson's army as a whole, manpower was stretched, and they were quickly discovering the benefits of cavalry as they went along. Orders duly arrived on 13th June for the Brigade to advance north that night. The main Brigade group was to advance along the "main track" and the yeomanry were to advance simultaneously along the west flank, in the hills, probing for enemy, flank guarding and attempting to link with 21st Brigade. The "main track" is recorded in the "Official History" (presumably of 25th Brigade) as "a nightmare of a march without lights by unknown corkscrew tracks and along the precipitous sides of the Lebanon Mountains".[10] The yeomanry column was in fact advancing through the scree-covered hills without benefit of this track. Nonetheless, attached to the yeomanry column, and under Johnson-Houghton's command, were: a troop of light tanks, a troop of the 6th Australian Divisional Cavalry in universal carriers, a section of anti-tank guns, a section of divisional signals to ensure there was no further breakdown in communication, and a field ambulance. It was a potent force, but it was hampered from the start.

Although the start-time for the main and yeomanry columns was 9.30, "B" squadron's eclectic combination of supporting arms took time to muster and the column did not cross the start line until after 2200 and even then quickly became disjointed as only the horses could progress off the track. They were further slowed down by the rather optimistic order to simultaneously liaise with 21st Brigade. Accordingly, 2nd Lieutenant Morgan-Jones's troop was sent as far as Kafr Melki and there waited for sufficient dawn light to ascertain if any sign of 21st Brigade could be identified. They duly returned with nothing to report. The rest of the squadron meanwhile pressed on. When Johnson-Houghton's command arrived at Heitoura at 7.30 in the morning, only two mounted troops had made the journey (Morgan-Jones was still to re-join them). In fact, the only vehicle which had been able to negotiate the rough hillside and keep up with the horses, was dispatch rider Trooper W.H.O. Fox's motorcycle. The fact that even he managed this was a rather singular feat.

By 0900 there were still only two troops of horsemen at Heitoura. Cunningham and his troop were therefore sent forward to gain some elevation. Meanwhile a dismounted group scaled a hill on the east flank. When all came back reporting nothing, it was once again apparent that the squadron were in front, alone and isolated. Furthermore, without the motorised divisional signals section, they were unable to communicate with anyone.

10   Verdin, *The Cheshire Yeomanry*, p.322.

When the opportunity for communication presented itself, Cunningham did go on to report that his troop had come under sustained machine gun fire from three different positions. It took him some time to disengage from this contact and get the information back to S.H.Q. Fortunately, the squadron hadn't needed to move in the meantime. Nonetheless, the extent of the opposition in front of the column deserved to be brought to the attention of Brigade. Johnson-Houghton therefore sent back two gallopers to inform brigade headquarters. Corporal Shickell and Trooper A. King were tasked with this ride, it by now being apparent that messages needed to be managed by pairs rather than individuals. The journey back gives the best indication of just how isolated "B" squadron's line of march had made them; not only did they need to negotiate the hillside route, but they had to take a detour of the enemy positions between them and the advancing Australians, who were behind rather than parallel with "B" squadron.

Although valuable for reconnaissance, the squadron was effectively shorn of its capability to fight large groups of enemy and to dominate ground. The entire machine gun troop was with the regiment in the 21st Brigade sector.[11] This however was temporarily solved when two Australian pioneer officers arrived at S.H.Q. They had arrived on foot from Jabaa in the direction of Jezzine. They were lost, and they were irate. They had lost contact with their men during the previous night's fighting and hoped that they might have attached themselves to "B" squadron. Johnson-Houghton explained to the officers that he had not seen them, but that if they were to be found then they could join him in a task. The Australians were keen to be involved in some fighting, and they willingly agreed to help; they just had to find their men first.[12]

That evening, the full complement of pioneers appeared at last. It was, according to Verdin, obvious that the officers wanted to do as much fighting and as little pioneering as possible. A plan of attack on a nearby position was duly agreed upon, with a dismounted joint attack supported by the pioneers. Leaving S.H.Q. at 0200 they found that the chosen enemy had withdrawn completely, to join the general withdrawal from Jezzine by the larger French force that night (taken after a hard battle by 25th Brigade). This was also the point at which 25th and 21st brigades were at their closest so far - two hours' drive apart. The size of this gap does show the unlikelihood of the squadron ever achieving the secondary task of linking up with 21st brigade before this point.

Now that the French had moved out, the squadron duly moved in and consolidated the position, and the Australian pioneers went off to look for another scrap. Besides taking new ground, the squadron acquired five horses left behind by the retreating Spahis they had been chasing since the start of Exporter. They could continue moving; but the dependency on vehicles in the planning for this phase had cost 25th Brigade

11 Despite the pleas of Major Johnson-Houghton to have a machine gun section attached to his force.
12 Verdin, *The Cheshire Yeomanry*, p.323.

an opportunity. The tethering of the attendant firepower to vehicles (to invert one of Churchill's phrases) had meant that none of that firepower was able to stick with the horse on the treacherous march. Equally, the designation of so many roles to "B" squadron meant that they were too dispersed when they reached Heitoura to do anything more than simply wait. If they had had a horse-mounted section of machine guns attached then they would not have had to wait for the Australian pioneers to carry out any fighting tasks. They would also, on reaching the Sidon road early on the 14th have been able to do serious damage to the retreating French force leaving the Jezzine sector.

The exertion required to keep up with and simply get into the position where they might have harried the French forces should be noted. A notable component of nearly all campaigns in fact is simply the effort needed to get to where a task needs to be carried out or might be needed to be carried out. It is nicely encapsulated in the labours of Trooper T.P. Nicholls who had been left behind on the night of the 13th to evacuate lame horses, to his immense frustration. Having eventually returned the lame horses, he then requisitioned a local Arab stallion, and without saddle or map, rode it back through Jbaa to join the squadron at Heitoura. The only guidance he had were the day-old tracks of the squadron on the broken ground. If anything shows the quality and the relish of the yeomen for their role, it is this. It also demonstrates the quality of their training under Chrystal, but more importantly, the quality of the raw material that the Territorial Army had been able to attract for service back in 1939.

By the 15th that human material was feeling hungry. "B" squadron had been away from its "B" echelon for two days – and it had exhausted its rations. Some officers in particular were struggling as they had made the mistake of not using the whisky bottle-sized ration pouches to carry the issue beef.[13] This problem however was solved by the local populace, who were clearly at odds with the French colonial regime. An Arab village welcomed "B" squadron, slaughtered three sheep, and served them mutton with chapatis in an olive grove. This incident demonstrates firstly the partial accuracy of Churchill and De Gualle's assertion that resistance to Maitland-Wilson's force would be reluctant – or at least that the indigenous population clearly resented the French occupation. Secondly, it further shows the capacity of the 1941 Cheshire Yeomanry to establish cordial relations. Whether it was because they paid them well is not revealed, but they certainly avoided antagonising the Lebanese and Syrians. The other notable point from this anecdote of Verdin's is that the horses aren't mentioned. Therefore there weren't any problems. There was generally a local water supply available, wherever the yeomanry found themselves in Exporter. For forage, it likely given the lack of mention to the contrary, that there was also generally adequate grazing available. The fact that the horses were therefore clearly being grazed wherever the yeomanry happened to bivouac, makes the cordial relationship with local people

---

13 Verdin, *The Cheshire Yeomanry*, p.324.

a notable achievement. But it may still have been facilitated with the exchange of money.

The last inference that the rations anecdote suggests, is that the yeomanry – especially "B" squadron – were working beyond "spec" and truly showing what a flexible force they were. When augmented with decent fighting power, they were becoming one of the most valuable assets in either of the two brigades they were involved in. On the 16th, they were once again lined up to protect the flank of 25th Brigade, this time with a section of light tanks and an artillery battery. As the previous 72 hours had demonstrated, any advancing column would be isolated and vulnerable from all sides. The flank guard had to be able to maintain a mobile screen at all times. The yeomanry's capacity to cross ground that vehicles couldn't, as well as their range, speed and self-sufficiency are salient features of all the cavalry deployed during the Second World War from the Wehrmacht infantry division recce patrols that remained constantly out on patrol, to the soviet fighting columns that remained behind enemy lines. 25th Brigade's commander now fully understood how to use his mounted unit.

The model for resupply was also now well-established. Essentially, the initial rapid advance across challenging terrain was carried out by the point troop or section, and then their route in covered by roadblocks and machine gun positions on the surrounding high ground. This then complete, B echelon brought up rations while any immediate local tasks for the squadron were worked through. The efficiency with which this model worked, does also give credence to the officers in the other squadrons, who felt that a regiment was too big and unwieldy a unit. As was being proved here, a squadron could still complete several tasks (admittedly at a stretch), cover or dominate a wide area, yet be resupplied quickly.

On the 17th the French carried out a ferocious counter-attack. This was to overlap with their earlier attack on and capture of Merjayoun where they routed the Australians and the Scots Greys. Now there was a sizeable French contingent in the rear of Maitland-Wilson's main force and with a home run to unprotected Palestine on the cards. The attacks inflicted horrific losses, on the 5th Indian Brigade at Merjayoun itself, and completely overrunning the Royal Fusiliers at Quoneitra. With the fighting against the Jezzine counter-attack following this, the 5th Brigade had by the 21 June lost 738 casualties.[14]

With a general retreat looming, 25th Brigade prepared to withdraw themselves from Hamsiye, down the same road they had advanced up three days earlier. One of the single greatest endorsements of the Cheshire Yeomanry in this campaign, is that "B" squadron were tasked to move into Jezzine and cover the brigade's withdrawal, with some tanks attached and under command. With the known strength of the enemy[15] this was expected to be a truly formidable task involving heavy casualties.

---

14 Verdin, *The Cheshire Yeomanry*, p.325.
15 Two battalions of Foreign Legion, one of Senegalese infantry, plus attached units. See TNA WO 196/1936: 17 July, Cheshire Yeomanry 1941.

Major Johnson Houghton and Captain Verdin observing the fight for Merdjayoun.

The decision to do this was made at a conference at 1700 on the 17th. While it was going on there was "heavy fighting on East flank."[16] That fighting was a newly arrived battalion of infantry sent by 7th Division to try and stem the tide. The war diary identifies them as "the 14th Battalion", Verdin as The Kings Own Royal Regiment. Whoever they were, their intervention stopped the French advance in its tracks in severe fighting; the withdrawal from Jezzine was therefore carried out by the French. "B" Squadron had been spared.

It was during this particular operation that the squadron saw, for the last time, the group of Spahis that they had been chasing ever since Adeisse, and had last nearly caught at Hansiye. The Spahis were seen retiring up a track towards the rear of the French positions. The fact that they were on a track, bunched together and moving slowly indicates that they did not believe they were under observation. Even so, they were clearly no disciples of Brigadier Chrystal. Captain Thomas of the Royal

---

16   TNA WO 196/1936: 17 July, Cheshire Yeomanry.

Australian Artillery made no mistake as he called in the fire mission. Although exact casualties were never confirmed, Lt Dawson counted 20 dead horses lying there the following day. Probably most of the unit had become casualties. It was a fearsome reminder on correct dispersal and tactical movement for cavalry.

The battlefield however was becoming very confused, and the Cheshire Yeomanry came close themselves to suffering a similar fate, also at Australian hands. The Australian artillery it should be remembered were holding off counter-attacks on a rapidly shifting battlefield. The sudden appearance of cavalry was a constant threat in country well-endowed with dead ground. One Australian artillery officer, Alwyn Clarke recaptured how the air of panic could so easily set in. He had been ordered to engage enemy cavalry by his battery commander. However, he had seen the supposedly enemy patrol close enough and was not convinced they were enemy: "I did get a good look at their faces - fair, sunburnt and with fair hair - more English than French". No-one else around him agreed, and Clarke had to refuse to follow a string of orders, even after the Brigade Major had run out of the door to grab a machine gun and the Intelligence Officer had passed out. "I was the only one at Brigade and Regtl HQ who was not convinced that they were French. There was such 'panic' everywhere that I hate to think what would have happened to the 'Cheshires' if I had been a few seconds later" - because Clarke had arrived only just in time to see the colouring and ensemble of the horsemen. Though in fairness he described them as "something from the film version of the 'French Foreign Legion.'"[17]

After this narrow escape, the squadron now spent six days holding the line between Jezzine and Hamsiye. Part of their sector overlooked a deep, thickly wooded wadi, and it was into this that the yeomanry sent constant patrols. The cover and nature of the ground made it ideal country for small cavalry patrols.[18] This also provided an opportunity for Captain Thomas to go out and locate the enemy batteries. Himself an adept horseman, he was able to ride out on several patrols and cover ground in a way that infantry patrols would simply not have been able to do as extensively. For the rest of this period, the prevailing note from the War Diary is "Status quo the same" and "shelling". Nonetheless, the patrolling was at least partly productive as it resulted in the capture of a French "M/C".[19]

It was in fact quite heavy shelling over a number of days, and the fact that only one man was killed does not do justice to the weight of bombardment the squadron headquarters and reserve troops were subjected to. The only man killed, Corporal J. Thurlwell was the squadron cook, and the signaller, Trooper G.T. Richards was

---

17 NCY 19/46: *Interview with Alwyn* Clark (publisher and author unknown), Cheshire Archives. See Appendix III.
18 This mirrors the effectiveness of the Italian cavalry in Abyssinia, which had used patches of woodland to move unseen and set up ambushes for the British motorised artillery columns. See Piekalkiewicz.
19 TNA WO 169/1936: Cheshire Yeomanry 1941. Presumably this means Mortar Controller.

very lucky to survive the severe wounds that he received. Neither of these were with the forward sabre troops. There were also two horses killed and several with minor shrapnel wounds – as ever the horses took most of the enemy fire. No-one was fully able to ascertain how the French artillery were able to inflict such accurate fire. While well-hidden Artillery Fire Controllers (AFCs), like Captain Thomas, could have remained well-hidden among the trees, Verdin has a more convincing theory. He proposes that it was the smoke from the farriers' portable furnaces that drew the attention of the French artillery. [20]

This may have been the case, but at the time it was only the second explanation. In the first instance, S.H.Q. thought that it might be the result of civilian collaboration. The war diary records that a patrol had been sent to a Monastery near Sabah on the 19th, where there was a "5th Column feared".[21] It had been noted that the monastery had a commanding view of the squadron's position and that the shelling seemed to follow the ringing of the monastery's bells. Both these signs of collaboration appear to have been coincidental. When Captain Verdin took a patrol to the Monastery on the 23rd, they seem to have been genuinely convinced by the Abbott. The Abbott is in fact referred to by Verdin as "extremely friendly"[22] and not only allowed them to search the monastery but explained the pattern of bell-ringing. He also showed them the monastery-full of refugees, the old and the sick, driven to seek refuge by the fighting. Captain Verdin chose to accept the Abbott's explanations at face value. The clergyman was clearly convincing, because he was not questioned again, even after the bombardment that killed Thurlwell. By now the squadron was fully equipped, Tommy guns and "much needed stores"[23] having been brought up by trucks under the command of Lt C. Funnel. Now stationary, it was also decided to reduce the risk to the horses – who couldn't climb into trenches during bombardments – by sending them back on the 23rd; the day after Thurlwell and the two horses were killed.

Morning of the 24th broke over the usual dawn stand-to routine. This completed, the yeomen then broke ranks to eat their breakfast. In the background the Roman Catholic Padre, Captain J. Kavenagh, added to the general hum of conversation as he celebrated Mass with the catholics of the squadron. Suddenly shots started to fall around S.H,Q. They were from Corporal Shickell's section, which was posted out beyond the monastery. Shickell's section had been manning an outpost – the monastery's hill provided an obvious and necessary place for one and were facing towards the direction of main enemy threat away from the rest of the squadron. But they had now turned around and were firing in the same direction as their own squadron base. They had good reason, and it was the Abbott who had so charmed Verdin four days earlier that had alerted them to imminent danger. He had, from his monastic height, caught sight

---

20   Verdin, *The Cheshire Yeomanry*, p.326.
21   TNA WO 169/1936: '19 June' Cheshire Yeomanry 1941.
22   Verdin, *The Cheshire Yeomanry*, p.326.
23   TNA WO 169/1936: '23 June' Cheshire Yeomanry 1941.

of a French fighting patrol silently approaching the squadron's headquarters. Having slipped through the wooded valley, they had climbed the hill immediately beneath S.H.Q. undetected, then worked round to appear on the track behind Major Johnson-Houghton's S.H.Q. This is when the Abbott had seen them; he immediately sprinted out from the monastery towards the nearby corporal Shickell, pointing behind him. Shickell looked, identified the threat and straight away opened fire with his men. The rounds flying past S.H.Q. alerted the rest of the squadron to the danger, who all opened up as well. So too did two light tanks hastily brought up from reserve. By the time these arrived though, the 40-man French patrol had started their withdrawal. The sharp eyes and quick intervention of the Abbott had undoubtedly saved many of the squadron. The only allied loss sustained in this engagement, was Captain Thomas's Universal carrier, which was burnt out. The French patrol lost one dead and two wounded. The Frenchmen were clearly formidable soldiers; they had planned and executed a very daring infiltration and done it by climbing ground that had taken horses three hours to ascend. Clearly they had been able to observe the squadron extensively and take careful note of their dispositions before approaching. The close wooded country that benefited cavalry so much, also benefited other reconnaissance soldiers too.

The narrow foiling of this surprise assault did not disguise the fact that the squadron needed to be redeployed – and quickly. A slightly wider dispersal of the squadron duly ensured, with S.H.Q. taking up a new position that they could share with a battery of 25 pounder guns. Dawson's 4 troop found themselves at Houranie. Their march out towards the new position yielded a moment of interest, when two French deserters presented themselves to the point section (indeed the point section for the entire brigade), whereupon they were sent down the line to Brigade.

"B" squadron was to be shelled heavily for 11 days. At one point the shelling was so heavy that Sgt Ashe's patrol was forced to press themselves to the ground for over an hour – the patrol had been caught out in the open and clearly the French gunners were determined to not let them escape. The fact that Ashe's detachment did escape, as did many other yeomen and horses in those 11 days is credited to the deficiencies of the old French artillery ammunition. These were fired from "75s", the pride of the French army in 1914. But by 1941, presumably old shells were still being used. The guns also had a low trajectory which meant the rounds tended to strike into the ground at a flat angle rather than come down from above and blow their shrapnel up and over a wider area. Regardless of the efficacy of the shelling, being subjected to it was a considerable strain, requiring great strength of will from the men. Another noteworthy point from these 11 days was the sang-froid displayed by the horses – which couldn't dive into trenches and were still vulnerable even when they were lying on the ground. The accounts from the members of the squadron on Jezzine ridge recount that, even when the shells were bursting among the horses, they did not bolt or stampede, and in fact made no attempt to break loose.

The preponderance of French shelling during this phase also shows a general French strategy in this sector, of essentially sitting back and letting artillery take over the defence. Aggressive counter-patrolling seemed to dwindle out. The total absence of French cavalry patrols allowed the yeomanry patrols to get bolder and bolder, pressing right up to the French lines, whereupon they could dismount and crawl forward until they could tell exactly where the guns were sited. One patrol near Beter got so close that they could report that the battery was sited inside a house, with the muzzles pulled back from the window to avoid detection from anything – except a determined close reconnaissance patrol. Captain Thomas was able to call in the fire mission.

On 2 July Brigadier Stevens was put in charge of the operations against the centre sector because he knew the ground well. Although Plant still retained direct control of 25th Brigade. Stevens decided that Cheshire yeomanry should take over the guarding/roadwatch role allotted to 2/27 Battalion, who could now be freed up for more fighting through tasks. It was shortly after this that the rest of the Cheshire Yeomanry were reallocated away from 21st Brigade. The impact this had on 21st brigade was felt immediately, however. On 8 July, the decision was made not to rush the attack on Beirut without adequate flank protection. The fact that this was an inevitable result of losing their flank protection, does suggest that the contribution of cavalry to the centre, and to securing the links between the Brigades was considered a worthier cause than enabling a quicker attack on Beirut.[24]

It is from this point that the stories of "B" squadron and the regiment combine, as from the 5 July most of the Cheshire Yeomanry were to operate together in the area of 25th Brigade. The brigade was now mobile again, and therefore the cavalry's role changed from reconnaissance patrolling, especially close-target recces, to screening the flank and patrolling the main axis of the brigade's advance – not to mention the laterals. The country was still difficult, hence the use of the cavalry for this role, and so progress was still relatively slow. The French were still fighting, and advancing towards them meant a different type of action from the stealthy reconnaissance of the previous few days. Patrolling the axis of an advancing brigade in these circumstances meant that the cavalry could expect plenty of fighting in the final days of the campaign, even after Damascus fell on the 8th, it did not trigger a general French collapse – at least not in 25th Brigade's sector, where the newly reunited Cheshire Yeomanry were being given ever greater rein. It was in fact a day of hard fighting for many of the regiment. A significant engagement was fought at Beikroum (see below), and the war diary for the 8th also reports that meanwhile "In the Jezzine sector Mr Dawson & his troop have been very active and today in an [intensely] independent engagement they captured a M.G. post and 6 men ... and a map of the area giving positions. Mr Dawson suffered no casualties & the 25th Brde and Brigadier Plant are very pleased with him."[25] There were three notable actions fought in this phase; two by Dawson, and the third fought by the rest of his squadron. Taken alongside the rest of the

24 AWM 52 1/5/14-0110 7: 8 July 1941, Australian Division General Staff Branch (7 Aust Div GS Branch).
25 TNA WO 169/1936: 8 July, Cheshire Yeomanry 1941.

regiment's activities, the North Somerset Yeomanry's dismounted assault on the Jebel Mazar and the final action fought by the Yorkshire Dragoons, these engagements show an array of capabilities in the fighting repertoire of Exporter's invading force and its mounted arm.

The original Cheshire Yeomanry war diarist, Capt. C.D.T. Phillips-Brocklehurst, provided plenty of detail – somewhat unusually for a war diary - for the particular actions of the Cheshire Yeomanry. The regiment it would seem were keen to document three very creditable actions performed by their men. The first occurred on the 6 July, with the regiment still too spread out to fight a battalion size engagement. "B" squadron were approaching Beikoum when two patrols from Lt Cunningham's 3 troop came under intense machine gun fire on approaching the village. The initial firing wounded three horses, and left Cunningham under no illusion about the seriousness of the obstacle he now faced. Cpl N.G. Ingram's section was left to observe the enemy position, and the rest of the troop pulled back to await further redeployment. As it was, the enemy retired during the night and the troop was then able to move forward into Beikoum. Despite this fairly easy tactical bound forward, there was still dangerous territory to be pushed on through, in the next bound forward. Advancing the next day out of Beikoum duly brought down machine gun fire upon the heads of Cpl Shickell's section, as it worked its way through olive groves on the right flank of the troop's axis of advance. As the position seemed to consist of four guns, Major Johnson-Houghton understandably decided that his squadron lacked the punch to topple this threat by themselves. The Australian infantry on their left flank duly agreed to lend the yeomen a platoon, commanded by their Lt Bishop, to help storm the position.

This entire operation was now under direct scrutiny from Brigadier Plant as he monitored the forward progress of his column. Plant personally ordered two officers, Captain Verdin and Lieutenant Dawson to reconnoitre new enemy positions north of the brigade, towards Baadarane, then fall back and get the rest of the squadron to hurry up, once they had secured the Beikoum environs. The two officers used motor transport to go ahead, while the supporting troop rode up behind them on horseback under Sgt Bradley. Verdin then left early, leaving Dawson and his troop to make a full recce, in order to return to the squadron. He left with serious misgivings about what Dawson was now being asked to do in a task most blatantly unsuited to cavalry.

Verdin however carried on back and found the rest of "B" squadron still pinned down inside Beikoum. First of all Bishop had not yet arrived, presumably because the infantry were too overstretched to provide any further reinforcements. Secondly, the yeomanry didn't have the firepower to press ahead by themselves. They lacked the heavy weapons and they were dispersed for reconnaissance. Furthermore an entire troop was detached from "B" squadron. But significantly, the terrain for the first time in the campaign was now preventing the yeomanry from deploying as cavalry. The valley ahead of them was strewn with heavy boulders. The only route through it suitable for horses was along a track on the precipitous valley's western-side. Every inch of this track was covered by French machine gunners. Not only this, but shell-fire from the east could be called down upon any point of the track too. A detour to the west was out of the question because of the boulders, and these themselves made an advance by infantry difficult enough. Nonetheless an infantry operation was the only choice left if the area in front of them was to be cleared in anything resembling a timely manner. In the meantime Johnson-Houghton resolved to make a final stab at clearing the French machine guns. Inevitably the horses were sent to the rear, but this made itself felt in the lack of manpower which had to be sent back with them as handlers. Meanwhile, the main body of the unit found that clambering over rocks in spurs was deeply problematic and that these had to be discarded. In some conditions, the horses and their accoutrements too easily became a nuisance.

The dismounted party tasked with clearing the machine guns in front of "B" squadron was led by Sergeant H. Green, and they worked their way silently over the boulders, grenades in hand. The coup de grace at Beikoum was delivered by Trooper Parry-Jones who launched the grenades into the cave in question. But there was no-one at home. The fact that the French had been able to escape without detection was itself ample evidence of the cover that any defenders of this valley would now enjoy. The issue therefore remained of how long would they stay and use this cover to fight on.

This seemed to be answered by the prodigious shelling that Beikoum village was subjected to that afternoon. With the obvious pointlessness of retaining horses for this phase, it was now just endured by the humans of the squadron left in Beikoum – and they could take refuge in trenches. Help however arrived in the shape of Lt Bishop and his platoon of Australians. No doubt frustrated by the time it had taken them to get through to the Yeomanry, the Australians elected to press on immediately with their attack that night. But just like the yeomanry before him, Bishop found himself pinned down by machine gun fire as soon as his point section had left the limits of the village.

The 8th dawned over Beikoum illuminating a multi-phase attack by the yeomanry and their supporting arms. Artillery bombardment fell upon the enemy positions from the off, and Bishop's platoon made an attack up the right flank with Corporal E.A. Cotgreave's section of yeomen reinforcing. This wave was in turn supported by a Hotchkiss section of Sergeant Ashe, Lance-Corporal E. Wright, and the newly promoted Lance-Corporal Greatorex, who had taken part in the previous sally under Sergeant Green.

It took a day of hard-fighting to clear the initial objective, the high-ground west of a village called Mazraatiech-Chouf. In the meantime Squadron H.Q. had been heavily shelled, mainly after Australian vehicles conspicuously arrived bringing up supplies. But reinforcements had also arrived, in the form of 1. Troop from "A" squadron. With vehicles so painfully visible, it was decided to bring up further supplies using Australian infantry pack-mules. Thus sustained, Johnson-Houghton could commit his command to more dismounted advancing. The yeomen continued to come under determined enemy machine gun fire, shelling and mortar fire. Verdin writes that these days at Beikoum resulted in deep frustration – and that this was the first time the squadron had felt such strain. It was at Beikoum, under frequent shell and mortar fire, with any forward movement frustrated by instant machine gun fire, that "B" squadron found its most difficult phase of the campaign. The experience was "to cure the military ambitions of most of its members."[26] Up until this point the prevailing mood had been one more of excitement.[27]

The shelling kept the squadron from advancing any further than Mazraat-ech-Chouf, and throughout the 9th, the forward positions did not move one bit, with heavy machine gun and mortar fire from a position just north of the village proving formidable. Furthermore, French soldiers could be seen on both flanks. S.H.Q. meanwhile was still some distance behind in Beikoum.

On the 10th, S.H.Q was informed that the enemy had counter-attacked and re-occupied Mazraat-ech-Chouf. Sgt Sutherland and 3. Troop therefore went forward to investigate further. The village had indeed been reoccupied again, but then evacuated once more, with only five men left behind, three of whom were wounded. They were promptly captured and sent down the line. The forward Hotchkiss sections then came under heavy shell-fire. So too did S.H.Q in Beikoum. However, it was quickly becoming apparent that the enemy were retiring while firing, and soon the yeomen could count to up to 20 between hearing the gun fire and the shell falling. This gave everyone more time to hide, and therefore there was greater freedom of movement. This was the first of the three actions recorded in the war diary. The entry for the 9th gives rather more on Dawson's "independent engagement". It was one of two engagements for 4. Troop; one fought on the 8th, then another on the 10th.

The six Vichy soldiers taken on the 8th listed in the war diary (mentioned above) were taken in a dismounted fight; while Dawson and 4. Troop's second action, on the 10th, was a battle involving on the British side; machine guns, mounted yeomanry, dismounted yeomanry, engineers, tanks and Bren carriers. This entire phase (between the 5th and 10th) saw the yeomanry, placed ahead of the main column, and fighting their way forward. The yeomanry with 25th brigade (less "A" squadron who were covering the laterals next to 21st brigade), and Brigadier Plant were in fact finding that most reconnaissance by itself was essentially futile, given the difficulty of crossing the ground undetected. 4. Troop's fighting proved to be hard-fought and problematic – but this was typical of 25th Brigade's experience in the hotly contested middle-sector.

Lieutenant Dawson meanwhile had been left on the 6th on the East flank, with orders to patrol towards Baadarane. Verdin's earlier described misgivings about this task were strongly felt by Dawson as well. Not only was the ground in front of him most formidable, but so too were the enemy numbers that he could see in and around Baadarane. Dawson's role of silent observation was brought to an end, when he noted enemy moving out of the village towards him; another French counter-attack was on. He promptly reported the situation to Brigade. However, nothing was done in time to prevent enemy reoccupying the very high ground that he had been observing them

26   Verdin, *The Cheshire Yeomanry*, p.344.
27   Verdin, *The Cheshire Yeomanry*, p.344.

from earlier that day. Dawson's 4. Troop would therefore have to go into action again and re-take it with support. The date was set for 8 July.

Ultimately they were to locate the most eastern point of the enemy defences, find out what strength was in these defences, and if needs be fight to find it out.[28] The advance could actually be conducted on horses as the ground here was suitable in places – thus it was only as they approached what they believed was the eastern most position that they then dismounted. The now-dismounted advance (under Cpl Laycock) came under machine gun fire from a position on the right front. Leaving Lance-Corporal H.J. Wright and his Hotchkiss section to give covering fire, Laycock and his men worked their way round the right. They then stormed the position, led by Laycock and the section Tommy Gunner H. Mildren. Their charge was so fast and unexpected that the only return from the Vichy soldiers was a single grenade that exploded in the wake of the charging yeomen. The supporting Hotchkiss jammed after only firing one round, meaning that this attack was completely unsupported. The position was nonetheless captured intact and without casualty, including a map detailing the rest of the enemy positions – and confirming that this was indeed the easternmost point. One enemy N.C.O. made an opportunistic escape as Laycock's men stormed in, and as he sprinted away the section all opened fire on him. They all missed. This was because their chests were heaving too much, after storming the position, to take steady aim. The miss was costly, because Laycock's newly-stormed prize was soon being shelled heavily.

Once the shelling had stopped, Dawson sent the prisoners back. The Senagalese infantry were marched back to the Australian lines carrying blanket wrapped bundles of captured weapons, while the yeomen rode. The Senegalese trudged along in the middle, wearing greatcoats and kit in spite of the heat. Immediately behind them the nearest trooper covered them with his drawn sword. It was an astonishing sight. The Australians, equally incredulous and impressed, greeted the unusual vision with laughter and cheering.[29]

This attack had now ascertained the easternmost limit of the enemy position before the major assault on the 10th against the high-ground overlooking Jezzine to Beit ed Dine. The next battle for Dawson would be a small part in this assault. After they had returned their prisoners from the battle fought on the 8th they then made their way to their forming up point and started to prepare. Once they were back in position though they were themselves soon under attack when French pilots strafed them in captured R.A.F fighters, still with British identification markings on them.[30] None of this troop were, however, injured. The preparation for battle continued. In theory

---

28 Verdin, *The Cheshire Yeomanry*, p.334.
29 Verdin, *The Cheshire Yeomanry*, p.336.
30 The war diary is amended to note the R.A.F believed these aircraft to have been captured in France. TNA WO 169/1936: 9 July, Cheshire Yeomanry 1941. This in turn suggests that the aircraft had been deliberately maintained in British colours all this time.

4. Troop were simply now to go forward dismounted alongside armour, to divert the attention of the defenders while an infantry company attack went on next to them as the principle attack. The tank was to be under Dawson's command.

The relevant war diary cites a straightforward concept for the attack. "The general plan" Captain Brocklehurst writes in the war diary "was to seize the high ground above Haret Jandal [sic] and then proceed to Aamatons [sic] as a second objective. "The troops available for this attack were (1) Mr Dawson's command, consisting of his troop, four tanks, six carriers [universal carriers roled as Bren carriers], (2) "D" Company 25th Battalion [D Company 25th Australian Infantry]." [31] These were designated as part of the overall operation though rather than specifically at the disposal of Dawson, as the diary seems to suggest. This force was to carry out a "flanking movement" on the right and west flank of a position that was vaguely described by the available information as a "small enemy post" at Haret Jandal and Aamatons as the main position of enemy concentration. "Not at all exact" noted Captain Brocklehurst pointedly in the diary.

As the enemy had blown the bridge, engineers were to make the crossing at Wadi al Jablaye fordable for tanks, while the artillery carried out a barrage that was to be "complicated and timed". When the barrage opened up at 2200, Dawson advanced to find that the engineers had been unable to make the crossing fit for tanks. This immediately threw the carefully laid plan into disarray. Dawson hastily reorganised his attack calling on a further two tanks plus carriers south of the Wadi to give covering fire; with the other tank and carriers personnel, and half of his troop dismounted on the right of the road. Meanwhile 1 section of Dawson's troop remained mounted on the left of the road.

"In spite of the M.G. fire the mounted section advanced right up to the first objective and the dismounted group started the ascent of the high ground above Haret Jandal." This would suggest that the galloping horsemen were too elusive a target for the French gunners. "Here M.G. fire, mortars and hand grenades pinned them [the dismounted section] to the ground… for the best part of an hour… these troops were so close to the enemy that they could hear the French officers and N.C.O.s issuing the fire orders and on two occasions hand grenades thrown by the enemy landed by our own men who threw them back again."[32] The position proved to consist of 4 concealed machine gun positions, not to mention the mortar support in depth. McCone's section was heavily engaged throughout, while Dawson moved from one position to the next as he tried to manage the battle, nearly always with Trooper K. Bowker in attendance – volunteering each time his troop leader set out on another run across the battlefield. Although the infantry battle on their flank was attracting much of the enemy attention, McCone's section was still hard-pressed, and Dawson and Bowker were attracting a lot of enemy fire as they moved about – one round passed through Dawson's trousers. Impressively, Sergeant Bradley was able to finally

---

31 TNA WO 169/1936: '10 July' Cheshire Yeomanry 1941.
32 TNA WO 169/1936: 10 July, Cheshire Yeomanry 1941.

extricate McCone's section from the inferno of suppressing fire they were under. And to do so without the section taking any casualties.

It was then that the flanking company of infantry informed Dawson that although they had taken their first objective, they had suffered heavy casualties with all but one of their officers down and needed Dawson to adopt a defensive position. Being so close to the enemy, forming a defensive position meant pulling back a little, but "retreat for Mr Dawson's command proved extremely difficult but was necessary in order to take up a good defensive position." "Eventually by crawling in ditches still under a whirlwind of fire they arrived at a position on the road where they could cover D Coy's retreat and hold this under heavy fire while the last man of D. Coy was evacuated.[33] Mr Dawson then left tanks and carriers to cover the bridge and withdrew his own exhausted men".[34] It was an arduous experience for both sides. That night, French and Allied withdrew from the battlefield.

Contact with the enemy was now lost, so Dawson was ordered the following morning to patrol up to Moukhtara. The mounted advance guard appreciated the need to swiftly locate the enemy again. Although they found that the road had been hastily mined by the retreating Vichy forces, they trusted in their rudimentary training and cleared the road themselves without waiting for the engineers to come up and do it for them. This contrasts with a very segregated approach to battlefield tasks in the British army, described by Anthony Beevor on D-Day. Beevor tells of a culture in British forces where engineers would flatly refuse to carry out an infantry role and vice versa.[35] Dawson then informed Brigade that road and mines were clear and pushed into Moukhtara itself; he and his men they found three wounded Senegalese who hadn't been able to retreat quick enough. This patrol was the last of "B" squadron's contributions to Operation Exporter.

In the aftermath, Dawson particularly recommended Sgt Bradley "for his coolness and efficiency he showed while leading his patrol to Haret Jandal under fire, capturing 2 positions and 2 A/T guns during the operations."[36] He also of course recommended Laycock for decoration after distinguishing himself again, and also Trooper Bowker for conspicuous gallantry while acting as both messenger and guide, while under heavy fire – a role Bowker had repeatedly volunteered for.

With so much heavy fighting occupying the attention of the authorities, it actually proved very difficult to receive an award in the middle sector that 25th Brigade fought through. As it was, the only yeomen to be officially recognised in these actions were Dawson and Bradley, who were both mentioned in dispatches. Unofficial, though well-earned, praise was also addressed towards the squadron farriers. Farriers significantly

---

33 It should be noted that the infantry had fought an extremely hard battle, and that Private J.H. Gordon was awarded the V.C. during it. The second V.C. to be awarded to the central column in Operation Exporter.
34 TNA WO 169/1936: 10 July, Cheshire Yeomanry 1941.
35 Anthony Beevor, *D-Day: The Battle for Normandy* (London: Penguin, 2009), p.142.
36 TNA WO 169/1936: 10 July, Cheshire Yeomanry, p.194.

helped the cavalry arm to stay self-sufficient and mobile, with "B" squadron's farriers having no support in the way that the rest of the regiment's farriers did. The technology and training of the farriers was little different to that of their forbears at Waterloo; their role is an example of the skilled work required to maintain fighting cavalry that was not transferable to other arms.

The North Somerset Yeomanry and the Yorkshire Dragoons

The recording of both these units' roles at the beginning of the operation is obscure and nebulous. Operational planning in May and June, evidently dismissive of horsemen at first, only accepted that one regiment of cavalry were required for Exporter. The Cheshire Yeomanry were therefore in from the first. But the tightly-stretched resources of Wilson's little army needed to maintain their lines of communication as they advanced into 'Syria'. The rest of 5th cavalry brigade were available, so they would do for this backstage role. It was in this spirit that the R.H.Q of the North Somerset Yeomanry were met by their new Australian brigadier on the eve of Exporter. Having been rushed up from fighting tanks in the western desert to now play a role in this side-show with diminished resources, Verney recalls he was a little harassed-looking:

> "Horses, huh?" he said, gazing gloomily round the camp. "We use them for rounding up sheep down under."[37]

Because Verney avoids naming him it is difficult to ascertain exactly who he is – the North Somerset Yeomanry are not officially on any brigade order of battle until Exporter was well underway. Nonetheless the fact that they were close to 21st Brigade suggests that he was brigadier Stevens, and that the North Somerset Yeomanry were a part of the overall operation from the start – even if they had more of a mopping-up role. Their listing on any brigade strength unsurprisingly happened during the same phase that patrolling the tricky "laterals" became the main effort for cavalry units, to the extent that the "Kelly Gang" were raised, and more horses requested (and denied). The "Kelly Gang" originally asked the North Somerset Yeomanry for 50 saddles (another request that was denied), and this cannot have been earlier than 2 June. Therefore, at least some of these yeomen were operating close to the 6th Divisional cavalry from whom the "Kelly Gang" were enlisted, near the front, from this date.

The nature of the North Somerset Yeomanry's war is more literarily captured in Verney's description of their main contribution as "a few bloodless and pleasant wanderings, which might be claimed as valuable patrol work."[38] Clearly he did not buy into the prevailing enthusiasm. On the evidence of the unit diary at this stage, Verney's cynicism does not seem to be misplaced. Especially as "A" squadron was still

---

37 Verney, *Going to the Wars*, p.87.
38 Verney, *Going to the Wars*, p.89.

at Alma Chaab on 17 June – whilst the rest of 21st Brigade had crossed the Litani on the 9th. On the 26 June meanwhile elements of "HQ" and "C" squadrons were in fact returning to Az Zib. Verney studiously avoids showing any sense of frustration in his still rather flippant analysis that "for nine-tenths of the Syrian campaign we played the part of camp-followers, guarding Vichy POWs or entertaining, in the best Yeomanry tradition, migratory Staff Officers."[39]

The war diary however reports on the 4th July that Lt Watson's patrol was coming under enemy artillery fire, close to Chebaa (the now notorious Shebaa farms area). By now they had clearly been moved into the 25th Brigade sector along with most of the Cheshire Yeomanry and at least some of the Yorkshire Dragoons and were listed as a division asset. With the move had clearly come a greater sense of energy and this was presumably precipitated by the realisation of any available cavalry's suitability for patrolling "laterals". The war diary for July records a comparative explosion in activity, with troop leaders and squadron leaders conducting personal recces in virtually every other line of text. Meanwhile, with the regiment widely dispersed as the list of tasks increased, Major Baker's "B" squadron activities become more serious:

> Major Baker gave orders to continue advance and to take a recce patrol to HASBAYA. His leading section were fired on 1 ½ miles out of Fohkar (Rachaya al Fokhar)… [shortly after 1730] orders were received for Sqn to advance to HASBAYA [a distance of about 5 miles].[40]

The report is cursory, recording then that the "enemy retired and at 2330 hrs orders were received for sqn to advance to Hasbaya. It had clearly been a determined enough firefight to bog down Bakers' men for so long. Their presence in a busy sector under the command of 6th Division, [from which Baker's squadron was in fact detached], the paucity of any personnel available by this stage of the campaign, and the undisputed freshness of the North Somerset Yeomanry even at this stage, all dovetailed into deciding the only substantial task for the remaining 236 men of the North Somerset Yeomanry.

A significant assault was to be mounted in their area. This was against the French forces holding the Beirut-Damascus road, which had three infantry battalions and a cavalry regiment astride it. The diary for this Vichy South-Syrian force is recalled in Gavin Long's *Greece, Crete and Syria* (1953).[41] It recounts from the French perspective that the first renewed attack against the highest point (the 1500m Jebel Mazar) "was driven back with a loss to the British of 194 prisoners, as a result of the 'vigorous resistance of troops who knew the ground thoroughly, the coolness of unit commanders who maintained resistance even when surrounded and the heavy, well-timed support

---

39   Verney, *Going to the Wars*, p.89.
40   TNA WO 169/1401: 4 July, North Somerset Yeomanry 1941.
41   Gavin Long *Second World War*, p.510.

of artillery.' A second British attack 'had barely begun when it came to a standstill.'[42] It was during this phase, when despite the influx of new troops the fighting was becoming no easier, that the North Somerset Yeomanry were approached. "The Divisional General himself drove up. He belonged to the rugged category of General [he was presumably Major-General Jon Evetts of 6th Division] …"

"My Division is putting in an attack up the road to Beirut at dawn the day after tomorrow, 11th July. We've had casualties as you've probably heard, and we can't cover our left flank – those hills you can see from here. I've no idea what's up there – rather less than a Regiment probably, but they've got some guns which could do us a lot of damage, unless they're given something to think about."[43] What he had in mind was therefore a diversionary attack on his south-western flank. The unit diary at this time records the position as Qatana, though this was demonstrably an approximation. Evetts, himself a light-infantryman by origin, presented his plan to Lt. Col Morton:

> Frankly, I'm a bit vague about what you fellows are trained to do, but the 'Yeomanry' sounds sporting... [can you do it?][44]

Whether he genuinely understood their capabilities or not, the North Somerset Yeomanry were fresh and in situ with a responsibility as cavalry to operate on the flanks. Nonetheless, the divisional staff were alarmed to find that these yeomen didn't have Tommy guns, or bayonets. In fairness, the Cheshire Yeomanry with all their fighting had only had some of their Thompson guns delivered to them in theatre, when they were in 21st Brigade's sector, dug in near Tyre and Sidon. The lack of bayonets though is more of a solecism, as one thing yeomanry had consistently been asked to do in every brigade involved, was to occasionally act as infantry on the assault. The North Somerset Yeomanry however weren't to ride into battle, or to carry sabres;[45] trucks were sourced from 5th infantry Brigade.

The North Somerset Yeomanry then advanced to battle in trucks and experienced their first casualties when the lead vehicle hit a mine. There were seven wounded in their lower limbs, including Verney's old troop sergeant whose legs were "shattered" [Sgt Edwards according to the casualty return].[46] This according to the war diary was at 2100 hours. "The unexpected explosion and the black smoke, twisted by the wind into monstrous shapes against the night sky, were terrifying. Any martial ardour I had worked up in myself evaporated instantly, like the smoke … yet, afterwards, Tom told me he remembered wishing he had felt at that moment as calm as I looked. Whereas

---

42 Gavin Long *Second World War*, p.510.
43 Verney, *Going to the Wars*, p.92.
44 Verney, *Going to the Wars*, p.92.
45 Sabres were specifically for use in the mounted reconnaissance role.
46 TNA WO 169/1401: 'Appendix 3 CO battle report', North Somerset Yeomanry 1941.

I admired Fergie Deakin [In reality Lt. Hynes who was killed in this action] who exclaimed cheerfully: 'Let battle commence …'[47]

"C" squadron lead, followed by "A" squadron, then RHQ, then "HQ" squadron. "C" squadron took the initial enemy fire, and thus became preoccupied dealing with this, the main objective. "A" squadron meanwhile were detailed to "deal with the flank".[48] "HQ" squadron followed "A" squadron and Colonel Morton went in company with "A" squadron. After comparatively little fighting the North Somerset Yeomanry were at the summit just as dawn was breaking, with what appeared to be a small fort at the end. Later we discovered it was a pretty big fortress cut out of the mountain top …" [49]

By 0500, one section having reached the fort, the attack was still going ahead. But it was running into formidable difficulties; the lead section having found that the entrance to Chaia fort was concreted and with small gun embrasures, a situation the war diary summarises:

> A troop of "A" sqn. endeavoured to move round left flank, held up by 2 L.M.G's [sic] and snipers from hills due west. 'Remained in position and took on L.M.G's in open and at fort. During this period mortar and rifle grenade fire was in constant operation from enemy positions … By 0730 there were "enemy L.M.G's … in strength to our front with snipers on high ground … North of Fort.[50]

The yeomen were very exposed, hot and tired. Verney recalled, "men sleeping, literally sleeping, with bullets spattering round them. We had done all that was required of us and the infantry had been successful. The difficulty was to get out – a long clamber down the mountain under shrapnel and machine-gun fire and a still longer march across the plain in range of their guns."[51]

The colonel reports that having manoeuvred his force into a position to inflict heavy fire on the fort (which they could not penetrate), they were in turn being subjected to far greater weight of fire from the French defenders. "Realising the likelihood of serious casualties by [illegible] remaining, resulting in depletion of the Regt. to no purpose, I therefore ordered the Regt to return to the foothills to reform. They were ordered to disperse to avoid casualties from the heavy shell fire which the plain and area surrounding was being subjected to, and make their way to Camp."[52] This order, according to the Medical Officer was issued at 1330,[53] the shelling having been

---

47 Verney, *Going to the Wars*, pp.95-100.
48 TNA WO 169/1401: Appendix 3 CO battle report, North Somerset Yeomanry 1941.
49 Verney, *Going to the Wars*, pp.95-100.
50 TNA WO 169/1401: Appendix 3, CO battle report, North Somerset Yeomanry 1941.
51 Verney, *Going to the Wars*, pp.95-100.
52 TNA WO 169/1401: Appendix 3 CO battle report, North Somerset Yeomanry 1941.
53 TNA:WO 169/1401: Appendix 7 Medical Officer to Adjutant, North Somerset Yeomanry 1941.

continuous since 0600. "Every Stretcher party [the colonel lists 17 stretcher bearers detailed for this operation] or runner who were sent out [sic] was fired on by L.M.G WEST of the position. It was absolutely impossible to contact anyone from the main forces during the operation."

The interminable communications failures faced during this operation are detailed vividly by the Signals Officer in his report, who had had to resort to using runners until there was a lull in the machine gun, artillery and sniper fire so that "after 45 minutes (0700) there was a lull and I was able to get the two sets round the back of the hill to a gully about 200 yards forward. For about one hour the shells were landing 1 1/2 to 2 miles away. Then they began to shorten their range considerably and from 0900 to 1200 hrs they were dropping either 100 yards ahead or behind us dotted all round. Finally they got our range completely and a direct hit was registered on one set and we were forced to leave the sets and retire … all movement being hampered by sniping from the hills opposite.

> At 1400 hrs I saw troops retiring off the hills about 1 1/2 miles away … and at 1430 made contact with the Adjutant in the middle of the plain and was informed that we were retiring.
>
> I returned to the road-head, split up the troop in small parties and N.C.Os and told them to make their own way back to Camp through the hills.
>
> Communication from the Regt back [by] the wireless was non-existent except for runners the journey for whom took so long as to be almost useless.[54]

Morton's own report adds a final detail that clarifies Verney's own account of the death of "Fergie Deakin". The colonel's report records in a footnote that during the withdrawal, Trooper J. McKenna of "C" squadron, saw 2nd Lieutenant M.A.J. Hynes of his own squadron lying badly wounded out "under intense L.M.G and sniper fire. Tpr. McKenna at once went out, picked him up and brought him in to his troop position."[55] By the time that the report was written on the 11th of course, Hynes had died of his wounds.

Although not the last casualties the regiment suffered during the war, this battle was the single biggest loss of men for the regiment, or indeed for any of 5th Cavalry Brigade. The biggest losses of horses are all attributable to the Cheshire Yeomanry.

For a sense of the full range that these cavalry units offered brigade commanders in this campaign, one needs only see the activities of the Cheshire Yeomanry and the North Somerset Yeomanry on the night of the 10th July. While the west-countrymen were redeploying from screening to putting in a dismounted attack; the Cheshire Yeomanry were reconnoitring then deploying to attack a battery position well-back

---

54 TNA WO 169/1401: Appendix 4, Signals Officer to Adjutant, North Somerset Yeomanry 1941.
55 TNA WO 169/1401: Appendix 3, CO battle report, North Somerset Yeomanry 1941.

in French lines and seriously threatening any approach. Dawson of "B" squadron meanwhile was coordinating mounted, dismounted and mechanised elements in another action.

Neither the Cheshire Yeomanry nor the North Somerset Yeomanry were to fight the last mounted engagement in Operation Exporter however. That was performed by "C" and "HQ" squadrons, The Queens Own Yorkshire Dragoons, the unit of the newly commissioned Grand National winner Bruce Hobbs.

The Last Battle

The Yorkshire Dragoons seem to have been taken no more seriously than the North Somerset Yeomanry at the start of Exporter. The Dragoons' role, as enshrined in their "Operational Order No.1"[56], had begun with tasks such as "Protection of R.A.O.C. [Royal Army Ordnance Corps] and R.A.S.C. [Royal Army Service Corps] Dumps in area ROSH PINNA[57] [in Palestine] Customs House." The sabre squadrons then being tasked with such roles as "Main Guard ROSH PINNA camp", and "Prisoner of War Camp Al MALAKIYA" guard.

The institutional blind spot towards the French resolve to fight therefore resulted in the Yorkshire Dragoons, starting the campaign in Pith helmets, doing a role eminently more suitable to the Palestine Police.

As with all senior officers in Exporter, it seems that the realisation eventually dawned that these quaint horsemen could be used to plug both the capability gap and the clearly exposed manpower gap of Wilson's army. Certainly by the time that the French counter-attacked, and Wilson's position looked critical, the Yorkshire Dragoons had become more closely involved – just as all cavalry had.

The strikingly increased workload of cavalry activity came to the attention of Lt.Col Blackburn of the Australian 2/3rd Machine gun battalion for one. Taking the 15 to 16 June for example, when Blackburn was in the Merdjayoun sector with 25th Brigade, there was a pressing need to secure crossings over the river Jordan. His unit was rushed to this task late on the 15th before any Vichy units could get to it. This had them careering down a hazardous road, through thickly descending mist, to find cavalry already in position. The horses had taken the short cut, away from the road, and they now handed the bridge over to the Australians. The following day Blackburn was ordered to aid Kuneitra. And here too he found cavalry. Going by their own proximity alone, this would have been the Yorkshire Dragoons as well.

At Kuneitra, the allied forces were in danger of collapsing in the face of a French counter-attack which had pitted around 1500 French with 27 medium tanks, 12 light tanks, field guns and armoured cars against a single British Battalion of the 1st Royal

---

56   TNA WO 169/1407: Operational Order No.1, Yorkshire Dragoons, January-December 1941.
57   In Palestine where most of the yeomanry units had been in training at some stage.

Fusiliers, supported by one captured 20mm gun, which was quickly out of action after a spring broke in the firing mechanism. Blackburn sent out a detachment to lure out the tanks until they were within range of the 2 pounder anti-tank guns. This relieving force was to occupy a grand total of 3 trucks. This is the plan outlined in both Colin Smith's *England's Last War Against France: Fighting Vichy 1940-1942*[58] and Gavin Long's *Greece, Crete and Syria* Vol II.[59] This detachment, soon learnt that the garrison had mostly surrendered and duly returned back, reaching Blackburn again at 19.15 hrs with a reinforcing patrol of Yorkshire Dragoons [presumably picked up along the way] and five escapees from Kuneitra in tow. The Fusiliers had surrendered at 1800. The Yorkshire Dragoons were now in theatre and starting to become involved in quite a range of tasks.

The Yorkshire Dragoons' war diary does catalogue this particular patrol, dated 16-18th June. It lists a composition of one officer, one sergeant, two corporals and ten other ranks, and two L.M.G.s with 500 rounds. It also details two police armoured cars, 60,000 rounds for the Queneitra [sic] garrison who according to the diary were at the time "in danger of being attacked". Their mission was to assist C company 2/3 and proceed to Quneitra [sic] to deliver the ammunition. The patrol committed to its secondary task quickly. It "reached the high ground S.E. of Tell Abou Nida at 0500 hrs. 17/6, and as the enemy were reported in the town of Queneitra, fire positions were taken up at Tell Abou Nida. 'At 0800 hrs. a mounted troop of enemy cavalry moved towards our position from Queneitra, it dismounted 1000 yards away. A sortie was made in the A.F.V.s [the police armoured cars] to try and cut off the enemy cavalry, they were dispersed and approx. 10 casualties were caused to the enemy. The A.F.V's [sic] then reported to the R.A. to give information."[60] Thereafter the patrol fought off an attack by enemy infantry, supported by the machine guns of 2/3 and the armoured cars were dispatched on a reconnaissance patrol. While they were away, the rest of the force knocked out two French armoured cars attempting to move out of Kuneitra. The [British] armoured cars then took part in the relieving attack of the "Queens"[61] on Kuneitra, which was met by shelling and mortar fire. Despite this the report records that the infantry entered Kuneitra at 1955 hours. The patrol stood to on the Damascus road on the morning of the 18th, out of Kuneitra, whereupon Australian Bren Carriers took over, while the ammunition that was originally intended for Orr's Fusiliers was handed over to the Queens. The patrol

58   Smith, *England's Last War Against France*, p.230.
59   Gavin Long *Second World War*, p.402.
60   TNA WO 169/1407: ' Patrol report 16-18 June' Yorkshire Dragoons, January-December 1941.
61   The 2/Queens, infantry battalion of 16th Brigade, whose flank the North Somerest Yeomanry protected when they assaulted the Jebel Mazar. They were new arrivals in theatre, having neither made it to Crete, as their transport was set on fire shortly after leaving Alexandria, nor to the Western desert, as "Operation Battleaxe" was quickly cancelled after heavy tank losses.

returned to the Dragoons R.H.Q. at Rosh Pinna at 1130 on June 18th. They had suffered no casualties, though the armoured cars attached to their patrol were mildly damaged by striking road blocks, and one bolt head had been shot off. A side show this may have been, but no-one could now say that the Yorkshire Dragoons were still bystanders. Or that cavalry in theatre were by now an unusual sight.[62]

This patrol had accompanied a small party in the teeth of heavy fighting and this shows: a) how far forward the Yorkshire Dragoons could and were on occasion being deployed just as the Cheshire Yeomanry were, and b) how effectively they could move across this terrain. Significantly they were accompanying a force with vehicles that presumably was finding it hard-going. The presence of cavalry in this sector would also have provided Lloyd with a screen to cover his rear in the case of any retreat – as indeed "B" squadron Cheshire Yeomanry had been required to do for Plant.

By 21 June there had been a complete 180 degree change in the High Command's view since that first conference in Egypt. When Exporter was being planned, the first proposed use of cavalry was the inclusion of a squadron. By the end of that meeting, those in attendance had accepted that a full regiment would be required. Three weeks of heavy fighting later, through Lebanon and Syria had done even more to reformulate this view, because on 21 June Damascus fell[63]. However progress in the western sectors was negligible. After Merdjayoun had been secured, Jezzine had held out and Lloyd had been able to fight through with 5th Indian Brigade for dreadful losses and despite being entirely surrounded. Soon after Damascus's defenders had finally surrendered. One the coast meanwhile, the ever-depleted 21st Brigade was fighting through one position after another, while its cavalry regiment were detached to secure the laterals. Nonetheless, the strategically isolated forces of Dentz were being whittled down without replacement. In contrast Wilson's force was growing by the day. With the addition of Habforce from the north and units like 16th Brigade coming in from the south, the allies were soon enjoying a 2:1 numerical advantage. This increase allowed firstly the securing of Jebel Mazar at the very end of the campaign, but also it enabled the concentration of a full division for the battle for Beirut. The new arrivals precipitated substantial remodelling of units, and Wilson decided for example to re-raise much of 1st Cavalry Division in its original brigade entities. The 4th Cavalry Brigade would consist of: those units that had been so suddenly and secretively transferred to Habforce on the 10 May; the lorry-mounted composite regiment that had formerly been named Todcol (Staffs and Greys); the Yorkshire Dragoons; Transjordan Frontier force (who had both mounted and armoured car units), and the Druse Legion. The Cheshire Yeomanry were kept with 7th Division at the insistence

---

62 The Kelly Gang were now operational as well, and the North Somerset Yeomanry were fully committed.
63 On the following day Syria received much less media coverage, as press focus was now on Operation Barbarossa.

of Laverack[64], who was now clearly an admirer of this particular unit. Supported by a mere one troop of anti-tank guns from 2/1st regiment, this force was to be spread across Palestine and Syria. Meanwhile the 5th Cavalry Brigade, which included the North Somerset Yeomanry, was to box in the still sizeable enemy presence in the hilly and inaccessible Jebel-Druse. They would also cover the Deraa-Damascus route (along which the Free French had advanced in the assault on Damascus) and – rather incredibly – also cover the western part of the Haifa-Baghdad route. The quelling of French resolve however was still far from complete; and there was to be action yet in the Jebel Druse.

It was not however carried out by any of the 5th Cavalry Brigade units. This being war, and one fought by an invading force in particularly challenging topography, the constant reshuffle was an ongoing phenomenon. The Yorkshire Dragoons for example stayed on near Kuneitra for a few days only – 60 of them actually took part in the final assault on Kuneitra on 18 June, supporting the second wave.[65] More generally though, they were garrisoning the Jisr Bennt Jacub and by now conducting rear area security operations. By the time that the operational lines had been tightened, Damascus taken and the French defenders facing eventual defeat, the Yorkshiremen were receiving their next set of orders. The Movement Order details their dispositions for a transition across to Ezraa – a cross country transfer that would severely test man and beast.[66]

Clifford Wrigglesworth of the Yorkshire Dragoons recalled this stage of the campaign for them: "We were sent into the Jebel Druse."[67] As the war diary accounts suggest, they had been far from idle so far, and as Wrigglesworth's squadron leader is quoted saying, the journey south-west had not been an easy one. "We had to sally forth from Al Malakaiya on horses, riding down to cross the Jordan north of Tiberius and up onto the Golan Heights. It was rough country, all stone walls and boulders, which was particularly tough on the packhorses who carried the Hotchkiss guns… At one place where we had to slither down a rock, take two strides and then hop over a little ditch, one of Bruce's [Bruce Hobbs's] packhorses slipped, fell over the ditch and lay there. We sent for the farrier who decided that the only thing to do was dispatch the animal, but the poor chap who looked after it was so upset that, in desperation, he pulled out his water bottle and poured water into the horse's ear, whereupon it sprang to its feet."[68] This was not easy country, and they were to find that the denizens knew precisely how to fight in it.

---

64 This was to be until 7th Division's approach to Damour had been completed.
65 This assault actually turned out to be surprisingly easy. The 2nd Queens advanced with bayonets levelled under the barrage of one 25 pounder – Blackburn's 2/3 and a detachment of Yorkshire Dragoons in the second wave. In all, only one casualty was inflicted on this force, by the fire of the retreating French rearguard.
66 Modern day Izra, some 80 km south of Damascus.
67 IWM 14139 recorded 1994-05-24, Interview with Clifford Wrigglesworth.
68 Fitzgeorge-Parker, *No Secret So Close*, p.89.

Their route through Ezraa took in the site of the most easterly of Verdilhac's thrusts back in mid-June, which had then completely cut off Lloyd's brigade column from Palestine. There was still very hard fighting to do (as the Somerset men could testify). Elsewhere, in the early hours of 11 July (the final day of hostilities) "C" squadron Cheshire Yeomanry were checking their weapons and saddles before forming up to attack a gun battery. Similarly committed to their cause, British forces only 24 hours earlier – despite the common knowledge that Dentz was in armistice negotiations – carried out a hard fought assault north of Jezzine which resulted in a Victoria Cross for Private James Gordon of the Australian infantry. It was now that the North Somerset Yeomanry came up against such hard opposition on the Jebel Mazar to protect the flank of 2 Queens. And their action was by no means the fiercest - some of this being carried out by on the Jebel Mazar operation by the Kings Own Royal Lancaster Regiment. The Axis forces seemed equally intent on fighting until the bitter end. Among other things, there was still a political agenda to fulfil.

Even after the five weeks of the Syrian campaign, that had seen around 400 people killed each week, many senior decision makers were still imposing debilitating degrees of political restraint upon the men acting out their orders in the field. Thus was found a patrol from the Yorkshire Dragoons, with the armistice only 72 hours away, sallying forth with orders not to become engaged with the enemy, and wearing solar topees because their steel helmets were stored on the squadron lorries.

The patrol in question, 2. Troop "C" Squadron Queens Own Yorkshire Dragoons left Bosra at 0445 hours (whilst 3. Troop and "C" squadron H.Q. proceeded to Samia) with their breathtakingly optimistic recommendations on sighting any enemy. There were political tensions here superseding the military one; presumably as Middle East Command hoped to only alienate Vichy France's colonial subjects from metropolitan France – rather than from themselves as well. There was, it must be admitted some logic in this. The Soueida area had been notorious as a hotspot of tribal resistance to French rule.

Now that British cavalry were in the area, they had to be wary of the fact that the indigenous inhabitants, whatever their feelings towards the French, were a highly capable adversary when they wanted to be. This was after all an area "Which the French washed their hands of because they couldn't control the tribesmen."[69] The French had tried to subdue them in the Great Syrian Revolt, resulting in the Druse annihilating 5000 of them at Salkand. "After that" summarises Wrigglesworth "they left them strictly alone … Very wild country; mountainous."[70] As the seemingly impossible guidelines on contact with the enemy show, any speculation about enemy forces in this area was bound to be highly unreliable.

In terms of terrain it was however well-suited to horse-soldiers, especially as this rocky outcrop was on the strategic flank, placing it even further within the remit of

---

69   IWM 14139 recorded 1994-05-24, Interview with Clifford Wrigglesworth.
70   IWM 14139 recorded 1994-05-24, Interview with Clifford Wrigglesworth.

cavalry. After all, the most likely antagonists here were likely to be cavalry themselves. Those French Druse antagonists could be identified by the red and white turbans they wore – unlike those who had joined the British and wore distinguishing black and white headdresses. "C" squadron was the outpost squadron in this new home for the Yorkshiremen and their horses, and they were to patrol the villages in the six-mile stretch between Soueida, with its old French fort, and their own position upon the Soueida road.

This long trek into their new operational zone now behind them, the area had to be secured with daily patrols. It was on one of these that the two aforementioned troops from "C" squadron were proceeding to Ed Dour, because the locals reported that the Druze cavalry had left on 8th July, shooting the Mukhtar's son before they did so.[71] Also it had to be established if nearby towns like Sejen were still occupied or not. It is therefore apparent that there was a painfully-drawn political backdrop to any operations in this area. Factor in the capabilities and ferocity the locals had demonstrated in the 1925 revolt, and high command's trepidation becomes more understandable.

No. 2 Troop were 800 metres from the road (so as not to be an obvious target) and watering their horses "when we were surprised by the crack of rifle shots and bullets pinging around us"[72] recalled the officer in charge of 2. Troop, Bruce Hobbs. "We dismounted and I sent the horses back [thereby reducing the troop by one man in four to lead the animals] while we got down behind cover and engaged the enemy."[73] The war diary version ponderously refers to "No. 2 Troop acting on orders not to get engaged, returned to Sqn. H.Q. who were with No. 3 troop …"[74] Hobbs's more informal account explains this disobeying of orders and elaborates by adding that "as I had been given strict orders not to get involved in any armed combat and we were obviously hopelessly outnumbered in any case, I said, 'Come on boys, out!' and, summoning the horses, beat an orderly retreat." He clearly didn't mention to his superiors that he had returned fire. This response and the lack of casualties at this stage duly allowed the war diary to claim that policy had been appropriately followed. But the Druse had other ideas.

Operational procedure was informed by the unreliable intelligence briefs that there would be no fighting, and in light of this "continual information"[75] the decision was taken to "remain in observation and see what action they decided to take." The Druse intention however was quickly becoming obvious. As S.H.Q. saw Hobbs's troop

---

71 TNA WO 169/1407: Report on Patrol to Samia and Sejen 10 July, Yorkshire Dragoons, January-December 1941.
72 Fitzgeorge-Parker, *No Secret So Close*, p.89.
73 Fitzgeorge-Parker, *No Secret So Close*, p.89.
74 TNA WO 169/1407: Report on Patrol to Samia and Sejen 10 July, Yorkshire Dragoons, January-December 1941.
75 TNA WO 169/1407: 'Report on Patrol to Samia and Sejen 10 July, Yorkshire Dragoons, January-December 1941.

emerging from the dead ground, to the sound of firing they could see "some of the red and white hats following… 'then more and more… they seemed to have turned out a whole regiment for us'"[76] At this point the Druze were seen to halt and dismount close by a fork in the Sejen and Soueida roads. The Dragoons detachment commander elected to withdraw to Samia "but just as the orders were being given, a strong attack developed on our right. No. 2 Troop engaged this attack."[77] This attack was guessed to be about a squadron and was firing on 2 troop with 4 Hotchkiss guns. Meanwhile another squadron came from Sejen and started to work around the left flank. The squadron leader, Simon Lycett-Green recalled in Fitzgeorge-Parker[78] that "they seemed to have … us in an encircling movement." Lycett-Green ordered his men to withdraw towards Samia "and this they managed to do by fighting their way back to the horses, and then finally withdrew under heavy L.M.G fire. The action lasted one hour, and the patrol arrived back in BOSRA at 1330 hrs."[79]

They had been under heavy fire and been given a masterclass in what expert cavalrymen could do. "In carrying out their attack, [the Druze cavalry] moved very swiftly round our flanks, and while covering us with L.M.G. fire they moved their sections (rifle) mounted. These did not hand over their horses, only dismounting in dead ground, taking a few shots and then remounting and carrying on. Their horses were very well trained to fire, several enemy fired from the saddle, and it was on these that we inflicted most casualties."[80]

By the end of the engagement the immediate report suggested that the Dragoons had lost one dead, one missing and one a prisoner, with 12 enemy Druze killed and one French, with an unknown number wounded. Such is the innate optimism of documents after such encounters that the very same page of the war diary has a handwritten postscript added 16th July detailing the Dragoons' casualties as two missing, both prisoner at Soueida, "returned to us on July 12". One of them had been wounded through the hand.[81]

A soldier called Meller [Miller in Fitzgeorge-Parker] had been in the last section to come out and his comrades had seen him "put his head up over a rock and a bullet went slap through his head.' He was wearing one of those ridiculous topees." When the French surrendered the following day, the Dragoons formed up in the square of

---

76 Fitzgeorge-Parker, *No Secret So Close*, p.89.
77 TNA WO 169/1407: Report on Patrol to Samia and Sejen 10 July, Yorkshire Dragoons, January-December 1941.
78 Fitzgeorge-Parker, *No Secret So Close*, p.89.
79 TNA WO 169/1407: Report on Patrol to Samia and Sejen 10 July, Yorkshire Dragoons January-December 1941.
80 TNA WO 169/1407: Report on Patrol to Samia and Sejen 10 July, Yorkshire Dragoons, January-December 1941.
81 TNA WO 169/1407: Report on Patrol to Samia and Sejen 10 July' Yorkshire Dragoons January-December 1941.

Soueida and the French garrison marched out. Amongst them, hatless, was Trooper Meller "waving like mad to us. He had only had his topee shot off!"[82]

Meller was fortunate; but so too were the rest of his regiment. The risk posed by the sizeable Druze presence in the Jebel-Druze was clear. But the events of 10 July 1941, and of the 1925-27 Syrian revolt also showed the calibre of horsemen the Yorkshire Dragoons had to fight against. The speed with which they enveloped the two troops of British cavalry was formidable, and so too was the standard of the training that both men and horses had received. The report in the war diary is sombrely clear on this.

However, the gravity of what might have been faced barely seems to have registered in the account given by Wrigglesworth, given in 1994. Asked about the French Druze cavalry he replies "Not very good" and that "the horses were more or less as good as ours".[83] Given the official account recorded at the time, it would seem that Wrigglesworth's memory in 1994 was at error. It could actually be that as a private soldier he was not in a position to appreciate how close his unit was to being surrounded and massacred (it was S.H.Q., a tactical leap further back and looking down, who could identify this). But then it could also be a combination of an old soldier's dogmatic dismissiveness of his enemy and/or of the importance of the campaign he was serving in. Wrigglesworth after all went on to serve in the desert, lose his leg and be captured. Hobbs himself went on to fight at El Alamein and win the MC. It might well be that men with these experiences later, did not look back on their mounted days as climactic stages of the war. Wrigglesworth's description of the encounter with the French Druze cavalry was of a "bit of shooting between their cavalry and ours." "One fella wounded but that was all". He was, it should be noted, in the same troop as Hobbs, whose men were nearly surrounded and came under sustained machine gun fire, while also being outnumbered during an engagement that lasted an hour.

The Wrigglesworth account generally is not as detailed or as enthusiastic as that of the Hobbs biography by Fitzgeorge-Parker. It is the latter that provides slightly more detail on the subsequent five months that the unit spent garrisoning the Jebel Druze post-armistice. They covered the area between the historically significant map points of the Beau Geste-esque old Crusader fort at Soueida, and Salkand (twenty miles away). It was a hotbed of political intrigue that the French had thoroughly failed to understand, imposing their own administration and bureaucratic philosophies on the vibrant local communities, and causing deep resentment. The Yorkshire Dragoons avoided this pitfall, maintaining the pre-existing *maisons de tolerance* – brothels. "Our Commanding Officer thought they were a good idea… so he kept them on and ordered the medical officer to examine and pass the girls."[84] Thus were the extant local conditions embraced.

---

82 Fitzgeorge-Parker, *No Secret So Close*, p.90.
83 IWM: 14139 recorded 1994-05-24, Interview with Clifford Wrigglesworth.
84 Fitzgeorge-Parker, *No Secret So Close*, p.90

Further cultural riches lay in the ancient vaults of Soueida's fort, where an officer's servant found the enormous wine vats left behind by the French. He attached a tube from one of them to his own bed, and was later found in deep, serene unconsciousness. And who could blame him? After all, Operation Exporter was over.

A final feat of endurance was still in store, however. "B" squadron Cheshire Yeomanry was asked to take part in the victory parade in Beirut. A signal honour. The plan was for them to make their way there by both road and cross-country, arriving around 2000 hrs the evening before, allowing them plenty of time to get into parade order. As their route involved crossing wadis that had had their bridges blown, this turned into a 15-hour march that got them in at 0600 the next morning, exhausted, unfed and field-soiled. At one point on the march one horse and rider had simultaneously fallen asleep, going off the edge of a four-foot drop into an olive grove. It says a lot for the durability of these horses that there was no serious injury. They had descended 2500 feet in 15 hrs, and now had less than two hours to briefly rest and eat before pressing on again to join the start line for the parade.

Thus the yeomanry did take their place on the ceremonial march, alongside Bren carriers and marching infantry, and beneath ceremonial fly pasts of R.A.F planes. The yeomanry's swords and buckles were presumably still blackened and saddles unpolished as they took their place. With "B" squadron representing the yeomanry (and generations of antiquity) on their horses, the rest of the regiment simply joined the crowd. This actually proved fortuitous as by eleven o'clock the band required to play the general salute for the assembled generals had not arrived. Blushes were spared when the Cheshire Yeomanry's R.S.M. Douglas, informally dressed in shorts, standing in the crowd, was prevailed upon to use a trumpet borrowed from some French Marines. Thus the generals were able to receive their salute.

After the painful hoop-jumping of the victory parade the regiment was released, no doubt buoyed by the praises General Maitland-Wilson addressed to their representatives in "B" squadron. Finally, they were able to escape to Beirut racecourse, with its umbrella pines, sandy ground and proximity to the sea. Men could relax, and the horses could romp and roll with freedom.

The Syrian campaign as reported by the *Illustrated London News*, 12 July 1941.

Conclusion

Appraising British Cavalry in Syria 1941

The 5th Cavalry brigade was a living example of the limited military resources available to Wavell, Maitland-Wilson and Laverack. It supported an Exporter force that had no medium tanks yet faced a defending force with some 90 of them. This resulted in a threat to laterals throughout much of the campaign and meant that the impact of what were actually quite limited counterattacks became substantial. The main value in these attacks was their propinquity to Palestine and the fact that the allied invasion which they splintered now had to immediately tend to the flank and rear of its columns with forces that it could ill-afford. Understandably variously arranged components of 5th Cavalry brigade needed to be deployed in increasing numbers.

It is clear that mounted cavalry made an important and valuable contribution to operation Exporter. The fact that as the campaign progressed, more cavalry were being brought forward, and mechanised troops were being re-roled is testament to this. But it is important to note that the conditions in what is nowadays Lebanon and Syria were specifically suited to the capabilities of cavalry in 1941. The roads were few and vehicles generally couldn't operate off them. Objectively these shouldn't have been surprises. What did seem to surprise most of those involved was how versatile cavalry proved to be in roles other than providing eyes and ears. They could quickly and surreptitiously seal off enemy positions, then clear them and have the ground in between vanguard and main column reconnoitred. They could have – in 1941 Syria – pushed on with little need for resupply as the horses could live off the Levantine countryside indefinitely, the men could often do so too, and their role normally didn't require a massive expenditure of ammunition. Improvements in technology, specifically radio communications and anti-tank weapons, would only have augmented this capability, not replaced it. Vehicles simply could not go where the yeomanry were needed to go on this campaign. The other key capability for which horses made the yeomanry well-suited was that of dominating ground; in either flank role or covering a retreat. It was however a capability of which the yeomanry were often denuded because of the paucity of Vickers guns available to them. Given the initial reticence about deploying any cavalry in early Exporter planning conferences, there was a significant revolution achieved in the perception of cavalry's capabilities by the end of 1941. This is shown by using the same measure; of senior staff planning conferences.

A New Role

In mid-1941, Middle East Command believed that if the Germans were to be successful against Russia, they would then soon try to enter Syria. This prompted a re-appraisal of existing resources there. Habforce, their time as lorried infantry now served, were to become armoured. But the surviving 5th Cavalry Brigade were not to simply become lorried infantry in their place as might have seemed logical; or even to be mounted in tanks as their designation within 10th Armoured Division immediately after Exporter might suggest. Assuming that the Germans were indeed to push into Syria, the 5th Cavalry Brigade were now to be tasked with remaining in the hills behind the German frontline and to act as saboteurs.

For this role the yeomanry started to train in explosives and furthermore, got their wish for further firepower – every regiment was to be equipped with a mortar troop. The mortar troops would be issued with four 3-inch mortars, the standard infantry battalion medium mortar. The French superb use of heavy mortars had given a particularly striking lesson to the allies, which combined with the French superiority in armour to offer serious obstacles to any allied progress, let alone success. The yeomanry could recreate some of this effect. Meanwhile, large supplies of ammunition, food and forage would be dumped in the Syrian and Lebanese hills, with the plan for additional replenishment by airdrop. The soldiers it seems were very pleased with the decision.[1] Cavalry were to be kept; their mobility harnessed for modern warfare as operational troops – and with them, all their capabilities and faults.

Criticism to the plan was voiced at the time, though this didn't get in the way of actually creating the new force. Of the conception for this eccentric role, eleven points were put into a paper – though sadly the title and publication details are lost. Verdin records the gist of it though one of the three remaining sabre squadrons was to be converted entirely to machine guns. Therefore, it would consist of three troops, each equipped with 4 of the excellent Vickers medium machine gun, thus giving the unit plenty of direct fire power. The remaining sabre troops would be enlarged slightly, and the anti-tank rifles would be discarded. The "H.Q." squadron would be bolstered by a Light Machine Gun troop. Thus the regiment would be bristling, not only with Vickers guns, but with Bren guns. The point of this would be to put up a fight against low-flying aircraft, just as "B" Sqn had.[2] The proposals were not discussed beyond this point – they were simply enacted and the cavalry began preparing for the new purpose in October 1941.

1   Verdin, *The Cheshire Yeomanry*, p.363.
2   Verdin, *The Cheshire Yeomanry*, p.364-5.

As the role was never carried out (German strategic failures in 1941 ended the threat to Syria) the significance of this plan being developed should principally be seen as a testament to the faith in cavalry following the operation. After all, cavalry had now been employed in modern warfare and made a very substantial impact without suffering many casualties. They could have achieved significantly more with greater firepower.

There was, it must be accepted, a sense of the optimistic rather than practical about this scheme. Cavalry could operate unseen at night but would have been horribly exposed to aircraft during the day, not least because the Luftwaffe had more machines at their disposal than the Vichy French. Then there is the fact that there were not to be any anti-tank guns issued – presumably because mountain territory was deemed to be impassable to tanks. And of course the operational isolation for units that required to be supplied by air drop with far more than simple infantry battalions required. So it may well be that cavalry wouldn't have been cut out for such a role. The fact the role was developed is probably best used simply as an endorsement of how effective cavalry proved in their traditional role, in the type of topography that has always suited cavalry well – regardless of the era.

Cavalry Vulnerability

In the regimental history of the Cheshire Yeomanry, Verdin wrote that "In spite of these criticisms, it was fully accepted at the time that the use of horsed cavalry had justified itself. As flank guards in the hills to the advancing columns, and as a quick means of obtaining information in mountainous country, it had no equal and proved invaluable."[3] These accomplishments were won in spite of the technology arrayed against the cavalry. The predominant reason for both the success of and the need for the cavalry was, as Verdin indicates, the terrain.

But the first part of Verdin's justification requiring analysis, is the first five words. The criticisms in question were: the vulnerability of horses to air attack and artillery, the lack of firepower and the reaction time of a cavalry unit when dispersed. Some of these faults could be easily rectified, some were less of a problem in the hilly country cavalry excel in, and only one in fact might be classed as an intractable feature of cavalry on a 20th century battlefield.

First of all there was the vulnerability to air. This had been well-documented from the previous war, and quite apart from the western front, the wide dispersal it consequently required of cavalry had almost led to the failure of the famous Beersheba charge by the Australian cavalry. Add to that the fact that planes had been improving in the interceding 24 years, and the odds would have been on the side of the planes, not the horses. Nonetheless, in Syria there was comparatively limited impact from air forces in mountainous country in 1941. This was particularly the case for aerial

---

3   Verdin, *The Cheshire Yeomanry*, p.347.

reconnaissance, which although effective for roads, simply could not pin point concealed enemy gun positions. After all, the most effective demonstration of this was done by horsed cavalry. On the rough hillsides it was also mainly cavalry, rather than vehicles or infantry which achieved the best results in reconnaissance.

British Cavalry in Syria in 1941 had escaped extensive punishment from aircraft for a variety of reasons. The paramount one however must be that they faced relatively few Vichy aircraft, and those that were in theatre were concentrating on firstly the Royal Navy, then the main columns of ground troops, rather than the will 'o the wisp reconnaissance screens of lightly armed and less potent cavalry that were in any case so difficult to hit.

The various escapes from aircraft recorded in the yeomanry annals and the *Manchester Evening Chronicle* may all seem miraculous, but the fact is that they consistently happened. Whether the soldiers disappeared into nearby olive groves, turned a tighter turn than the plane and galloped away; or simply grouped together and fought off the aerial attacker with concentrated fire – the ability to escape serious losses proved unfaltering. Partly it was due to the wide dispersal that the yeomanry so strictly observed, unlike their Vichy counterparts. However, wide dispersal did mean that only small units could be handled effectively. In fact the consensus seemed at the end of the campaign that one squadron operating as an independent command, with an attached Vickers gun section, was ideal for such country.[4] But for emphasis, it must be repeated that the British cavalry did face relatively few aircraft.

With the threat of artillery there are similar themes in evidence, at least with moving horsemen. Once shelling started, horsemen were able to disperse and ride fast, so there were remarkably few shell casualties. The Spahis that Captain Thomas of the Australian artillery so quickly dealt with were very unlucky; they were trapped and ranged so there was no near miss or ranging shot to warn them. Ultimately though, the British cavalry were never seen so closely bunched together. Another point about the shelling in this campaign is that much of it was done by low-angled 75mm field guns of Great War vintage, whose shells went straight into the ground and blew their shrapnel in a limited arc. Higher angled shells, or starburst shells would have caused significantly more damage, as they did throughout the remainder of the Second World War (not to mention the Western Front during the First World War). But even with the elderly French guns, shelling was a significant problem for static troops, or rather for their horses, as the men were invariably in trenches whenever stationary for more than a few hours. This then led to another problem.

When the sabre troops were stationary, horses inevitably had to be kept at some distance behind, along with the handlers. This meant that starting the next task took a long time. This was however a necessary evil that had to be embraced. Nonetheless the yeomanry's natural advantage in dealing with both air and artillery threat was that small parties of horseman moving along the sides of precipitous slopes or where

---

4   Verdin, *The Cheshire Yeomanry*, p. 347.

they could rapidly melt away into undergrowth, were a challenging and less valuable target to engage. Both these means of avoiding aircraft became redundant if the units weren't moving and had for some reason been identified – such as when smoke from the farriers' fires were spotted.

The next problem with cavalry remaining stationary was unit reaction time. "There is, however, a great disadvantage when horses are kept a long way from the troops they serve in that the latter cease to be readily mobile."[5] These reasons are:

1. The time required to reunite men and horses.
2. The need to re-saddle the horses.

The latter could not be avoided because seven stone saddles couldn't be simply left on the horses all day on the off-chance that they might suddenly become needed. Even toughened up animals with lots of training required a rest for their backs. These drawbacks were amply demonstrated in the episode of the Cheshire Yeomanry at Sabah Monastery, when a surprise attack was foiled by the quick reactions of the Abbot and Corporal Shickell. In the fight back, the nearby light tanks were the first reinforcements on the scene – they merely needed to have the ignitions turned on, where the horses had to be untethered and saddled before being pressed into a gallop.

The 5th Brigade cavalry certainly demonstrated impressive patrolling range and flexibility – whether with the Cheshire Yeomanry attached to 21st or 25th brigades or the Yorkshire Dragoons around Jezzine and the river Jordan. But they also brought along some notable limitations. That they were able to overcome many of these, should not obscure the likelihood that cavalry would potentially be vulnerable to a more numerous air force, and to more modern artillery. Extensive use of either would presumably wear them down with no means of response – as the Axis forces were able to prove against groups of Partisans time and again. This problem becomes significant when one considers that their designated role after the 1941 Syrian campaign was to operate as mounted saboteurs in the enemy's rear area. Another innate problem that horse units brought with them was that when stationary for prolonged periods – as cavalry boxed into a section of hill country by extensive Wehrmacht anti-saboteur operations might be – they were not able to exploit their innate advantage of operational mobility.

Where Soviet cavalry divisions on the Eastern front were highly flexible, the British 5th Cavalry brigade was not flexible as the lack of firepower limited their uses. They were highly mobile and that's where the advantages began and ended. This undoubtedly offered their senior commanders a useful capability in 1941, and with rearming could have become a much more multi-dimensional force. A fact not lost on those who planned the subsequent cavalry role and duly re-equipped them. Cavalry were therefore a good solution for Laverack going forward, because such

---

5   Verdin, *The Cheshire Yeomanry*, p.345.

problems as the lack of firepower could indeed be easily solved. Signals problems could be addressed too, or at least partially. This became apparent in the planning for defending against the envisioned German invasion of Syria in 1942. It was of course clearly recognised that had the cavalry possessed more firepower they would have been a far more effective advance guard. They would never have been held up at Heitours for four days for example. Therefore the French would have had to withdraw immediately and had to fight the rest of the force in daylight at Jezzine. This would have exposed them to flank attacks from the Yeomanry's "B" squadron. As tempting as it might be to hypothesise on the would-be achievements of a better equipped cavalry arm, it must be remembered that the lack of firepower which so handicapped the yeomanry was as inevitable a product of the War Office parsimony towards cavalry cavalry, just as the existence of the cavalry units was.

Nonetheless, they had done their bit when asked. The dominant factor in assessing the impact of cavalry in the British order of battle, is the official recognition of what they were there to do. This goes beyond Laverack's initial conferences before Exporter – to the very reason that the War Office still retained cavalry in 1941. The rationale was explained in C.I.G.S. Field Marshall Milne's 1927 note to the then Secretary of State for War; cavalry were required while the army otherwise lacked the fast-moving troops needed to protect it (i.e. provide a flank guard) and offer a close reconnaissance role, which no amount of aircraft, even with the most modern technology, could offer. At the end of Exporte Major-General Allen of 7th Division personally thanked the Cheshire Yeomanry for the "the high standard of efficiency of the regt, enabled it to play a valuable part in the successful operations."[6]

The Overall Picture

The invasion of Syria only happened because forces had been withdrawn from the assault in the Western Desert. This had meant that neither enterprise was properly resourced; Battleaxe failed and Exporter was "unduly long and costly".[7] Nonetheless both were the product of Churchill's instinct to attack to restore momentum – an approach that ultimately helped swing the war. Both factors lead to the inclusion of the yeomanry in operation Exporter. Naturally, with more assets available to Wavell and his subordinates, Exporter would have gone ahead without any cavalrymen on the British side. The French would still have used them too, however the key to Dentz's battlefield successes was not horsemen but skilful combinations of mortars and armour. These tactical factors, combined with the allies' operational failure to concentrate on a single thrust for much of the campaign proved significant. The product was a very slow-moving invasion, and greater numbers, such as those that would have

---

6   TNA WO 169/1936: Appendix M G 15/1/957, Cheshire Yeomanry 1941.
7   Gavin Long *Second World War*, p.524

been available later, would have mitigated against French technical superiority even without the influence of the yeomanry.[8]

The yeomanry themselves did well in Syria but would never have survived long in the Western Desert of 1940-42 or the congested Normandy Bocage of summer 1944. But they were uniquely well-placed to enhance any force subject to British doctrine fighting through mountains at this stage of the war. Furthermore, the innate quality of the personnel in the yeomanry ranks meant that all the roles available to them in the summer of 1941 had been firmly "gripped". It is not therefore such a surprise that the allied planners after Exporter allocated 5th Cavalry brigade their saboteur role for defending Syria. As Verdin concedes, the idea now of expecting horsed cavalry to do their new role barely seems credible.[9] Yet the role was duly drawn up and allotted on 15 October. The use of horses with their relatively silent movement at night would be very effective, and allow them to operate far from base, with large quantities of explosives and mortar rounds packed on their horses. In this sense the plan was logical.

8   Gavin Long, *Second World War.*
9   Verdin, *The Cheshire Yeomanry*, p.632.

Epilogue

"Please Take Care of Him"

The available historical literature demonstrates that the Germans failed in each of their objectives for 1941. As the threat to Syria accordingly passed, so did the need to retain horsed cavalry. Any unit in training for a future role, had to have hard proof that it would surely be needed. Otherwise, there were shortages in the immediate vicinity to be made up for. Clearly, 5th Cavalry Brigade's mounted saboteurs were in line for a re-role. On the 13 February 1942, a regimental exercise for the Cheshire Yeomanry was ended with a trumpet sounding an officers' call. The men holding commissions duly made their way to the Orders Group.

The Colonel was badly shaken – his body language showed it. With face and voice strained by emotion, he informed the assembled officers that they were to be converted from cavalry to signallers. The rest of the brigade was to lose its horses as well. Lt Col Dennis revealed that the C-in-C Middle East himself had written a letter, informing him that the Cheshire Yeomanry were to give up their saboteur role and become a line signals regiment instead – the need for signallers in the Middle East theatre was desperate.

The news was taken glumly and an air of misery pervaded the Cheshire Yeomanry for some time. They were no longer to be a combat regiment, or to be in a role traditionally associated with elitism. Their regional, cultural and regimental identity, recently reaffirmed so efficiently and so against the run of expectation was now gone. So too would the means of that identity – the horses that they had invested so much in and become so demonstrably attached to. In the days that followed, Lt Col D.G. Williams of the Royal Wiltshire Yeomanry sent a letter of condolence.

A previous sense of social snobbery had maintained the yeomanry's sense of distance for some 150 years. In the heat of war, that had no doubt become harnessed as well, but the cavalry had become key operational assets, sometimes with the most frontline role that any unit in theatre could have. Every step of the way they had maintained a skill-set that no-one else in the army could readily be re-roled to, unless like the "Kelly Gang" they had all previously been horsemen. It seemed that the role of signallers was going to be a mundane, and comparatively drab role that anyone could have been allocated to. The weight of the blow to these yeomen can be understood. Similar emotions were repeated that week across the rest of the brigade. The North Somerset Yeomanry were also to become signallers, and the Yorkshire Dragoons were to crew dummy tanks to fool German air reconnaissance.[1]

Whatever the true source of the misery so evident in February, it was as nothing to the emotions felt on the 25 March 1942. This was the day the horses left, bound for the now anachronistically named "remount" depots at Natanya and Tel Mond. The movement order was received from the Headquarters at Jerusalem on the 24th. Sudden and perfunctory as so many administrative tasks may seem in an army – and especially at war – the emotional impact of this particular document was profound at the time. It is fitting that the parting of a cavalry regiment and its horses, so soon after campaigning together, can be retold by an able chronicler who served with his own horse during that campaign in his family regiment. Verdin recounts "There are some scenes in life so fraught with emotion that they defy adequate description. One of them is the final parting of a cavalry regiment with its horses… try and imagine the feelings of a cavalry soldier who waters and feeds his horse for the last time knowing it will never return." Soldiers wept. The soldiers who had tended to their animals for the last time that morning stood silently and glumly at the gate until the last dust clouds of the horse party had faded from sight.[2]

The Cheshire Yeomanry's commanding officer rode with the horse party. The group passed back over the ground that the regiment had come to know very well indeed as they exercised and trained under Brigadier Chrystal the previous year. Each place name was also imbued with millennia of cavalry history – Jenin, the plain of Esdraelon, Musmus Pass – as well as of the recent memories accrued by the regiment as it had trained. On the 27 March, the horse party staged at the Tulkarm Plain (which had been their home for 4 ½ months); for the final night. The march across the plain became slower and slower as the riders guided their horses to the end of the journey, "as if clinging desperately to every minute which remained with the horses."[3]

But their fate was ineluctable, and those now designated to take over the horses waited. It was a consolation that the waiting hands into which the horses now passed, were those of the RAVC; skilled in handling animals. Whether the horses had become bewildered or not, they could not have failed to pick up on the air of depression pervading the column. The deft skill and care of the RAVC men was therefore paramount in the handing over.

When the horses had arrived with the regiment at Whitwell back in 1939, many had come with notes attached to their head collars. In March 1942, at the remount depots, many had new notes attached to their head collars. Most simply gave the names and said, for example, that as an old hunter and yeomanry mount, this animal

---

1   Verdin, *The Cheshire Yeomanry*, pp.370-1
2   Verdin, *The Cheshire Yeomanry*, p.374.
3   Verdin, *The Cheshire Yeomanry*, p.375.

was used to being treated well, and that he/she should be put down as humanely as possible. This was the fate for a significant number of horses. After all, many simply did not take to being retrained to pull GS wagons. But it is difficult to say exactly whether this was the fate of most of the animals. Horses and mules were needed, and a notable number of 5th Cavalry Brigade's horses were certainly retrained as draught animals by the RAVC, whose regimental history suggests (but only suggests) that possibly most were thus deployed in Sicily and Italy, as well as around the Middle East. However the evidence is merely indicative, rather than substantive. It does seem though that many were kept on, and in the hands of the British army until the end of the war. At this point it seems that nearly all of the army's horses and mules in the Middle East were shot. We do not know what happened to those in Italy, although there are anecdotes of many being given to local farmers. Apparently, however, a contingent of horses from the Yorkshire Dragoons were spared this fate and passed onto the Arab Legion and Transjordan Frontier Force to continue as cavalry mounts.[4] For the human element of 5th Cavalry Brigade, there was their own retraining to get on with. The process begun in 1920 was finally complete and the anachronism was over.

How the War Ended

As any signallers could have told the cavalry, their new role was an important one that required a high level of training. Furthermore, with vast distances to maintain communications over, the work was vital and depended upon those doing it to do it very well. The yeomen adjusted to this accordingly, flourishing in their responsibility to maintain communications over vast swathes of Sahara on their own initiative. They were less happy about going onto be a very small, and in truth fairly dispensable, cog in congested, already well-developed North-West Europe later on. However, when the war did end there was still some determined celebrating to be done. The journey was over, and the soldiers had all played their part, sharing a notable stage of the war with their horses. The four-legged yeomanry now long-gone, it was down to the humans to do the celebrating, on a scale of drunkenness that eclipsed even that of the horse parties' Marseille hell-raising in 1940.

One of Verdin's few lucid memories of the night of VE Day 8 May 1945, was of signing a movement order sending Lt. Dawson to Britain immediately in a Motor Torpedo Boat. It would allow him to get there in time to watch the Newmarket 2,000 guineas. Dawson used it too. It took him a week to get back, because the crew of the M.T.B he hitched a ride with stopped off at Yarmouth to pick up extra gin.

[4] Cheshire Archives (NCY) 19/57: Syria: The Last British Cavalry Action – Part 2, Information from Tom Louch, formerly Sergeant in the Yorkshire Dragoons as cited in Denis C Bateman's (publisher unknown)

The excesses induced by the relief of surviving such a war were clearly considerable. And the fate of other yeomen is a sobering foil to those stories of well-oiled exuberance on the night of VE Day. Lt. Shaw had been captured in the western desert; Clifford Wriggelsworth was wounded, captured and had his leg amputated in an Italian field Hospital; John Verney overcame his distaste for the army, later parachuting into Sardinia, winning the MC and getting captured, before escaping in December 1943 and serving in the invasion of North-West Europe. Bruce Hobbs, with the rest of the Yorkshire Dragoons, went onto fight at El Alamein as infantry and win the MC. He survived the war intact. Each idiosyncratic biographical thread combines to weave a tapestry of the Second World War. That tapestry includes the threads belonging to "Blighty", "Rufus", "Little Nell", "Vixen" and thousands of others. Not all of those threads willingly took their place in this great weave, or indeed survived it. But help form it they did, as well as they could do.

Appendix I

Allied Chain of Command, Syria 1941

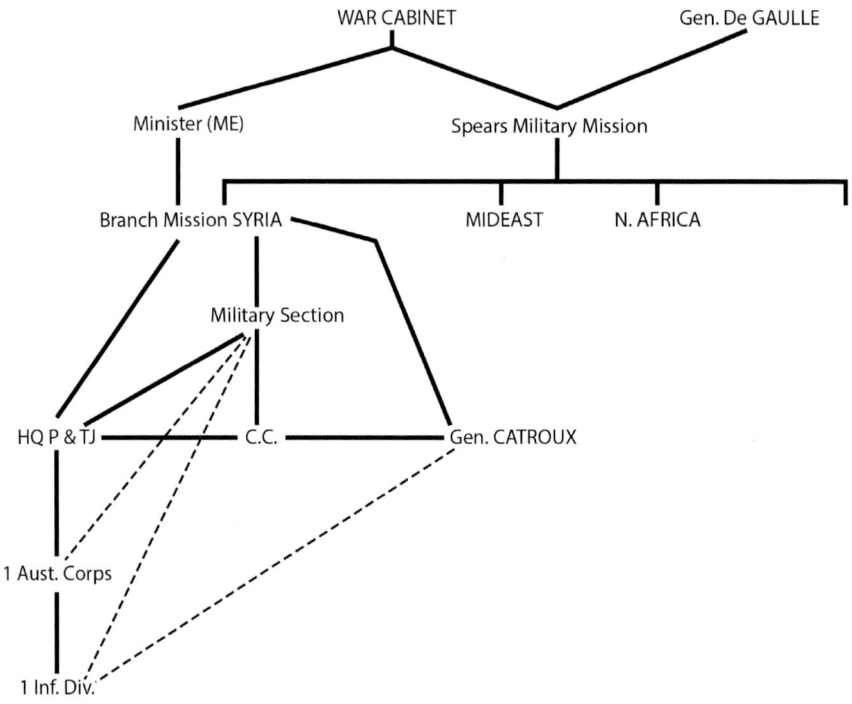

Appendix II

Syria Branch – Spears Mission

Headquarters.
Head of Mission   Gen. Spears
Attd. Mr. Hamilton

Secretary (GSO II)   Major Smith-Dorrien
"   " (GSO III)   2/Lt Wells
Attd (from Spears Mission)   Capt. Barton
                                2/Lieut. Lord Oxford[1]

Military Section.
GSO I   Lt. Col. BARTER
DAQMG   Maj. SHAPLAND
DAD Tn   Not yet appointed.
Air Section.   Wing Comdr De Sibour RAF
Naval Section.   Capt. Morse, R.N.
Press & Propaganda, Censorship,
Finance & Economic   Brig. Walsh
                                (PLAN OVERLEAF) [sic]

Distribution
GOC
BGS
G
I
A
Q
File
WD (2)
Spare (12)

---

1   Note the difference in abbreviations for 2nd Lieutenant Wells and 2nd Lieutenant The Lord Oxford.

SECRET
1 AUST CORPS INTELLIGENCE SUMMARY No. 53[2]

Compiled from information received from 1200 hrs 12 Aug to 1200 hrs 13 Aug 41

a. Items side-lined in the margin will NOT be reproduced in any form.
b. Information contained herein is for circulation down to Lt. Colonels' commands only.

ATTITUDE OF VICHY FRENCH:

The following extract from a report by the Security Officer attached to the Embarkation Board is of interest. It is to be borne in mind that the Security Officer, F.S. Officers, and N.C.O.'s [sic] engaged on this work have been in close and friendly contact with all ranks of the Vichy French for some weeks past and were present at their embarkation and departure from BEYROUTH.

Morale of T.F.L. : (Troupes Fancaises du Levant -ie.VICHY FRENCH)

a. There is no pro-German feeling whatever. Again and again, Officers have said that the sooner they are fighting the Boche the better.
b. Anti-British feeling does not run deep. Our invasion of SYRIA is considered an act of aggression, but the French officers admit they do understand our reasons. What is resented is:-

1. Our dealings with the French Fleet.
2. Our reference to PETAIN.
   The T.F.L believe that PETAIN is whole-heartedly anti-German and is patiently waiting his time.

a. The hatred of the T.F.L. for the Free French is bitter, and vice versa. Incidents such as firing on volunteers for the Free French should not be considered either as anti-British or pro-German. The Free French are blamed for having entered SYRIA and fought their own compatriots when they might have stayed in Africa and fought the Boche. In the feeling of one side for the other there is all the cruelty and passion of Civil War".

---

2   AWM 52: I Corps docs: 10 July 41 1/4/41 Corps, I Australian Corps General Branch (I Aust Corps 'G' Branch).

SECRET
1 AUST CORPS INTELLIGENCE SUMMARY No.54[3]

Compiled from information received from
1200 hrs 13 Aug to 1200 hrs 14 Aug 41

a. Items side-lined in the margin will NOT be reproduced in any form.
b. Information contained herein is for circulation down to Lt. Colonels only.

— — — — — — —

PART II – SECURITY

ATTITUDE OF VICHY FRENCH: A person, hitherto found to be reliable, expressed the following views:-

Quite a number of his acquaintances who were pro-British previous to our occupation of SYRIA, had swung against us, and his explanation was that powerful 5th columnist activity was rife in BEYROUTH.

A cousin of his, a member of the Vichy Forces, informed him that he had no intention of joining the Free French, as in his opinion, the British forces would be incapable of holding SYRIA when the Germans attacked. This view was shared by the majority of Vichy forces.

His cousin also commented on the fact that their camp was placed in between two De Gaullist camps, with the idea of obtaining converts. In his opinion, no greater mistake could have been made. In fact, it only served to antagonise them further.

Signature
Lt-Col.
GS 1 Aust Corps
DISTRIBUTION as per summary No.28.

---

3   AWM 52: I Corps docs: 10 July 41 1/4/41 Corps, I Australian Corps General Branch (I Aust Corps 'G' Branch).

Appendix III

Lieutenant Alwyn Clark Recollection

Arriving at Brigade and Regtl HQ, I noticed men racing around with machine guns and rifles and, as I walked towards the stone hut of our RHQ I saw a truck backed up to a window and the Sig and Pay Sgt's [sic] throwing filing cabinets, typewriters, maps etc, in a great panic, into a truck and I heard our 'I' officer on the phone, "For Christ's sake Freddie (our Bty Commander) do something about it, ten rounds gun fire a thousand yards past that tomb on the ridge" and as I entered through the door, "Thank God. Someone from the guns. Here! Take over" as he shoved the phone into my hands. Conscious of his order – 'ten rounds gun fire' and not being able to see where the rounds would land, or know the target, I immediately ordered over the phone to the BC 'STOP', the emergency order to stop firing.

An infantry officer (the Brigade Major) standing immediately behind the 'I' officer explained "We are about to be attacked by the French Spahis." They are assembling for the attack just over the ridge.' I asked, "Position of our troops?" He replied, "The Cheshire Yeomanry are advancing along the ridge but they are not due for another two hours."

I ordered one round to fall just this side of the ridge, near where the French would have to pass in charging down onto our HQ and, as "shot" came over the phone about seven horsemen dressed just like the film version of the "French Foreign Legion" came over the ridge heading for the spot where the shell was supposed to land. Luckily it arrived first, about 25 yards in front of the horsemen who scampered back over the ridge. I did get a look at their faces – fair, sunburnt and with fair hair – more English than French. Immediately after, about 50 to 70 of them came over the ridge, only 100 yards away, another look and I said to the Brigade Major, "The Cheshires!"

"Couldn't be" he said, "Must take charge of that machine gun!" and stormed out the door on the run, expecting me to carry out his orders of "ten rounds gun fire." Another look … I was convinced that they were the Cheshires and refused to order the ten rounds gun fire as they rode over the exact spot on which the ranging round had landed and on which all the guns were laid, ready to fire. They disappeared back over the ridge. About ten minutes later the Bty Commander was on the phone again

(I had to answer because the IO had collapsed onto his stretcher and couldn't be awakened) "The French we fired on are now out in the open and only 600 yards from the guns. Permission requested to engage them over open sights!' I replied, "DO NOT, repeat DO NOT, engage, as I think they are our own Cheshire Yeomanry." A few minutes later and a very agitated and frightened Bty Captain. "The French are only 200 yards away and a threat to our guns, can I engage them over open sights?" Again I answered, "DO NOT engage, unless they first commit a hostile act against the guns as I still think they are our own Cheshire Yeomanry."

I was the only one at Brigade and Regtl HQ who was not convinced that they were the French. There was such a "panic" everywhere that I hate to think what would have happened to the Cheshires if I had been a few seconds later, both at the corner and arriving just in time to hear the order "ten rounds gun fire." The point was this – I was only a junior lieutenant [sic] – as Liaison Officer – I was only a messenger boy at RHQ, with no authority, especially to order my own Bty Comdr, or to refuse to carry out the orders and requests of the infantry Brigade Major. This was made abundantly clear to me when I had to report to Regtl HQ at Jezzine. But that is another story.[1]

1   Alwyn Clarke: NCY 19/46 Cheshire Archives.

Appendix IV

North Somerset Yeomanry Casualty Return Following the Assault on Jebel Mazar[1]

DIED OF WOUNDS		
2/Lieut. M.A.J. Hynes. "C" Sqn.	10-7-41	
409720 Sgt. Koomen, W.J.M. "A" Sqn.	"	
5046820 Ck/Cpl. Coulson, S.H. "HQ" Sqn.	"	
WOUNDED		
403012 Tpr. Grant, A.B. "C" Sqn.	"	Leg amputated.
323218 Tpr. Brooks, G.R. "C"	"	Sh.wds. kneck & thigh [sic]
552880 Tpr. Routledge, G "A"	"	War neurosis.
318624 Tpr. Billett, D. "A"	"	Contusion – ankle
318364 L/Cpl. Rugg, A.W. "A"	"	" " R& (indecipherable)
419691 Sgt. Edwards, N. "A"	"	Wounds to feet.
410245 Tpr. Bryant, L.B. "A"	"	Sh.wds. rt. ft.
403387 Tpr. Field, W.H. "A"	"	Contn. ankle R.
328292 Tpr. Petherbridge, R.J. "A"	"	Contn. ankle.
550713 Tpr. Johnson, R.N. "A"	"	Contn. ankle Rt.
398270 Cpl. Otridge, D.J. "HQ"	"	Sh. Wds. Back.
318495 Tpr. Pugh, L. "C"	"	War neurosis.
404349 Tpr. Bowes, J. "A"	"	GSW Buttock.

1 TNA WO 169/1401: North Somerset Yeomanry.

5106605 Sgt. Ayres, E.E. "A"	"	GSW Head
325969 Tpr. Russum, H.N. "HQ"	"	Compd.fr. leg. rt.
318368 Sgt. Louis, W.A. "A"	"	GSW left thigh.
324173 Tpr. Harbutt, R.F.C. "A"	"	GSW shoulder rt. And leg L.
MISSING 15 O.R's missing. "C" Sqn:- Sgt. Poole, L/Cpl. Wicks, Cpl. Shipp. Tprs. Freeman, R.P. Harrill, R.H. Warren, V.H. Davis, Aw.W. (934), Farr. Jones, G.T. (118). Bemmet. "A" Sqn:- L/Cpl. Eggleton. Tprs. Warner. Osborne (727), Mitchell, D. Case D.A., Dance, R.J. *The various mistypes and inconsistencies are as per the original document.		

Appendix V

Postscript

HQ 7 Aust Div 24 Jul 41
Letter to I Aust Corps

"The Cheshire Yeomanry, commanded by Lt-Col D W Williams, were under command 7 Aust Div during the recent operations in SYRIA. It is desired to place on record the valuable services rendered by Lt-Col Williams and the excellent work carried out by his regt.

In the early stages the regt cleaned up a large number of the frontier posts, and the regt, less one sqn, then ... right flank protection to the adv of the 14th Aust Inf Bn Gp. Subsequently it moved across difficult country via ... And then west in on the enemy's left flank at the Litani. The other sqn protected the left flank of the 25 Aust Inf Bde Gp in the early stages of the attack and subsequently moved to the Jessine area.

Later the regt was concentrated under 25 Aust Inf Bde Gp and operated in the area Mtolle –

***

Lt-Col Williams was ever ready to co-operate and this, plus the high standard of efficiency of the Regt., enabled it to play a valuable part in the successful operations.

Allen Maj-Gen GOC 7 Aust Div[1]

"After the campaign was over there were no regrets that it had been used."[2] The basis for this is expressed in a note from Lt. Col Williams to all ranks of the Cheshire Yeomanry, dated 17 July 1941, addressed from R.H.Q., "In the Field":

> I wish to congratulate all ranks for the big part the Regiment has played in bringing the Syrian Campaign to such a successful conclusion. The Australian

---

1   Appendix M G 15/1/957.
2   Verdin, *The Cheshire Yeomanry*, p.247.

Forces with which we have been operating cannot speak highly enough of the Cheshire Yeomanry, and the Higher Commands have all told me, personally, how sorry they are that we are no longer under their command. It has not come as a surprise to me that the Regiment has done so well, but it is none the less gratifying and we have certainly put Horsed Cavalry back on the map. I am proud of having commanded the Regiment in this campaign.[3]

3   NA: WO 169/1936: Cheshire Yeomanry 1941

Bibliography

Primary Sources

Cheshire Archives
NCY: 19/57 Syria: The Last British Cavalry Action Part 1, Denis C. Bateman
NCY: 19/57 Syria: The Last British Cavalry Action Part 2, Denis C. Bateman
NCY: 19/46: Interview with Alwyn Clarke

Imperial War Museum Department of Sound Records
IWM: 14139 recorded 1994-05-24 'Interview with Clifford Wrigglesworth'

The National Archives (TNA)
WO 169/1396: Cheshire Yeomanry War Diary, January-December 1941
WO 169/1401: The North Somerset Yeomanry, January-December 1941
WO 169/1407: Yorkshire Dragoons, January-December 1941

Australian War Memorial
WO 52 1/5/14 Divisions: 7 Australian Division General Staff Branch (7 Aust Div GS Branch)
AWM 52: 1/5/14-0110: 7 Australian Division General Staff Branch (7 Aust Div GS Branch)
AWM52: 1/5/14/11: June 1941, Exporter Force
AWM52 1/4/1: I Corps docs: 1 Australian Corps General Branch (1 Aust Corps 'G' Branch)
AWM52 8/2/25/7: 25 Infantry Brigade: July-August 1941

Hansard
HC Deb 10 October 1939 vol 352 cc146-8

Interviews and Correspondence

Robert McIntosh (2018), 'Horses of I Cavalry Division WWII'. E-mail (4 April 2018)

Government Publications

War Office, *The Manual of Horsemastership, Equitation and Animal Transport 1937* (London: HMSO, 1937)

Official Histories

J.E. Edmonds, (ed.), *Military Operations France and Belgium 1918*, Vol V (HMSO: London, 1945)
Falls, Cyril. (ed.), *Military Operations France and Belgium 1917*, Vol. I (Macmillan: London, 1940)

Secondary Sources

Anglesley, Marquis of, *A History of the British Cavalry, Vol. VIII, The Western Front, 1915-1918; Epilogue 1919-1939* (Leo Cooper: London, 1997)

Badsey, Stephen *Doctrine and Reform in the British Cavalry 1880-1918* (Ashgate: Farnham, 2008)
Bierman, John and Smith, Colin, *Alamein: War Without Hate* (London: Penguin Group, 2002)

Falls, Cyril, *Armageddon 1918* (Weidenfeld and Nicolson: London, 1964).
Fitzgeorge-Parker, Tim, *No Secret So Close: The Biography of Bruce Hobbs* (Pelham: London, 1984)
Flanakin, Len, *The Teddy Bear Lancers* (Warwick: Warwickshire Yeomanry Museum Trust, 2010)
French, David, *Raising Churchill's Army: The British Army and the War against Germany 1919-1945* (Oxford: OUP, 2000)

Guderian, Heinz, *Panzer Leader* (London: Penguin, 2009)

Harrison-Place, Tim, *Military Training in the British Army, 1940-44: From Dunkirk to D-Day* (Abingdon: Routledge, 2000)
Hay, George *The Yeomanry Cavalry and Military Identities in Rural Britain, 1815–1914* (London: Palgrave Macmillan, 2017)
Holland, James (ed.), *An Englishman at War: The Wartime Diaries of Stanley Christopherson DSO, MC, TD: 1939-1945* (London: Bantam Press, 2014)

Liddell-Hart, B.H. (ed.), *The Soviet Army* (London: Weidenfeld and Nicolson, 1956)
Gavin Long *Second World War 1939-1945, Vol. II – Greece, Crete and Syria* (Canberra: Australian War Memorial, 1953)

Piekalkiewicz, Janusz, *The Cavalry of World War II* (Orbis: London, 1979)

Ranfurly, Hermione, *To War with Whitaker: The Wartime Diaries of the Countess of Ranfurly 1939-1945* (London: Heinemann, 1994)
Roberts, David, *The Storm of War* (London: Penguin, 2010)

Segev, Tom, *One Palestine, Complete: Jews and Arabs under the British Mandate* (London: Abacus, 2002),

Taylor, A.J.P., *England 1914-1945* (London: Folio Society, 2000)
Travers, Tim, *The Killing Ground: The British Army, the Western Front and the Emergence of Modern Warfare 1900-1918* (Allen & Unwin: London, 1990)
Travers, Tim, *How the War was Won: Command and Technology in the British Army on the Western Front, 1917-1918* (Routledge: London, 1992)

Verney, John, *Going to the Wars* (London: Collins, 1955)
Verdin, Sir Richard, *The Cheshire (Earl of Chester's) Yeomanry 1898-1967: The Last Regiment to Fight on Horses* (Birkenhead: Willmer Brothers Limited, 1971).

Winton, H.R., *To Change an Army: General Sir John Burnett-Stuart and British Armored Doctrine, 1927-1938* (Lawrence, Kansas: University Press of Kansas, 1988)

Journals and Periodicals

Anon., 'Interview: U.S. Special Forces ODA 595', *Frontline*, no date <https://www.pbs.org/wgbh/pages/frontline/shows/campaign/interviews/595.html>
Bennington, Stuart and Cullimore, Hugh, Hidden in the Archives: Australia's Second World War "Kelly Gang", *Australian War Memorial*, 2018 <https://www.awm.gov.au/articles/blog/wwii-kelly-gang>
Correll, Diana Stacey, How the horse-soldiers helped liberate Afghanistan from the Taliban 18 years ago, *Military Times*, 2019 <https://www.militarytimes.com/news/your-military/2019/10/18/how-the-horse-soldiers-helped-liberate-afghanistan-from-the-taliban-18-years-ago/>
Cheshire Live, Last Post sounds for bugler Dougie, *Chester Chronicle*, 2014 <https://www.cheshire-live.co.uk/news/british-army-veteran-who-led-7183656>
Dowell, Stuart, Charge of the Fake Brigade: An Enduring myth of WWII is that Polish cavalry charged German tanks. They didn't, *The First News*, 2018 <https://www.thefirstnews.com/article/charge-of-the-fake-brigade-debunking-the-myth-of-the-wwii-cavalry-charge-against-german-tanks-2131>
Miller, Joyce Laverty, The Syrian Revolt of 1925, *International Journal of Middle East Studies*, 1977
Stevens, Sir Jack Edwin Stawell (1896–1969), *Australian Dictionary of Biography*, <https://adb.anu.edu.au/biography/stevens-sir-jack-edwin-stawell-11763>

Wallace, Samuel, Stirrups to Steering Wheels: The Issues of Cavalry Mechanisation in the Interwar Period, *The Society for Historical Research*, 2017 <https://www.linkedin.com/pulse/stirrups-steering-wheels-issues-cavalry-mechanisation>

Theses

Badsey, Stephen. D, Fire and the Sword: The British Army and the Arme Blanche Controversy 1871-1921, Cambridge University, 1982.
Salmon, Roger, The Management of Change: Mechanizing: The British Regular and Household Cavalry Regiments 1918-1942, University of Wolverhampton, 2013

Index

A

Adchite, 104–5, 110
Adeisse, 128, 135
Armoured cars, 81, 83–84, 87, 118, 151–53

B

Baadarane, 140, 142
Baadi, 126–27
Balfour Declaration (1917), 64–65
Beikoum, 140–42
Beirut, 86, 88, 105, 108, 111, 114, 124, 139, 148, 153, 159

C

Camels, 66–67
Cavalry mechanisation, 185
Churchill, Winston, 45, 72–77, 80, 82–83, 87, 91, 93, 133
Columns
    central, 121, 145
    main, 87, 91, 103, 115, 117, 128–29, 142, 161, 164
Cunningham, Lieutenant J.W., 126–27, 131–32

D

Dakar Raid, 77
Damascus, 86, 88, 112, 139, 154
Dawson, Lieutenant G.B., 126, 136, 138–40, 142–45, 151, 170
Dentz, General Henri Fernand, 76, 87–88, 93, 98, 102-3, 105–6, 110, 115, 120, 122, 124, 153, 155, 166

E

Elijah, 52, 54

F

First World War, 36, 44, 64, 164
Formations/Units
    I Australian Corps, 115, 174–75, 180, 182
    6th Australian Division, 83, 87, 114, 120, 146-48
    7th Australian Division, 86-87, 89
    1st Cavalry Division, 35–36, 40, 43–45, 49, 51-52, 54-55, 63, 68, 71-72, 75, 79, 81, 83, 87, 112, 153
    4th Brigade, 51, 55
    5th Brigade, 55, 70, 79, 81, 142, 165
    6th Brigade, 56, 69
    21st Brigade, 86, 89, 93, 101, 110-13, 117, 128, 131-32, 139, 142, 146, 148, 153
    23rd Brigade, 114
    25th Brigade, 86, 93, 101, 110-11, 114, 116, 120-23, 125, 128-32, 134, 139, 142, 145, 147, 151, 165
    5th Indian Brigade, 87, 112, 134, 153
    2/16th Australian Infantry, 102
    2/27th Australian Infantry, 102, 122
    2/31st Australian Infantry, 111
    1st Royal Fusiliers, 110, 134
    Cheshire Yeomanry, 35–40, 44, 47–49, 61–63, 69–71, 73–76, 86–95, 97–98, 100–102, 105–9, 111–23, 125–27, 129–37, 139–40, 142–48, 150–51, 162–69, 176–77 180–81, 184
    Household Cavalry, 50–51, 55, 63, 72
    North Somerset Yeomanry, 34–35,

40–41, 47, 49, 57, 59, 69, 72, 74, 86, 90, 93–94, 118, 146–51, 153–55
Royals, The, 51, 55, 63, 84, 106,
Royal Scots Greys, 51, 55, 62, 67, 72, 87, 91, 110, 134
Royal West Kent Yeomanry, 34
Royal Wiltshire Yeomanry, 35, 51, 168
Sherwood Rangers, 34, 43, 48, 51, 56, 60, 62, 65, 70-71, 74
Staffordshire Yeomanry, 51, 74, 87, 91
Warwickshire Yeomanry, 36, 40–41, 50–51, 56, 67, 70, 81, 118
Yorkshire Dragoons, 34, 36, 41, 51, 86, 93, 118, 140, 146–47, 151–58, 165, 169–71
Arab Legion, 170
Druse Legion, 153
Glubb Pasha's Guides, 81
Habforce, 79, 81, 87, 89, 111-12, 114, 120, 153, 162
Kelly Gang, 118, 146, 168
Todforce/Todcol, 87, 110,
Transjordan Frontier Force/TJFF, 115, 153, 170
French Foreign Legion, 112, 136, 176

G

Galilee, 57

H

Haifa, 51–52, 55, 69, 79, 81, 90
Haret Jandal, 144–45
Hasbaya, 147
Heitoura, 131, 133
Horsemastership, 41, 46–47, 68, 72, 183

I

Iraq, 52, 76–77, 79–83, 87, 111, 118

J

Jezzine, 97, 110–11, 115, 117, 122, 132, 134–36, 143, 153, 155, 165–66
Junior officers, 34, 37, 68

K

Kuneitra, 108, 110, 151–52, 154

L

Lavarack, Major General John, 89, 111
Light Horse Militia, 119
Litani River, 63, 84, 87, 93–94, 98–103, 104–8, 115, 117–18, 128–29, 147, 180

M

Maitland-Wilson, Lieutenant General Sir Henry, 87, 91, 99, 102, 107, 110-11, 116-17, 121, 131, 133-34, 146, 151, 153, 159, 161
Manual of Horsemastership, 41, 46–47, 72, 183
Mazboud, 114
Mazraa, 121
Merdjayoun, 87–88, 111–12, 114, 117–19, 121–22, 125, 135, 153
Merjayoun, 106, 110–11, 134
Mers-el-Kebir, 77
Moukhtara, 145

N

Nazareth, 90
North Africa, 52, 77, 79, 81, 83

O

Operation Battleaxe, 81–83, 87, 152, 166
Operation Exporter, 86–87, 90, 92–93, 97, 100, 102, 110–13, 117–18, 145-46, 151, 153, 159, 161, 166–67

P

Packhorses, 128, 130, 154
Palestine, 44–45, 47, 51–59, 61–75, 77–78, 80, 82, 86–87, 107, 110, 151, 154–55
Patrolling, 103, 119–20, 129, 136, 139, 146–47

Q

Queneitra, 118, 152

R

Remeiche, 93

S

Samia, 155–57
Second World War, 73, 80, 164, 167, 171
Sejen, 156–57
Soueida, 156–58
Spahis, 59–60, 89, 93, 97–98, 101–2, 105, 128, 135, 164
Spears Mission, 173, 175
Suez Canal, 81–82
Syria, 77, 80–84, 86, 89–91, 111, 146–47, 153–54, 161–64, 166–68, 170, 172, 174–75, 180, 182–83

T

Tell Abou Nida, 152
Training regime, 55–56

V

Vichy, 59, 77, 82–83, 85, 87–89, 163, 174–75

W

War Office, 39, 41, 44, 62, 72, 166, 183
Wavell, General Sir Archibald, 79–80, 82-84, 88, 90-92, 111, 114, 161, 166